GIORDANO BRUNO

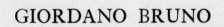

GIORDANO BRUNO

HIS LIFE, THOUGHT, AND

MARTYRDOM

BY

WILLIAM BOULTING

AUTHOR OF "TASSO AND HIS TIMES"
"ÆNEAS SYLVIUS," ETC.

"To love Truth for Truth's sake is the principal
part of human perfection in this world, and the
seed-plot of all other virtues."—LOCKE.

LONDON
KEGAN PAUL, TRENCH, TRUBNER & CO. LTD.
BROADWAY HOUSE. 68-74 CARTER LANE, E.C.
NEW YORK: E. P. DUTTON & CO.

PREFACE

THE life of Bruno has been written in English more than once, and he has had many excellent commentators. No one can now write about him without availing himself very largely of the solid and scholarly work done by Tocco, Fiorentino, Berti, Brunnhofer, McIntyre and others. The apology for the appearance of the present work must be that some facts, unrecorded in England, have come to light of late years, and also that a few usual, almost unavoidable inaccuracies require correction. Moreover, I have tried to follow the development of Bruno's thoughts in the order in which he declared them; and, on one or two points, I find myself compelled to differ from the conclusions of this or the other commentator.

Most of Bruno's works have been published in the editions of Wagner, Lagarde, and Gfrörer, well edited for their day. Different libraries contain different editions, when any are to be found in them. Even the British Museum, although it possesses a fine collection of rare, original impressions, does not contain all the volumes of the complete State Edition, and lacks that one which contains the works which were discovered in manuscript. To give the paging of any particular edition might therefore prove less convenient than the plan I have adopted of giving those indications for reference which are supplied by the subdivisions of the works themselves, except in the case of the published manuscripts.

v

Those who wish to verify a reference will thereby readily do so and may discover that reading the context is not a wholly unprofitable task. I have given minuter detail as to other works from which I have drawn or which throw light on the subject-matter.

W. B.

CONTENTS

GIORDANO BRUNO

CHAPTER I

BIRTH AND PARENTAGE—BOYHOOD

A TRAVELLER, curious to try the local line which runs
eastward from Naples, after journeying a few meandering
miles through a generous and beautiful country-side, will
find his train halting at the little city of Nola. Should he
descend, he would not come across anything strikingly
picturesque or architecturally memorable. There are few
vestiges of the remote past; even the mediæval cathedral
is a restoration. On an eminence, a ruined fortress still
dominates *Campagna Felice*—"the happy fields"—as the
inhabitants call their plain; and, as of old time, the vineyards are lavish in the production of "mangiaguerra," a
thick black wine. The sky is very lucid; the air sweet
and soft; the eye may range over the rich and varied
plain to Monte Somma (which hides Vesuvius) and to
other guardian hills.

Outside the walls of Nola there stood in the mid 16th
century, Cicala, a hamlet of "four or five houses, none
of them too imposing;"[1] and here, in 1548,[2] there was
born to a soldier in the service of the Spanish masters of
Naples, one Gioan Bruno and his wife, a man child. The

[1] Bruno, G; *Spaccio della bestia trionfante, Dial. I. iij.*
[2] Berti, D; *G. B. da Nola, sua vita e sua dottrina,* 1889, *App.,
Doc. vij.*—Auvray, L; *Mem. d. l. Soc. d. l'histoire de Paris et de l'Ile
de France, t. xxvij, p.* 288 *sqq., sub* 7*th December.*

A

infant was destined to become a precursor of modern
science and philosophy, to cast a search-light into dark
places and bring forth hidden things; it was his fate to
wander, an excommunicated and fugitive priest, through
many lands, impelled, heedless of self, partly by a restless
nature but chiefly because of a certain missionary zeal for
truth and desire to set the intellect free from the fetters
of authority; he was to endure strange vicissitudes in
penury, years of solitary suffering at the hands of the
Inquisition because he claimed "philosophic freedom in
thought and speech," and, finally, to pass from its cruel
dungeons "a flame to the flames." He was born in the
very year which saw an outbreak at Naples against a
contemplated introduction of the Spanish Inquisition.

Bruno tells us that his mother's name was Fraulissa.[1]
She was of a family called Savolini or Saulini. Probably
Fiorentino[2] was right in connecting her singular baptismal
name with German mercenaries, whose Italian wives may
very well have been so called; and certainly some of the
multitude of mercenary troops drawn from beyond the
Alps had settled in the neighbourhood.[3] As to the social
status of the Bruni and many similar problems, much has
been conjectured and no certainty achieved. It would seem
probable that the family was very far from being wealthy,
but had some claim to gentility.[4] The Bruni may have
been a branch of the noble family of that name at Asti.

[1] Berti, D; *loc. cit.*

[2] Fiorentino, F; *Dialoghi Morali di G. B. Giorn. Napol., N.S.*
1882, *fasc.* 19, *p.* 44. Great circumspection is required in regard to
this paper. In consulting the Registers, Fiorentino somehow contrived to confound the year 1545 with the year 1563! It should be
read side by side with the monograph *Bruno e Nola* by Signor
V. Spampanato, *Castrovillari,* 1899.

[3] See the reference to Il danese, etc. in Bruno's *Spaccio, Dial.
I., iij.*

[4] *J. Bruni Oratio Valedictoria.*

The child was christened Felipe (Philip). Perhaps his father named him after the heir to the throne of Charles V, as it would become a loyal soldier to do. We shall see how he came by the name of Giordano.

Gioan Bruno would seem to have been a caustic critic of life; for his son tells us that when, after supper, a friend declared that he had never before felt so happy, Gioan retorted: "that is because you have never before been so frivolous."[1] Probably Gioan was a man of parts; for it is accepted by most of the best authorities that he counted Tansillo, the Neapolitan poet, courtier and cavalier, among his friends.[2] Tansillo, although not born at Nola, came of Nolan stock; he never stayed long at Nola, but made a few hurried visits thither.[3] Felipe may have seen more of him, later on, at Naples. Anyhow, many works show how deeply Tansillo impressed his mind during the plastic years; he introduces the poet into his dialogues; he adopts Tansillo's style in his own poems, and he often equals his master, though, usually, he falls short of him in grace, smoothness and elegance; he even incorporates a little of Tansillo's work with his own. Any passing visit paid by Tansillo to Nola would produce a strong impression on the little lad; for the good folk around were of a different order.

In the cottages hard by dwelt certain members of his mother's family.[4] He tells us of a certain Scipione Saulino

[1] Bruno, G; *Eroici Furòri, P.I., Dial. II.*

[2] McIntyre, for example, accepts it. Cpr. McIntyre, J. L; *G. B.*, London, 1903, *p.* 5.

[3] Fiorentino; *loc. cit.* Luigi Tansillo, 1510–1568, was a favourite of Pedro de Toledo, Viceroy of Spain, and of his son, and was their companion on land and sea. At first he wrote with unbridled licence, whereby he incurred the displeasure of the Church; but he made his peace with the authorities and produced some excellent poetry, which was disfigured, however, by many faults of the style then in fashion. Before the Viceroy's death he was given a post in the Neapolitan Custom-House. Cfr. Rosalba, G; *Studi di lett., Nap.* 1903, *pp.* 166 *sqq.* [4] Fiorentino; *loc. cit.*

who went once a year, on Good Friday, to his crony, the
curate, to confess. Absolution was freely given, and, when
the year came round again, " Father," he would say, " to-
day's sins finish up the year "; whereupon the good priest
would reply, " And so does to-day's absolution. Go in
peace and sin no more." [1]

The rustics of the neighbourhood were a home-spun
people, rough and ready of tongue and of caustic wit. They
took the facts of life with unsophisticated directness and
retained very ancient usages, celebrating the vintage with
classic obscenity and shocking the Viceroy thereby.[2] Although degraded by centuries of misgovernment and oppression, the southern Italian had not lost his intellectual vigour
or his readiness to abandon himself to the enjoyment of
simple pleasures, as if all creatures were dwelling in the
sunrise of eternity. The Nolans were markedly superstitious, even for a credulous age. They beheld spirits in
deserted places—by an ancient temple and where the bodies
of the plague-stricken had been buried ; poltergeists played
tricks on them, and Bruno records how, when a child, he himself beheld spirits on hills where beeches and laurels grew.[3]

The quick eye of the child noted the peculiarities of his
neighbours and the small events of his life; and he never
forgot them. Years afterwards, when in exile, he introduces
the honest, kindly folk of Nola, not without irony, as interlocutors in his dialogues [4]; he delights in recalling many
details which he had observed—the produce of his father's
garden, the melon-plot of Franzino, the smell of burnt hair
when Vesta, the wife of Albentio, used curling-tongs, and
how she would shake her head ; he remembers hearing the

---

[1] Bruno, G ; *Il Candelajo, Atto V, sc. xix.*

[2] Miccio, S ; *Vita di Don P. di Toledo, Archiv. Stor. it, ix, p.* 23.

[3] *De Magia, Op. Lat. III, pp.* 430, 431.

[4] *Spaccio ; Il caballo.*

cuckoo when at Antonio Saulino's, the pupping of his bitch, the spoiling of a gown by Messer Danese, the tailor, and how he saw Paulino, given to blasphemy, stoop to heave up a great shovelful of earth and break the red string which held his breeches up. Character after character, incident after incident, crowd in on his memory: he may have had personal experience of the bugs which infested the wooden bedstead of Costatino.[1] The lad's eye was alive to beauty too ; to the pure sky, tremulous with excess of light, the mystery of the shadowy hills, the bounty of the corn-laden plain. In exile he recalls the glory and glamour of the world which were given to his childhood, and is never weary of thinking of " the golden fields of Nola ";[2] his birthplace ever remained for him a place " blessed of heaven;"[3] he ranks the rich Campagna with Araby and the garden of the Hesperides,[4] speaks of himself and was known as " the Nolan," and calls his philosophy the Nolanese.[5] Other Nolans felt like Bruno. Ambrogio Leone tells of one who, returning home after only two or three days' absence, cast himself on his native soil and kissed it with unspeakable rapture.

The observant child had often gazed across at Vesuvius from vine-bearing Cicala and noticed how bare and forbidding it looked. But one day his father took him thither, and he found its slopes covered with luxuriant trees and bountiful vegetation, while Cicala, in its turn, had become dark and dim and distant. " Astonished at the strange change," he writes, " I became aware, for the first time, that sight could deceive."[6] The seed of doubt was sown ; he would soon ask : " What are the grounds of certitude ? "

[1] *Spaccio; Dial. III, iij.*
[2] *Eroici Furori, P.I., Dial. II.*
[3] *Causa, Dial. I.*
[4] *Orat. Valedict.*
[5] *Cena delle Ceneri.*
[6] Bruno, G ; *De Immenso, IV, iij.*

Influences of the *genius loci* could not fail to affect an impressionable, imaginative child. To every Italian child the past calls with living voice; antiquity is real; sometimes it lulls to sleep, sometimes is a rousing force; it is never, as with the Northern child, a dull dream concerning men who were never really alive, whose voices come as the hollow croakings of Shades. Now, Nola was a poor little place but it had been a great and noble city; it was one of the most ancient in Italy; it was the Uria of the Etruscans. The citizens boasted loudly of their descent from a Calchidian Colony. Thrice had Hannibal been repulsed from the gates. Nola had been the chosen home of Roman wealth and fashion; the great Augustus died there. True, of its massive walls, its twelve gates and its two amphitheatres nothing remained; ancient marbles were built into cottage and pigstye and vineyard-wall; but the labourer's spade often opened up some sepulchre crowded with the famous funeral urns of Nola, and his plough would reveal the long buried treasures of ancient coin and medallion. The little Bruno saw many a classic custom observed at wedding feast and popular festival and even in religious rite. He would hear of famous citizens, of whom Nolans were very proud, such as Ambrogio Leone, the scholar, and Giovanni da Nola, the sculptor.[1] Felipe Bruno moved among a people who derived their life-blood from Etruscan and yet more ancient sources, from Greeks, Romans, Teutons, Moors and Spaniards; they were quick, astute and versatile, very human, as volcanic as their soil, debased, but not so degenerate as they became after three more centuries of misrule.

Such were the influences we know of which moulded the mind of little Felipe in his earliest and most formative years.

[1] Berti, D ; *Vita di G. B.*, 1889, *cap. I.*

We do not know in what manner he was educated at Nola, but he must have been a promising pupil, for, at about the age of eleven, he was sent to Naples " to study humane letters, logic and dialectic " [1] : in other words, Latin language and literature, probably some Greek, philosophy, and the modes of effective reasoning and expression.[2] He may have lodged at an uncle's house. One Agostino Bruno was a weaver of velvet in Naples at the time. He attended the public lectures of Il Sarnese, probably one Vicenzo Colle of Sarno, who published, later on, a work called " The destruction of the destructions of Baldwin, which, moreover, the destroyer has fulfilled " [3]—an extraordinary title, designed, as was customary, to hit the eye of the reading public. Besides these public lectures, " I received," he says, " private lessons in logic from Fra Teofilo da Varano, an Augustinian monk, who afterwards lectured on Metaphysic in Rome." [4] Bruno also told an acquaintance, in 1585, that an Augustinian monk, whose name the hearer did not catch or did not remember, had been his main teacher in philosophy.[5] It is noteworthy that in two of his works [6] he calls the interlocutor who expresses his own opinions, Teofilo. Bruno claimed to be a " lover of God " himself ; [7] but it would be quite in his manner to discharge at the same time some sense of obligation to Teofilo da Varano ; and Bruno was not one to be unmindful of the few

[1] *Cfr.* Berti, *op. cit., Doc. vij.*

[2] *Cfr.* McIntyre ; *op. cit., p.* 121, *note i.*

[3] *Destructio destructionum Baldovini, quas quidem destructor adimplevit. Neap., Matth. Cancer,* 1554.

[4] *Doc. vij.*

[5] Auvray, L ; *Mém. d. l. Société d. l'hist. d. Paris et d. l'Ile de France, t. xxiv, pp.* 288–299, *sub Dec.* 7.

[6] *Cena ; Causa.*

[7] *Triginta Sigillorum explicatio ; Ad excell. Oxon. Acad. Procancellarium.*

benefits he received.   It is clear that the very young scholar received an impetus towards speculative thinking from Fra Teofilo.   But independent thinking had well nigh ceased to be in Italy; and in most of the Protestant centres of learning also.   The contests between the Papacy and the Reformers had led to the vigorous enforcement of opposed dogmas throughout Europe, and throughout Italy the edicts of Trent ran under the protecting shadow of the neighbouring Vatican.

Bruno tells us that, when a boy, he studied the works of Peter of Ravenna on memory.[1]   The scholars of the Renaissance had discovered how much the ancient orators employed dodges for remembering, and they studied the mnemonics of Quintus Cornificius, which they and Bruno attributed to Cicero.[2]   They directed their attention to the subject; for a good memory was a precious possession even after the art of printing by type was discovered, since books were very dear and, owing to a want of developed organization in the book-trade, were hard to come at and often had to be fetched from afar.   Peter of Ravenna's "Phœnix"[3] went through several editions.   Cornificius and all the older writers made use of visual memory, since that is stronger than auditory memory in most people, and taught how to imagine some vacant space, such as a temple, and fill it with suggestive images, thus using the principle of the association of ideas,[4] which Aristotle had written of.[5] Later, Bruno interwove the mnemonics of Peter Ravenna

[1] *Triginta sig. explic.*, *sub Tabula.*

[2] *Cantus Circæus.* But P. Manutius, who published the *Rhetoricum ad C. Herennium lib. iv.* at Venice in 1564, declared the authorship to be uncertain.

[3] *Fœnix* Dom. P. Ravennatis *memoriae magistri* Ven. 1491.

[4] Cfr. Middleton, A. E; *Memory systems, old and new. N. Y.* 1888.

[5] Aristotle, *De mem et remin.*, *c.* 2, 451*b*, 18 ; 452*a*, 14.

and other authors, who followed Cornificius closely, with his own psychological and metaphysical conclusions, and his knowledge of the subject proved to be useful as an introduction and means of livelihood in city after city, and especially in France and Germany, where much attention was given to the subject and where fresh books on memory were produced for each generation, at least, during the 16th century.[1]

What career should he follow? Education was difficult to obtain and very expensive. The times were troubled. Neapolitans were beggared by the heavy taxes imposed to put down the Protestant revolt against Philip in the Low Countries; the civil administration was abominable; the police and even the judges were corrupt; brigands infested the country-side and increased the desolation which earthquake, famine and pest had brought about. What Bruno now witnessed or heard of branded itself in his memory. " If [Hydra] long for carrion," said he, when in England, " let him go stay in the Campagna or the highway between Rome and Naples, where so many robbers are quartered; for there at every step he will have more sumptuous banquets of fresh flesh than in any other part of the world."[2] Even high society was infested by cheats and thieves; the kingdom was riddled with heresy, and heretics were pursued and exterminated with barbarous cruelty. Turkish buccaneers raided the coast, burning and slaying and capturing women and children for the slave-market.[3]

The lad was in love with learning; thought he had caught a glimpse of the " high white star of Truth "; there

---

[1] Vide *Allgemeine Encyclopädie d. Wissenschaften u. Künste. Hrsq. v.* J. S. Ersch *u.* J. B. Gruber etc. *sub Gedächtniss.*

[2] *Spaccio, III, ij.*

[3] Giannone, Pietro ; *Ist. Civile del regno di Napoli,* 1723. Giannone only just mentions Bruno as "a visionary."

was but one refuge for a youth with no great means—the cloister, with all its opportunities and lettered ease. The Church was very wealthy : it possessed two-thirds of the landed property in Naples. And the order of Dominic the Spaniard was the most powerful and rich of the monastic bodies and enjoyed the full support of Philip and his counsellors. In his fifteenth year, a time of life when it was impossible for Felipe to comprehend anything like the full nature and implication of monastic vows and obligations or the real spirit of the cloister, he entered that Dominican Order of which the first requirement was intellectual submission. He would be trained by men who were called " hounds of the Lord " and whose special function was to uphold doctrine and to scent out heresy as dogs are employed to scent out truffles.[1] This was the first of the long series of sardonic ironies which Fate had provided for Felipe Bruno.

[1] Dominicans, so called from their founder, S. Domingo, on account of their special work, were punned on in the famous line " Domini canes Evangelium latrantes per totum orbem." Inquisitorial functions were attached to this order of " Preaching Friars " rather more than ten years after S. Domingo's death, which took place A.D. 1234.

CHAPTER II

MONASTIC LIFE AT NAPLES

BRUNO was admitted, as a probationer, to the monastery of St. Domenico by the Prior, Ambrogio Pasqua.[1] The vast building is perched on an eminence, and its silent cloisters and pleasant courts seem to invite to a life of quiet study and reflection. It is full of memories of the great Dominican, Aquinas, the "Angelic Doctor," who dwelt and taught there. According to monastic usage, Felipe was re-named Giordano. Possibly this name was given to him because of the promise he displayed; for it had been borne by the second general of the order. Hardly any one was called after the baptismal river in the sixteenth century; though in the sixth, when the Jordan figured as a river-god in more than one new baptistery,[2] it was used in christening as a very appropriate appellation.[3]

After a year's discipline in religious exercises, Giordano proved sufficiently docile to be allowed to make his vows in company with a "convert." He passed from the society of probationers to that of the professed ; but remained under the same superior and was called a novice until he became a priest.[4] He would seem to reveal the secret of those years when he writes : "The authority of directors, barring worthier and higher matters, whereto he was

---

[1] *Doc. vij.*
[2] E.g. S. Maria in Cosmedin and S. Giovanni in Fonte at Ravenna.
[3] Hodgkin, T; *Italy and her Invaders*, 1892, *v. I, pp.* 24, 25.
[4] Berti, D ; *op. cit., p.* 39, *n.* 3.

naturally impelled, putteth his mind into fetters, so that, from being free in manhood, he becometh a slave under a most vile and subtle hypocrisy."[1] The reverberations of independent thought still lingered in Southern Italy; nor, perhaps, did convent-walls wholly shut them out. He frankly told his judges at Venice that he "began to doubt the doctrine of Three distinct Persons in the Trinity from the age of eighteen; and, indeed, Augustine declared the term Person to be new in his time; but I have never denied the dogma—only doubted."[2] His acute and vigorous intellect was already at work, framing a philosophy, translating the Son as Intellect and the Holy Spirit as Love.[3] He was naturally of frank character, and his incautious honesty soon landed him in difficulties. " My master," he told the Inquisitors, "when I was a novice, in order to frighten me, drew up a process against me, for having given away the images of St. Catherine of Sienna and, possibly, St. Anthony, and retained a crucifix only ; whereby it was imputed to me that I despised the images of saints ; and also for having told a novice, who was reading the account of the 'Seven Joys of the Madonna' in verse, that he should cast it aside and read some other book instead, such as the 'Lives of the Holy Fathers'; but my master tore this document up the same day."[4] The stricter discipline ordered by the Council of Trent had not yet taken effect in the monastery; and so little cause of offence did the fathers find in Bruno (who was a close student, and whose converse was probably chiefly with books) that he became subdeacon and deacon in due course and was admitted to the priesthood in 1572, he being then 24 years of age.[5] Before he became a priest he had the confidence and

---

[1] *Eroici Furori, P.I, Dial. I., after 1st poem.*
[2] *Doc. xi.*   [3] *Ibid.*   [4] *Doc. xiii.*
[5] Berti, D ; *Vita di G. B., ed. of* 1868, *p.* 72, *n.* 1.

boldness, not merely to write a satiric allegory, for which he chose the title of "Noah's Ark" (there being a work of devotional mysticism by Hugo de Sancte Victore bearing the same name),[1] but to dedicate it to Pope Pius V, who then wore the tiara ; and he presented it to him,[2] probably when he was summoned to Rome. For, the monks could not fail to talk about the brilliant man they had secured ; Bruno had devoted some attention to mnemonics, and his reputation reached the Papal Court. Later, an acquaintance in Paris entered in his diary: "Jordanus told me that Pope Pius V and Cardinal Rebiba summoned him from Naples, and he was brought to Rome in a coach to set forth his Artificial Memory. He recited the Psalm *Fundamenta*[3] in Hebrew, and taught something of this to Rebiba."[4]

"Noah's Ark," the first fruit of his genius, has disappeared. We know that he crowded the ark with all manner of creatures, each probably symbolizing some human virtue or folly. The animals struggled for the seat of honour—the poop—a current metaphor for the faculty of Reason; the Gods granted the distinction to the ass; but he ran some danger of losing it, because his was a case of hoofs, not horns.[5] The gist of this early work may be preserved in two later books ;[6] but not even the temerity of Bruno could have submitted the audacities of one of these[7] to the severe scrutiny of Michele Ghislieri.[8] Berti and others think that Bruno's comedy "The Chandler" was

----

[1] McIntyre ; *op. cit., p.* 11.
[2] *Cena, Dial. II* ; *Cabala, Epist. Dedic.*
[3] *Psalm lxxxvj.*
[4] Auvray, L ; *Opus cit., sub Dec.* 21.
[5] *Cena, Dial. ij.*
[6] *Cantus Circœus; Cabala del Cavallo Pegaseo.*
[7] *Cabala con l'aggiunta de l'asino cillenico.*
[8] Pius V died 1572, the year in which Bruno became a priest.

written, although not revised and finished, during this monastic period.

Bruno says: " Being at the time at a monastery of my order, called St. Bartholomew, in the city of Campagna, some distance from Naples, but in the Kingdom, I chanted my first mass there; and I continued to wear the Dominican habit, celebrating mass and the divine offices under obedience to my superiors and the Priors of monasteries, wherever I was, up to the year 1576." Doubtless he diligently searched through the library of every religious house of which he was a temporary inmate. He could have found but little in common with his monkish associates, except that some of them would possess a tincture of that learning on which the " Angelic Doctor," who cast distinction on their order, had set his seal.

Even candid, courageous Sarpi tells us that he found himself compelled to wear a mask.[1] Bruno's was a very penetrable disguise. The habit concealed a fierce intellectual flame: it had burst forth once; it could not but show itself again; " the cowl does not make the monk." Here was a man of vast spiritual energy, of singularly open character, one not to be scared by legend or suppressed by authority, resolute to know at first hand, strong-headed if not headstrong, and brave to rashness. Soon the monks of St. Dominic had a taste of the " essence " of their young priest. Now that he was in full orders, and therefore less under direction, he indulged in a frankness of speech which speedily brought him into serious peril. At this time Arianism had found foothold in the South, and many had departed from " the fixed highway to the Infinite and Eternal." Bruno told the Inquisitors : " One day, during a discussion with Montalcino, one of our order, in the company of other fathers, he said that heretics were ignorant

[1] Sarpi, Fra Paolo; *Lett. I, p.* 237.

folk and used no scholastic terms; whereto I replied that
indeed they did not set forth their conclusions in the
scholastic manner; but they came to the point, as did the
fathers of the Church"; and then Bruno proceeded to
show, as an example, that Arius was not without some
kind of support from St. Augustine.[1] "I shewed the view
of Arius to be less dangerous than it was commonly taken
to be; for it was generally understood that Arius meant
to teach that the Word was the first creation of the Father;
and I explained that Arius said the Word was neither
Creator nor Created, but intermediary between the Creator
and the creature, just as the spoken word is an intermediary
between the speaker and the meaning he sets forth; and
that, for this reason, it is called the First-born before all
creatures; through which, and not out of which all things
are; not to which, but through which all things return to
their final end, which is the Father."[2] It is unfortunate
that the Founder of Christianity and His Apostles were as
silent about such high matters as if they had been agnostics,
while the Fathers gave vague and contradictory answers to
those important questions which the Roman Church had
by this time definitely and precisely answered with one
theologic scheme, the Eastern Church with another, those
unsuccessful disturbers of Christian peace, the earlier
heretics, with more, and the Protestants with several new
ones. Bruno, who had read the Christian fathers and the
Schoolmen carefully, was in the right; and Montalcino
appears to have reported the conversation at head-quarters.

This was not the sole count against Bruno. "The Provincial drew up a process against me on certain charges
of which I remain wholly ignorant; but I was told that he
was proceeding against me for fresh heresy, and was
reviving the affair of my novitiate; and I misdoubted I

[1] *Doc. xiij.*   [2] *Doc. xi.*

should find myself in prison."[1]   Bruno was no longer in
the hands of the Director of Novitiates, but, as priest,
answerable to the Provincial Father.   A charge of heresy,
therefore, might be fraught with very serious consequences.
The Papal States, which adjoined the Kingdom, were the
only possible refuge.   "So," he continues, " I left Naples
and went to Rome"; thus commencing a life of turmoil
and ceaseless wandering through Europe, which was to
endure for sixteen years, to be followed by nearly eight
years of imprisonment, and to end at the stake.

[1] *Doc. xiij.*

CHAPTER III

DISCIPLINE OF BOOKS

I. CLASSICS, ARISTOTLE, THE SCHOOLMEN ETC.

BRUNO must have been a marvel of intellectual industry. Interested in all things, burning to know, he must have put every spare moment at the monastery to good purpose; for his education was vast and varied. A good memory helped him; though sometimes one finds it, like the equally excellent memory of Macaulay, a trifle inaccurate; certainly he owed more to nature than to the systematized mnemonic art in which he believed. He spoke Spanish,[1] like all the cultivated people of the "Kingdom." Latin, of course, was a living language, spoken by every educated monk and scholar. Bruno's works give evidence of a wide range of reading in the Roman classics, and they contain many quotations from the Roman poets, especially from Lucretius, Virgil and Ovid. But his eager, romantic mind did not allow of being moulded by such studies into classic reserve and equipoise. He acquired an intimate acquaintance with the literature of that graceful, unlaboured daughter of Latin —his own tongue; that he commanded the great poets, Dante, Ariosto and Tasso, references and quotations in his works show; but he especially valued the sugared conceits and strained manner of Tansillo and the decadent Neapolitan school. The one play he wrote indicates the study of Bibbiena and Aretino no less than of Plautus and Terence.

He knew Greek, and shows a mastery of Aristotle in

[1] *Cena, Dial. II.*

the original unequalled by any scholar of his time. Aristotle was part of a Dominican's education, for Albertus
Magnus and Aquinas had effected the Church's acceptance
of the Stagirite as "topmost authority," "worthiest of
faith and obedience."[1] Petrarch, indeed, dared to say
that, after all, Aristotle was only a man ; and, recently,
Cornelius Agrippa, who lived and died in the bosom
of Mother Church, had attacked Aristotle; so had Ramus
and others ; but all recent onslaughts on Aristotle's authority were regarded as inroads on orthodox belief. Not
merely did Bruno possess a masterly knowledge of Aristotle,
but, by reason of his bent towards natural science, he
made close acquaintance with the chief classical and
Arabian commentators, translations of the latter having
been published not long before. At first he accepted the
cosmology of this most logical and comprehensive of
thinkers ; and certainly Aristotle's teaching would impress
on him the need of an attentive observation, which that
master did not always carry out. The more observant
scholars of the sixteenth century were aware that men
have not more teeth than women,[2] or two more sutures
in the brain-pan ;[3] that they have more than sixteen ribs,[4]
and that the back of the cranium is not an empty space.[5]
When Bruno studied Copernicus he came to regard the
Stagirite as a clog to human progress. Unlike Aristotle,
he cannot be charged with "moderation to excess": he
accused that "master of those who know"[6] of relying
on his own invention more than on fact and of being a
desiccated sophisticator of truth, perhaps instigated by unworthy motives![7] Imbedded in Aristotle's writings, Bruno

[1] Dante ; *Convito, iv*, 6.
[2] Aristotle ; *Hist. Animal., ij*, 3, 501, *b*, 19.
[3] *Ibid, j*, 8, 491, *b*, 2.   [4] *Ibid, j*, 15, 493, *b*, 14.
[5] *Ibid, j*, 8, 491, *a*, 34.   [6] Dante ; *Inferno, iv*, 131.
[7] *Causa, Dial. iii* ; *Dial. v*.

found fragments of the earlier thinkers of Hellas, who interpreted the Cosmos quite differently; for they had not based their science on uncriticized impressions of sense. Moreover, how should the static view of the Universe, held by the Ionians, be reconciled with its mobility, taught by the Eleatics, or the monism of Parmenides and Heraclitus with the pluralism of Anaxagoras and Leucippus? Sooner or later, he perceived that the atomic hypothesis of Leucippus and Lucretius, modifications of which, accepted by men of science rather more than two and a half centuries after Bruno's time, have proved so fruitful in speculation, went some way towards the required adjustment of such opposite views; and that it was of inestimable importance.[1] Aristotle had abandoned the right path; he had lost sight of the stupendous spectacle opened up by the ancient astronomy and reintroduced, in part, by Copernicus; he had missed that implication of Heraclitus which Cusanus discovered—how contraries condition one another, both negating and affirming at the same time, and how they pass over into one another. Close study of Aristotle made Bruno a rebel, while fragments of a yet earlier philosophy became fruitful in his own.

He read the Arabian thinkers of the tenth, eleventh and twelfth centuries with enthusiasm; for they exhibited something of his own growing passion for physical science; a passion which, possibly, may have been fanned by the "Academy of the Secrets of Nature" (the first scientific society ever formed in modern times), which was started in Naples A.D. 1560, and the influence of which is pretty sure to have penetrated into the courts and cloisters of San Domenico. He gave attention to the doctrines of Averrhoes (whom he greatly reverenced),[2] Avicenna, Avempace, Algazel, and, above all, Avicebron. Averrhoes'

---

[1] *De triplici minimo et mensura.*   [2] *Causa, Dial. iij.*

reasonings as to an endless creation, proceeding from within, and not imposed by an external deity,[1] and as to the individual mind forming part of a universal spirit remained with him;[2] but the servile assimilation of Aristotle by the Arabians soon ceased to commend itself.[3] Of Avicebron's "Fountain of Life" he had only indirect knowledge; but he gathered its drift from comments and quotations, and perceived thereby that the Aristotelian categories of Form and Matter cannot be regarded as ultimate, but require an underlying unity.[4] From Algazel he learned how much habit has to do with the formation of belief; that sacred writings concern practice, not theory, and, consequently, employ the unscientific conceptions, current at the time, to enforce moral truth only.[5]

He had to read the Fathers of the Church, who were regarded as important elements in the education of a Dominican monk, whose intellectual discipline lay in subtle distinctions and metaphysical refinements of thought. In this respect the schoolmen excel; no men have exhibited such subtle discrimination: it was they who built up the triple wall of Catholic defence. The schoolmen, therefore, were studied by Bruno, whose acute mind appreciated the power and profundity of men who were so seriously handicapped by authority and by the jealous watchfulness of Religion. Some years later a Parisian scholar noted in his diary: " He (Bruno) ranks St Thomas above all in his *Summa Contra Gentiles* and *Questionibus Disputatis;*"[6] and, six years later, Bruno said: " I have nothing but

---

[1] *Ibid., Dial. iv.*   [2] *Eroici, P. I., Dial. V, viii.*
[3] *Causa, Dial. iii.*
[4] *Causa, Dial. iij.* For Bruno's indebtedness see Wittman, Michael; *G.B's Beziehungen zu Avencebrol, Archiv. für Gesch. d. Phil. Bana xiii, p.* 14.
[5] *Eroici, P. II., Dial. iv, following poem* 71.
[6] Auvray, L ; *loc. cit., sub Dec.* 7.

respect for the doctors of the Catholic Church, and especially for St Thomas Aquinas, whom, as I said before, I have ever valued and loved as mine own soul; and, as witness to the truth of what I say, you may read in my book *De Monade* these words, ' Thomas Aquinas is the glory and illumination of all kinds of theologians and of peripatetic philosophy.' "[1] Aquinas commanded his respect mainly because he was one who sought for a coherent body of truth, completing the work of his master, Albrecht of Köln. Aquinas hammered the logical works of Aristotle and Christian dogmas into one whole; nay, more, it was he who made an even bolder attempt than that of Albrecht to condense all the knowledge of his time into an encyclopædic statement. The great spirit of Aquinas still seems to haunt his ancient home in Naples and still impresses itself on the best monks of his order. Bruno also admired Albrecht of Köln (Albertus Magnus) and declared that " he had no equal in his time and far surpassed Aristotle." [2] Perhaps he rated this great schoolman so high [3] because of his little book on Alchemy; a subject which embraced much of the very inconsiderable knowledge of nature which men possessed in the thirteenth century.

But, except as an intellectual whetstone, such study is the least fruitful; and the inadequacy of formal logic to scientific investigation (useful as it proves for the detection of deductive fallacy) was soon apparent to Bruno. Over and over again in his works he expresses his scorn for the barren logic of the Peripatetics; for they not only blindly follow Aristotle, but they misconstrue him and avert their eyes from gazing at natural things. Could Aristotle

[1] *Doc. xij.*   [2] *Oratio Valedictoria.*
[3] It is worth noting that Dante places Albert, the universal Doctor, with Thomas the Angelic Doctor among the spirits of the Wise (*Parad.*, *x*, 97–99).

have been summoned from the grave he had been with Bruno.

Perhaps it was as a part of his theologic education that Bruno applied himself to Hebrew. We know that he recited the 86th Psalm in the original before the Pope;[1] he uses Hebrew letters as symbols, and would appear to have attributed some mystic significance to the language.

II. THE NEO-PLATONISTS

When the literature of Hellas reached Italy in the previous century, the soil was ripe for its reception. Scholasticism had exhausted itself. Men were weary of dead distortions, desiccated dissections of reality, and they turned their eyes from the mediæval museum to Plato, " the dove cleaving the thin air," and to Plotinus, " the eagle soaring over Plato's tomb." They listened no longer to tired, wearisome voices from the cloister, and they hailed Plato and Plotinus as heavenly messengers. Plotinus and the Alexandrian scholars, repelled by Aristotelian formalism, tried to grasp the flow of life, its passion and the source of its passion, by insight rather than by discursive thought; and, what they achieved, they strove to express in allegory and metaphor; for they felt the impossibility of putting ultimate reality into logical form.[2] Ficino and his fellows translated Plato and the Neo-Platonists, and Bruno read these translations as well as the Platonic writings of the translators. We know from his character and from his Neo-Platonic works[3] how he must have lived in his own enthusiasm and found spiritual nourishment in thoughts too vital, not merely to

---

[1] *Cfr. p.* 13.

[2] Zimmermann, R ; *Gesch. d. Æsthetik, Vienna,* 1858, *p.* 123.

[3] Notably from the *Eroici.* Also from *De Umbris* and *Sigillus Sigillorum.*

be put by the syllogistic method of the schoolmen, but even to be quite definitely expressed.

A modern writer has justly observed that Plotinus is " the greatest individual thinker between Aristotle and Descartes."[1] Much in Neo-Platonism fascinated Bruno, especially the conception of the universe as a process of production from One who suffers no loss thereby,[2] and Plotinus' explanation of the lower by the higher ;[3] much Alexandrian thinking became an integral part of his own philosophy, often transmuted and improved, however.

St Clement had declared that " we cannot discern what God is so much as what He is not "; Cusanus had taught the same thing, and Bruno accepted the final limitation of human reason and experience and Plotinus' doctrine of a being above discursive thought, above good and evil and beauty, and above the distinctions, within the Will, of power and freedom and necessity. For our thought, being discursive, is imperfect.[4] The Absolute produces Mind contemplating itself ; i.e., it is self-conscious ; and from Mind proceeds the Soul of the World.   This is the trinity of being, and The One participates in all ; souls, separate in space and time, being present to one another in the Soul of the Whole.[5] The Soul of the World is not in time, but, just as light (which in Plotinus' and also in Bruno's time was supposed to suffer no loss in transmission) passes by gradations into darkness, so does the Ineffable pass, without loss, through gradations of being ; and, even as privation of light

---

[1] Whittaker, T ; *The Neo-Platonists, Camb.*, 1901, *p.* 34.

[2] Plotinus ; *Enn., V*, 1, 6.

[3] *Ibid., Enn., V*, 9, 4.

[4] *Ibid., Enn. V*, 1, 9 ; *V*, 4, 1.—Bruno, *Sigillus*, P. *I*, § 16 ; § 30 ; P. *II*, § 11.—Compare the profound and original thought of our English philosopher Bradley ; *Appearance and Reality*, and its reflection in Taylor, A. E ; *Problem of Conduct.*

[5] *Enn., iij*, 9, 3 ; *v*, 1, 1.—Bruno, *Sigillus*, P. *I.*, § 31.

is darkness, so is the privation of God evil;[1] though even in evil there is a rational order which issues in good.[2] Although individual souls are comprised and co-present to one another in the Soul of the World, they are separate in lower spheres. Having descended from the Absolute, they ever tend to return to Him[3] "who is at once thine innermost self and thine unattainable desire."

Plotinus further perceived that life is no mere collection of particles; he makes the unextended, individual soul form its own body; it dwells wholly in every part which it animates; for, can a part act vitally when separated from the whole to which it belongs?[4] The individual soul is the cause of its own thought and action, but is determined in its context.[5] The universe and its souls are in activity without beginning or end; all things being traces or shadows, in vastly differing measures, of the Supernal. Bruno maintained this doctrine of shades, vestiges, throughout his life.[6] Like Plotinus Bruno accepted universal animism; so did every thinker of his own time; in fact, the view dated from Thales.[7]

"The common mark of all Alexandrian philosophy is that it regards divine revelation as the highest source of knowledge."[8] Porphyry tells us that Plotinus was rapt into ecstatic vision of the Absolute four times, being united with Him; and that he (Porphyry) had the experience

---

[1] *Enn.*, *v*, 1, 1; *v*, 1, 6; *vj*, 7, 9.—Bruno, *De Umb.*, *Int. I, IV*; *Sig. P. I*, § 32.

[2] *Enn.*, *iii*, 2, 18.—Bruno, *Sig. P. I*, § 32.

[3] *Enn.*, *iv*, 4, 36.—Bruno, *De Umbr.*, *Int. VII; Eroici, passim*.

[4] *Enn.*, *iii*, 6, 4; *iv*, 3, 21; *vj*, 4, 5.—Bruno, *De Umb.*, *Conc. v; Causa, Dial. II; De triplicis min., I, iij*.

[5] *Enn.*, *iij*, 1.—Bruno, *De Immenso, Cap. x*.

[6] *De Imag. Comp., Cap. j; Cap. iv*.

[7] Aristotle; *De Anima, I*, 25.—Cicero; *De Natura Deorum, I*, 10.

[8] Windelband, W; *Hist. Phil., tr.* Tufts, *London*, 1896, *p*. 219.

once.[1] Plotinus writes of this emotional and mystical union wherein there is absorption in sublime tranquillity, and thought is still.[2] There is, he says, "a flight from the alone to the alone." The soul suddenly becomes pure intellect; but after intellectual discipline. Bruno accepted such experiences as miracles of faith; but held that one may, by strenuous effort and by the study and contemplation of Nature, penetrate lower "shades" and reach the rapturous light.[3] But such illumination is rational as opposed to the alogical illumination of the pure mystic.[4]

Through translations, or more directly, Bruno became acquainted with Philo Judaeus, Porphyry, Jamblichus, the pseudo-Orpheus, the pseudo-Hermes and other masters of the Alexandrian school. These authors were deeply

[1] Porphyrius; *De Vita Plotini.*

[2] *Enn.* ; *v*, 3, 17; *v*, 8, 11; *vj*, 7.

[3] *Cabala, Dial. I; Eroici, Parte I, Dial. II; Parte II, Dial. II.*

[4] All mystics, whatever their country, period or religion, seem to agree as to the main characteristics of their experience. Self-consciousness ceases; the subject of the experience feels himself lifted out of self and out of thought. To some, this beatific vision would seem to come suddenly ; to others, only after preparation. The condition is less rare than is supposed ; and it is most frequent in people of very high mental endowment and practical common sense. These excellent witnesses all declare that intellectual activity disappears and is replaced by a single emotion, a feeling of one-ness with the Absolute. Tennyson frequently experienced something of the kind ; he speaks of it as a "waking trance," which would come upon him from boyhood up, when he was alone, and which he could frequently bring on by repeating his own name : "All at once as it were, out of the intensity of the consciousness of individuality, the individuality itself seemed to dissolve and fade away into boundless being, and this not a confused state, but the clearest of the clearest, the surest of the surest, utterly beyond words, when death was an almost laughable impossibility ; the loss of personality (if so it were) *seeming* no extinction, but the only true life." There would seem to be a far-off approach to this condition experienced by a few exceptional people during the administration of anæsthetics ; but no psychologists, mental pathologists or specialists in hypnotism would seem to have given the subject much attention.

permeated by the Pythagorean doctrine of the mystical nature of numbers; and this fascinated Bruno, who was instructed in the mathematics of his time.[1] Jamblichus and other Neo-Platonic writers had a strong drift towards the occult, and with this tendency the Neo-Platonists had profound sympathy. Pico della Mirandola exhibited a craze for the Cabala,—that curious collection of rabbinistic mysticism to which the ninth and thirteenth centuries gave birth. From such sources as Pico, Bruno absorbed what these writers conceived that they knew of the lore of Chaldea, Assyria, Persia, India and Egypt. There was little or no idea of the historical development of thought, and every man dragged in each and every writer who could be supposed to support his own convictions, and would quote them all as of equally authoritative value. Moreover, as in the time of Dante, natural facts and even words were held to contain symbolic significance and to be adumbrations and indices of truth. Bruno did not escape from these intellectual habits, which were universal. He drew much mystical lore from Heinrich Cornelius Agrippa[2] of Nettesheim (1486–1535). Agrippa's work on the "Vanity of Human Knowledge" led him to take an ironical interest in "asinity."[3]

III. RAYMOND LULLY

In early youth Bruno began the study of one whom he calls "an untutored hermit, filled with divine genius";[4] one who, so he thought, builded wiser than he knew. Raymond Lully of Minorca (1235–1315), known as "the Enlightened Doctor," was a contemporary of Duns Scotus,

[1] Bruno; *De Monade, passim.*
[2] Agrippa, H. C ; *De occulta philosophia, fol., Coloniæ,* 1533.
[3] Bruno, *Il Cabala con l'aggiunta de l'asino Cillenico.*
[4] *De Lampade Combinatoria.*

the "Subtle Doctor." He gave up the life of a man of pleasure for Franciscan severity, and set himself to study in order to qualify himself for persuading the Moslem of the sweet reasonableness of Christianity. Lully's spirit was unconquerable, and the strange happenings which he encountered in many lands surpass the most extravagant imagination of the novelists of adventure. His zeal for the Faith burned as strong as that of Bruno for philosophic truth, and the example of Lully may have been a spur to Bruno in his youth and may have sustained him later in his chequered and nomadic life.

Lully found time to leave behind him 321 works on all branches of knowledge.[1] Of these the most important was his "Great Art" (*Ars Magna*). Scholasticism found Lully indifferent to it; but he believed he could prove the truth of Christianity by reason.[2] His attempt to do so was judiciously condemned by that great dictatorship in Theology—the University of Paris. Since Lully was a Franciscan, his works proved distasteful to the rival Dominican order, who set to work, and in 1376 a Bull of Gregory XI condemned his works as heretical. But this was said to be a forgery, and was formally annulled by Martin V (1376). The Spaniard's system was highly valued by many distinguished thinkers in the 16th century; but, two years after Bruno left Naples, Lullism was once again attacked as heretical.

The spirit of Neo-Platonism still breathes in "The Great Art," and the work is regulated by Pythagorean teaching as to the mystic nature of numbers. The art is based on the theory that, from certain given ideas, it is possible to disengage all ideas which are implicitly contained

---

[1] Antonio, Nicolas; *Bibl. Hispan. vetus; Hispan. scrip. ad a.* 1500; *cur. Bayerio.*

[2] Lullius, R; *De Articulis Fidei.*

in them, and so to track and discover knowledge. Lully
sets down for us what he considers to be those objects of
knowledge which are indisputable and universally accepted
and acknowledged, and also the methods of procedure by
which our intelligence operates. He then places in a
circle, called the key to discovery, nine fundamental questions which may be asked. Within this circle, which may
be regarded as fixed, are five other concentric circles, which
can be made to revolve, each one independently of the
others, and each of these circles is divided into 9 compartments. By following given rules of a simple character, the
middle term of any syllogism was held to be discoverable.
For speed in working, the circles and their compartments
were indicated by symbols. Bruno saw in this art the
germs of that complete and symbolic logic at which Lully
aimed; a vision which also aroused the hope of Leibnitz
and which occupied much attention during the last quarter
of the last century. He found it invaluable for the purposes
of artificial memory, and the first and last of his printed
works, as well as many of the volumes which lie between,
are devoted to improvements in Lullism. His mastery
of the "Enlightened Doctor" proved useful to him as an
introduction to scholars and to seats of learning.

IV. CUSANUS

Cusanus (Nicolaus Chrypffs of Cues, 1401–1464), the
son of a fisherman on the Mosel, became a cardinal and the
close friend of Æneas Silvius (Pius II). One of the most
remarkable men of his age, he was the earliest of those
speculative dogmatists who lie midway between Scholasticism and Critical Philosophy. Bruno owed to this remarkable mind his own strongest philosophic impulse and many

of his own views;[1] he speaks of Cusanus as "divine" and
"a great discoverer."[2]   Cusanus, as became a bold and
independent thinker, tried to rationalize theology, and made
more than one attempt to expound the Trinity as three
abstracted aspects of God and His universe, which are one.[3]
He held that sense-impressions are united in the activity
of thought; yet knowledge at its best and highest is merely
an image of being; and therefore can only approximate
towards, and can never be identical with Reality.   At best,
knowledge is as the polygon, which, while it remains a
composite figure, can never become a circle.[4]   Cusanus
declared the relativity of all knowledge; but, by intuition,
men can rise above antimonies and hold contraries together
in a unity; and when we do this we are doing, in our
finite measure, what God does.   By this doctrine of intuition, Cusanus saves himself from scepticism.   Yet, though
he is content to utter "O altitudo!"[5] and finds God incomprehensible, he declares Him to be all things, and that He
could not be other than He is; this gave rise to accusations
of pantheism.   The negation of greater imperfection, says
Cusanus, is nearer truth than is the negation of the higher
attributes.   In other words there are degrees in truth and
reality.[6]   The universe is the unfolding of what, in Deity,
is unity; just as a line is the unfolding of a point.   If we
reflect, we shall find that to a true maximum nothing can

---

[1] The indebtedness of B. to Cusanus is exaggerated by F. J
Clemens in his *G. B und Nic. v. Cusa, Bonn,* 1847; but, in spite of
its prejudice, this remains a valuable work.

[2] *Spaccio, I, j, at beginning; Infinito, III; Oratio. Valedic.*

[3] Cusanus, *De docta ignorantia,* i, 7; ij, 7; *Alchoran,* 6, 7, 8; *De
possest.*

[4] Cusanus, *De docta ignorantia.*

[5] "I love to lose myself in a mystery, to pursue my Reason to an
O altitudo," Sir T. Browne, *Religio Medici.*

[6] *Cfr.* the modern view of Bradley, Appearance and Reality,
c. *xxiv.*

be added; from a true minimum nothing can be taken
away; man can perceive therefore that, in Ultimate Reality,
maximum and minimum coincide.[1]   The universe is boundless in space and time, and the centre of the universe is
precisely where the observer stands in it, a doctrine to
which Bruno was much indebted.   Nature is animate and
articulated; everything being a more or less imperfect mirror
of the universe in its own place, and preserving itself in
relation to and community with other things.[2]   In conscious
experience there is indivisible continuity; but in things
there is an indivisible minimum.[3]   All these views of
Cusanus reappear in Bruno, often enlarged and enriched.
Cusanus' teaching that reason unfolds itself in numbers[4]
strengthened Bruno's Pythagorean tendency.   The German
saw that the universe can, at least in part, be explained
scientifically by the application of mathematics to the
results of observation; and Bruno is his eager pupil.   It
was probably the study of Cusanus which set him on the
track of the infinity of the universe of innumerable worlds
and of the interpenetration of everything in the whole.[5]
There was as yet no really philosophical or scientific
method: only an eager questioning of experience; but
Cusanus made the first attempt since the days of Greek
science to explain the universe on scientific principles.
He foreshadowed the law of inertia, and declared, in 1436,
that the earth is in motion;[6] but since we have no fixed

[1] Cusanus; *De docta ignorantia; De sapientia libri tres. Cfr.*
Bruno; *De triplici minimo.*
[2] Cusanus; *De ludo globi.*
[3] Cusanus; *De idiota, iij. Cfr.* Bruno; *De triplici min; De
monade.*
[4] Cusanus; *De conjecturis; De visione Dei. Cfr.* Bruno, *De
monade.*
[5] Clemens, F. J.; *op. cit., pp.* 142, 143.
[6] Cusanus; *De reparatione Calendarii.*

point from which to observe this, its movement cannot be measured.

The mysticism of his countryman Eckhardt reappeared in Cusanus,[1] and reinforced Bruno's own mystical tendency.

V. COPERNICUS AND LATER THINKERS

Not a century after Cusanus, in 1543, Nicolaus Copernicus (1473–1543) expounded the theory that the earth revolves round the sun, though he did not extend his conclusions, which he drew from mathematical considerations, to the sidereal heavens. Bruno got hold of Copernicus' work.[2] Probably it was in the monastic library; for it had been dedicated to Paul III at the entreaty of friends who feared what might otherwise follow, and one Osiander, a priest of Nuremberg, wrote a preface, in which he protests that the work is not presented as truth, but because it furnishes improved practical utility for astronomical computation.[3] Bruno knew that this mendacious apology for speaking the truth was not written by Copernicus, who had asserted his right to deal with the problem in his own way.[4] The thoughtful pondered over Copernicus' book, perceiving that he had applied Ockham's razor and dealt a blow to the bad method of multiplying hypotheses to explain observed facts of the same kind. It was irrational to suppose that Nature does not proceed straight to her goal. The new theory administered a shock to the fashionable Aristotelian physics and cosmogony, built on sense-perceptions, and, in time, it came to be heartily accepted and extended by Bruno, who had so early begun to doubt the

---

[1] Cusanus ; *De venatio sapientiæ.*
[2] Copernicus; *De orbium cœlestium revolutionibus.*
[3] It is obvious that Osiander was no pragmatist !
[4] Bruno ; *Cena, Dial. III, Seconda prop. di Nundinio.*

deliverances of sensation. There was general resistance to the new view. Those with the spirit of the Renaissance in them felt that a blow was struck at their exaltation of humanity; the pious opined that the fall of the official science of the Church might bring down much more. For Bruno, the vivid and realistic pictures of Dante were replaced by another kind of realism, colder perhaps, but only colder to the unimaginative, appealing less, perhaps, to ordinary human sympathy, but far more powerfully to intellectual vision. He was prepared to trust Reason and follow her whithersoever she might lead ; and he saw that, if the importance of man as a being was diminished, his intellect, which could hold the whole solar system in its grasp, gained infinitely in dignity.

Bruno read "The Nature of Things," by Bernardino Telesio (1509–1588). Local patriotism would prepare him to appreciate the writings of a man who, born at Cozena, had founded the Cosentina Academy at Naples. Telesio insisted on the importance of observation and took for his motto, "not by reason, but by sense." But he admitted that the mind co-operates with sensation.[1] Bruno calls him "the most judicious Telesio."[2] Girolamo Cardano (1501–1576) was another writer whom Bruno valued for his appreciation of physical enquiry. He used much superstitious information which can be traced to Cardano, or to the writings of that half-mad genius in motley, Aureol Theophrast Paracelsus (1490–1541). Paracelsus attracted Bruno because of his attempt to determine the chemical constitution of things ; because he held all creatures to be emanations from a world-soul,[3] and because he taught a doctrine deduced from this, that throughout the whole choir

[1] Telesius; *De rerum natura.* *Cfr.* Sensini, T ; *Sul pensiero filosofico di G. B.*, 1907, *p.* 13.

[2] *Causa, Dial. III.*

[3] Bruno ; *Causa, Dial. III.*

of heaven and furniture of earth there exists a subtle sympathy. Although Pietro Angelo Manzoli (Palingenius) held the universe to be infinite, he did not produce much effect on Bruno. Indeed, it seems doubtful whether Bruno ever read this Ferrarese poet, for he speaks of him as being a German.[1]

Bruno was vastly interested in the mathematics of his day, and, later, gave the subject much thought and evinced considerable originality in it, sometimes of a mistaken kind.[2] Indeed, like Bacon he had " taken all knowledge to be his province." Most of his acquisitions must have been made during the quiet years at Naples. Henceforth he was a wanderer, earning his bread; and what small leisure befell him was given up to creative work.

[1] *Oratio Valedic.* For the effects of these later writers on Bruno's mind and work, see Tocco, F ; *Fonti più recenti della f. del B., Acad. dei Lincei, Rendiconti ser., j, pp.* 503 *sqq;* 585 *sqq.*

[2] *Cfr.* J. B. Nolani *Articuli centum et sexaginta adversus mathematicos ; De monade; De triplici minimo.*

CHAPTER IV

WANDERINGS THROUGH ITALY. NAPLES TO GENEVA
(1576–79)

IT was a common thing in those days for monks to wander
from district to district and even from country to country.
By this means the individual monk was enabled to see men
and cities and enlarge his mind, while, at the same time, he
got exercise and improved his health; the monastic community, too, benefited by interchange of ideas and was
enlivened by news from the outer world. The doors of a
monastery were always kept wide open to a wandering
brother of the order; so Bruno, escaped from Naples, would
find no difficulty in obtaining hospitality. He boldly claimed
it at the actual headquarters of his order. The church of
Santa Maria sopra Minerva stands on the site of a ruined
temple, opposite another which has only been robbed of its
gilded tiles and its gods: it and its famous monastery confront the yet more famous temple of Agrippa.

He was not left there long in peace. "I learned," he
says, "that, after I left Naples, certain works of St
Chrysostom and St Jerome containing the forbidden annotations of Erasmus, which I had secretly used and thrown into
the privy when I came away to prevent their being found,
were discovered."[1]

Erasmus had "laid the egg of the Reformation"; in
1527, Edward Lee, afterwards Archbishop of York,
extracted twenty-one heretical opinions from his writings.

[1] *Doc. xiij.*

The veneration due to the saintly fathers of the Church had not prevented the Congregation of the Index from prohibiting the works of Chrysostom and Jerome, so here lay a two-fold fault.

Mocenigo, who, later, denounced Bruno to the Inquisition, made a curious statement. Bruno "told me that the Inquisition sought a quarrel with him in Rome on 130 points, and that he made off while they were being presented because he was credited with throwing the informer, or the man whom he believed to be such, into the Tiber."[1] The Inquisitors absolutely ignored this statement; so, clearly Bruno was innocent of the crime. Mocenigo was a spiteful person, not over scrupulous or exact in his statements, while Bruno was no liar or vain braggart. It is difficult, however, judging from other statements made by Mocenigo, to believe that this one was wholly a gratuitous invention. The recently discovered manuscript-diary in the Biblothèque Nationale contains the following passage. "7th Dec. [1585]. Jordanus came again. . . . He has been an exile from Italy eight years, as much by reason of a murder committed by his brother, whereby he incurred hatred and peril of life, as to escape the calumnies of Inquisitors, who are ignorant men, and, not understanding his philosophy, declare him to be a heretic."[2]

Probably the man who made this entry was Guillaume Cotin, Librarian to the Abbey of St Victor. If so, he was old and ill at the time. Whoever he was, the diarist did not always catch Bruno's remarks, or his memory failed him. But he was a scrupulously precise person. If he cannot catch a name, he leaves it out ; if he suspects that it is incorrectly caught, he erases it.[3] Possibly a brother of

---

[1] *Doc. I.*
[2] *M.S. Fr.* 20309, *fol.* 354, *V. sqq.*   Auvray, L. ; *op. cit., sub* Dec. *7th.*   [3] Auvray, L. ; *op. cit.*

Bruno was concerned in some "taking off" so common in Italy, and especially common in Southern Italy, in those days. But, if so, how did it affect Giordano? Was it connected with the citation for heresy? Was there danger of vendetta? Was there influence at work, or something connected with the case which would fatally weight the minds of Bruno's superiors? It is an inviting puzzle; but the data are imperfect; and ingenious and plausible hypotheses are nearly always exploded on the discovery of fresh facts.

He contrived to get away from the gathering storm. He cast his monkish garb aside, resumed his baptismal name of Philip and was no longer known as Jordanus while he remained in Italy.[1] He made his way over the three hundred miles or more which lay between Rome and the Republic of Genoa, where bloody faction-fights and the long struggle of the various classes of the city for mastery still prevailed. The Genoese, whom Dante denounced as barbarians,[2] were ever more famous for their quarrels and commercial enterprise than for their encouragement of learning, and there was little inducement to a scholar to remain in that unquiet city. He observed one thing with scornful amusement: it so struck him that he refers to it twice.[3] "At Genoa I saw the monks of [S. Maria di] Costello exhibit a tail with a veil over it, and making folk kiss it, saying, 'don't touch: kiss it; this is the holy relic of that blessed ass which was made worthy to bear our God from Mount Olivet to Jerusalem. Worship it, kiss it—and give alms. Ye shall receive an hundred fold[4] and inherit eternal life.'"[5] Bruno must have been accustomed to miracles in Naples such as the liquefaction of the blood of

---

[1] *Doc. xiij.*　　　　　　　[2] *Inferno, xxxiij,* 151-3.
[3] *Il Candelajo, Atto I, Sc. i.; Spaccio, III, ij.*
[4] *Mark, x.* 30.　　　　　　[5] *Matth., xix,* 29.

St Januarius, which still continues to take place four times yearly, and we shall find him ready to accept strange things as due to natural causes, not yet explained. But this base, mercenary fraud was too much for his credulity: it symbolized the "asinity" he despised.

On the Riviera Ponente, between thirty and forty miles from Genoa, lies Noli. It is a quaint, ancient little coast-town, at the head of a rocky gulf, embosomed in vineyards and backed by picturesque mountains which almost encircle it and are close beyond its high walls. It was then a prosperous little place, governing itself under the protection of the Genoese Republic. "Here," says Bruno, "I supported myself during four or five months by teaching grammar to children [1] and the sphere to certain men of condition." [2] The subject of Astronomy was then called "The Sphere," because the earth was supposed to be the central kernel of a series of transparent spheres, enclosing the sun, moon, planets and fixed stars—*spheres* for the metaphysical reason that the circle is the perfect figure. These spheres were supposed to revolve round the earth with uniform motion, because that is the most perfect rate of velocity. Such questions as the exact situation of heaven and the precise nature of the divine ideas embodied in the skies were included in teaching "The Sphere." It was a popular subject for writing about and lecturing on, and ladies as well as men read papers on it at the literary clubs—the Italian "Academies." Probably Bruno taught these "gentlemen of condition" more concerning "The Sphere" than was expected from him.

For reasons which he does not give, he turned back a few miles to Savona, the former rival of Genoa, and, even then, a busy port. It probably provided Bruno with little more than pleasant prospects amid gardens of orange and

[1] *Doc. vij.*   [2] *Doc. ix.*

lemon trees; for, at the end of fifteen days, he made for Turin, the capital of Piedmont.[1] There is a curious story that a fourth process against the fugitive monk was issued at Vercelli by the Genoese Republic.[2] The statement is far from inconceivable, but it comes from a suspected source; it is said to have been derived from the sentence of the Inquisition, a document which was non-producible at the time the assertion was made.[3]

Turin was then under Filiberto Emmanuele, one of the most enlightened monarchs of a line which, during ten centuries, has proved itself the astutest of the ruling houses of Europe. The reigning duke fostered both science and literature, and, a few years before, had reconstituted the University, making it one of the first in Italy. No town in Europe is built on so regular a plan as Turin is: Bruno found it a city of delight,[4] " but, getting no satisfactory sustenance there, I came down the Po to Venice, where I put up a month and a half in Frezzaria"[5]—the lane of shops at the end of the great piazza, opposite St Mark's.

To the eye, all was bright; the carvings on splendid palaces gave evidence of the taste, the wealth and the pride of Venice; every uncarved wall was resplendent with the noble designs of some great master, wet and new, or, at least, still unflaked and unfaded, and the canals below reflected their gorgeous hues. But Venice was in a terrible state within. For two long years plague had devastated the city, carrying off 42,000 people, the aged Titian among them. Venice offered a fairly safe asylum from the Inquisition, however; yet how should Bruno live? In that frank

---

[1] Doc. ix.

[2] De Martinis, Raffaele; G. B., Napoli, 1886, p. 12.

[3] Cfr. Atti della R. Acc. delle sc. mor. e pol, Napoli, XXIV, pp. 468–69; Archiv. f. Gesch. d. Phil., iv, pp. 348–50. See also chapter XX of this work.

[4] Spaccio, III, ij.   [5] Doc. ix.

succinct account of his days which he gave to the inquisitors, we read : " Whilst there, in order to furnish me with a few pieces to live on, I got a book printed, entitled ' The Signs of the Times.' But I shewed it first to the Revd. Father Master Remigio of Florence,"[1] a monk of Bruno's own order, who had gained distinction because of his learning and his version of the Psalms.[2]

Probably Bruno now made up his mind to try for better fortune in France, where Italians were well received and Italian influence was paramount. He continues : " Leaving Venice, I went on to Padua, where I found some Dominican fathers of my acquaintance. They persuaded me to wear my habit again, showing me that it was more convenient to travel with than without it. With this idea in my mind, I went to Bergamo and had a robe made of cheap white cloth, and over this I wore the scapular which I kept with me when I left Rome."[3] It was common enough for monks to doff the habit and don the gayest attire ; but they were bound to retain the scapular : to cast this aside was regarded as a very serious offence.

On the road to Bergamo, while resting at Brescia, he seems to have found a monk shut up because he had given way to a prophetic impulse : the poor brother thought himself a great theologian and spake with tongues. Bruno gave him vinegar and polypod and restored him to the brethren, " the same ass that he was before."[4] So did Æneas Silvius cure a demoniac with a little necessary medicine.

We know that he visited Milan, for he tells us that it was in that place that he first heard of a future friend and helper,

[1] *Doc. ix.*
[2] *Scriptores Ordinis Prædicatorum, II, p.* 259, referred to by Berti, *pp.* 71–72 of the edition of 1868.
[3] *Doc. ix.*   [4] *Sigillus Sigillorum*, § 48.

Sir Philip Sidney, "that very illustrious and excellent cavalier, whose acute spirit, not to speak of his renowned manners, is so rare that it were difficult to find his like out-side Italy; or within it."[1] Sidney had been travelling in Italy two or three years before, unattended by the usual bear-leader; he studied at Padua and, at Venice, got Paul Veronese to paint his portrait. Italy was the indispensable but highly dangerous finishing school for the courtier in manners, letters, art and life. Roger Ascham tells us that the Englishman usually returned "worse transformed than ever was any in Circe's Court," and that during the nine days which he himself spent in Venice, he found "more liberty to sin than ever I heard tell of in our noble city of London in nine years." Sidney wrote to Languet that if the Turks should conquer Italy "its vile allurements would so ensnare them that they would tumble down without being pushed." Sidney appears to have been one of the very few who "listened to the enchantment of the Siren's song untouched."

Bruno made his way over the snows of Mont Cenis with the intention of trying his fortune at Lyons. At the end of the long, deep, inhospitable valley along which the mule-track wound above the rushing waters of the Arc, he came to an inviting, fertile region, where, built beside two rivers and between two hills, lay the capital of Savoy. A Dominican monastery was built at Chambéry thirty years before; but he found no very kindly reception thereat. He complained to an Italian monk who chanced to be there at the time and who replied, "I forewarn you that you will get no civility in these parts, and, the farther you go, the less you will find of it."[2] Whereupon, Bruno decided to leave the route for Lyons and take the one to Geneva.

[1] *Cena, Dial. II.*   [2] *Doc. ix.*

CHAPTER V

AT GENEVA, LYONS AND TOULOUSE

FOR three years Bruno had sojourned in various Italian States, receiving hospitality in spacious, dignified monasteries or under the homelier shelter of some kindly Italian roof. Nowhere were the refinements of life wanting. Across the mountains, he found a stern, rough folk, who knew not the use of the fork or the amenities of the table. The guest at the inn was called upon to share his bed with more than one bedfellow, and might consider himself fortunate if he arrived at the inflexible hour for the common meal, and had neither to forfeit it nor to tarry for it.

At Naples, Bruno read St Augustine in secret, so we may suppose that he felt some interest in his writings. The austere and naked theology of that Father had been strengthened and hardened by John Calvin. That remarkable fugitive from France to Geneva had carried with him even more of the vigour of the legislator than of the dexterity of the controversialist. Conscientious in his rejection of a mediating priesthood, he nonetheless was visited by no scruples when he established at Geneva that worst of theocratic governments—the tyranny of a board of theologians. His sectaries established and maintained the outward form of a "city of God," less accomplished, less broad-minded, and even more coercive than ever Rome was; and, when Calvin died, his mantle fell on a man of like mind—his fellow-exile, Théodore de Bèze of Vézelay. Hardly more than twenty years before

41

Bruno's arrival, Calvin's perfervid zeal for petty theological
doctrines persuaded him to betray Miguel Serveto y Rives
to the Inquisition, and when Servetus escaped and sought
an asylum in Geneva, it was Calvin who sent him to the
stake.   Under Bèze, drastic discipline was dealt out to
anyone who offended against the most meticulous article
prescribed by the autocratic congregation of theologians
who formed a state within the political state and were
supreme over it.[1]

Nevertheless Bruno knew that Geneva opened her
gates to those who sought refuge for conscience-sake
and that independent thinkers from his own beloved Italy
had found asylum and established an Italian evangelical
church there.   It dated from 1542.   Bruno put up at a
hostelry and inscribed his name at the Academy.   One
may still read in the Rector's Register the name " *Philippus
Brunus Nolanus, sacræ theologiæ professor*, 20 May 1579,"
written in Bruno's bold firm hand.[2]

The presence of a wandering monk would excite little
surprise in most places.   It was quite usual to encounter
such travellers, who might wish to visit libraries, or who
found the atmosphere of their monastery uncongenial.
But a monk in this abode of the saintly elect could not
fail to attract attention; although Catholic princes sometimes passed through the city and even visited the most
distinguished of the exiles, the Neapolitan Galeazzo
Caracciolo, marquis of Vico and nephew of Pope Paul IV.
Di Vico had forsaken wife and children for faith's sake
and had been regarded by Calvin as a pillar of the church.

---

[1] *Cfr.* Bolsec, H. ; *Hist. de la vie etc. de J. Calvin, Lyons,* 1577.—
Bonnet, J ; *Lettres françaises de J. C, Paris* 1854.—Roget, A ; *Histoire
du peuple de Genève etc.* 1870-83.—Brunnem, K ; *M. Servetus, Berlin,*
1865.—Rilliet, A ; *Rélation du procès contre S., Geneva,* 1844.

[2] It will be observed that Bruno retains his baptismal name in the
Protestant city.

Indeed, Calvin dedicated one of his works to him. Di Vico was a kindly and honourable man, zealous for doctrine, but ready to welcome and aid any distressed fellow-country-man.[1] It was not long before he paid Bruno a visit.

"He asked me who I was and if I had come there to stay and avow the religion of the city. I then gave an account of myself and of why I had left my order, and added that I had no intention of professing the faith of the city, for I did not know what it might be; and that my object was to dwell in freedom and safety rather than anything else. The Marquis advised me to cast away my monkish garb at any rate. So I made trunk-hose and other gear from some stuff I had by me, and he and other Italians gave me a sword, hat, cloak and other needful clothes and other things that I might support myself by correcting proofs. I remained two months thus employed, going sometimes to hear Italians and Frenchmen expound and preach. I listened oftenest to Nicolo Balbani of Lucca, who expounded the epistles of Paul and preached the gospels."[2] Balbani was pastor of the Italian church and a great friend of Di Vico.

It would not need the insistence of his new friends to induce Bruno to read the works of Calvin. His inquiring mind led him to dip into all the chief writers of the Refor-mation. In the record of his trial at Venice we read the frank declaration: "I have read books by Melancthon, Luther, Calvin and other heretics beyond the Alps, not to acquire their doctrine or for improvement, for I think them more ignorant than myself, but out of sheer curiosity. I have never kept them in my possession—I mean those who professedly treat of matters opposed and repugnant to the

---

[1] *Cfr. Specimen Italiae Reformatae, una c. Syllabo Reformatorum Ital., Lugd., Bat.,* 1765, *p.* 205.—Berti, *op. cit., ed. of* 1886, *p.* 91 *sqq.*
[2] *Doc. ix.*

Catholic faith; while I have indeed kept by me other condemned works, such as those of Raymond Lully and other
writers who treat of philosophical matters. I scorn both
them and their doctrines." [1]

But, on his arrival at Geneva, before he knew much about
Calvinistic administration, he may have flirted with the idea
of joining the Reformed Church. John Vincent told Cotin
(if the diarist were he), rather more than six years later,
that "Jordanus said [to the Genevese] he would have
attached himself to their religion had they not so dishonoured
him." [2] Probably Vincent got this on hearsay; but it is
likely to be true. We shall deal with the "dishonour"
directly. Bruno did not vex himself overmuch with the
vain disputes of theology. He conceived it to be his business to try to get at the truth of Nature by reason,
and he confessed to his judges that he was no theological
expert.[3] But theology can be undermined by philosophy
and physical science. Bruno's intrepid zeal for truth landed
him in difficulties when little more than two months had
elapsed from his arrival in Geneva. One of the evangelical
shepherds of the city was Antoine de la Faye of Chateaudun,
a man who had taken his medical degree at Padua five years
before and was a refugee.[4] Most likely Aristotle was the
subject of dispute. How long Bruno continued to accept
the authority of Aristotle, we do not know; but he came
after much thought to perceive the errors of his Cosmology
and Physics.[5] Ever a fighter, a valiant knight-errant of
Truth, he was as impulsive and imprudent as courageous.
Rebellion against accepted views is always strangely limited
in its extent, and the governing body of the Genevese

---

[1] *Doc. xij.*   [2] Auvray, L ; *op. cit., sub* 15 *Mar.* 1856.
[3] *Doc. xij.*
[4] Haag, Eugène et Emile ; *La France Protestante*, 1846–59, *t vj,
pp.* 185, 186.   [5] Bruno ; *Infinito, Dial. I.*

reformers retained not a few of the prejudices of their fore-
fathers ; they regarded Aristotle as hardly less authoritative
than Holy Writ. Théodore de Bèze told Pierre de la
Ramée that they had resolved not to depart one jot or tittle
from the judgements of Aristotle ; and among those who
supported this decision was de la Faye, who, just now, was
lecturing at the Academy on Philosophy.

If, as a passage in Genevese records would seem to indicate, it was on Aristotle that Bruno attacked de la Faye,
he began a warfare at Geneva which occupied the best
years of a rebellious life—a determined and persistent effort
to upheave the dead load of obsolete authority and give
freedom to the human spirit once again. He felt, to use the
language of Bacon, that the ancient cosmology was " no
match for the subtlety of Nature." [1]

The consistory of theologians sat watchful for the slightest
offence against the stringent moral and theological code
they chose to institute.[2] On Thursday, August 6, 1579, we
find Bruno and one Jean Bergeon laid by the heels. It is
recorded in the Registers of the Consistory that Bruno had
caused Bergeon to print " certain objections and invectives
againt M. de la Faye, reckoning twenty blunders in one of
his lectures." (The twenty blunders became multiplied by
five in Parisian gossip.[3]) " It was resolved that he should
be examined after dinner." Then Jean Bergeon pleaded
that the Italian had persuaded him of the wholly philosophical bearing of the matter ; he was given a day's imprisonment and fined 50 florins.

The next day Bergeon sent up a petition asking the Council
to pardon his transgression. He had " been led astray by
the monk, who affirmed there was nothing in it against God

[1] Bacon ; *Nov. Org., xiij.*
[2] Fairbairn, A ; *Camb. Mod. Hist., II,* 368.
[3] Auvray, L ; *op. cit., sub* 20 *May,* 1556.

or the Council." His fine was reduced by half, "on account of his small means." Bruno seems to have been visited in his cell by the pastors and one Michael Varro, a lawyer who dabbled in mathematics and natural science and had written on motion. The lawyer's hobby strengthens the surmise that the quarrel arose about Aristotle. Bruno acknowledged that he had offended. The council sat again on Monday, 10th Aug., and decided that he should be set free, but he must beg pardon of God, the law and the insulted professor; he must acknowledge his offence before the Consistory and tear up the libel. So, on the 13th August he appeared, as required, before the Consistory " to acknowledge his transgression in that he had erred in doctrine and called the pastors of the Church of Geneva pedagogues." But a surprise awaited the good pastors: he would " neither excuse himself nor plead guilty, for the matter had not been truly reported. He believed the story came from Pastor Antoine de la Faye. Asked whom he called pedagogues, he made many excuses and assertions that he was persecuted, setting forth conjectures and fresh accusations, but nevertheless admitted he was here to own his misconduct in traducing the pastors. Was admonished to follow the true doctrine. Said he was ready to receive censure. Seeing that he calumniated the said de la Faye, and accused him of saying a thing which he did not say, and had no wish to repent his doings, but urged that he had done right, it is recommended that he shall make a complete apology and acknowledge his transgression; otherwise, that he be forbidden the sacrament and be brought up again before the governing board, who are entreated not to endure this kind of person, one who disturbs the school, and who shall straightway be compelled to acknowledge his offence. Replied, that he repented of his offence, would amend his speech, and, further, admitted having calumniated Pastor de la Faye. The said remonstrances and prohibition of the sacrament made, and he sent away remonstrating." On Thursday, Aug. 27, " Philippe Brun, student, residing in this city, begs for the sacrament, which had been forbidden him . . . acknowledging that he had greatly offended. It was decided that he should be thoroughly reprimanded and allowed to partake of the sacrament. The said reprimand to free him from his transgression; for which he humbly rendered thanks."[1]

These entries in the Genevese Register would seem, at first sight, to prove that Bruno conformed to a regulation of the City whereby students were compelled to sign the Calvinistic Confession of faith. It has been shown, however, that this regulation, framed in 1559, ceased to be enforced in 1576. After the latter date, only membership of the community was required; and Bruno fulfilled this condition by putting in an appearance at the Italian Evangelical Church. The sentence of exclusion from the sacraments would appear to have been merely a formal one—one that we find repeated at Helmstadt a few years later on a similar occasion. It does not necessarily imply that Bruno was ever a communicant. But it would carry with it the stigma of heresy and be productive of highly inconvenient, if not serious, consequences. When on trial for his life he gave an open and manly account of his career and opinions. It is true that here and there he slides over a fact capable of being turned against him; now and then he puts a little theological whitewash, as the times required, on his opinions. But any unprejudiced reader must regard his statement, taken as a whole, as being a model of plain, straightforward statement. In it we find him saying: " I often went to hear heretics preach or dispute [in Protestant countries] rather through curiosity

[1] *Registres du Consistoire : vol. de* 1577–79, *in* Dufour, T ; *G. B. à Genève*, Schuchardt, 1884.

as to their ways than because I found them inviting; nor had I satisfaction; so that after the reading or sermon, when the time came for the sacrament and the distribution of bread in their style, I went about my business. I have never taken the sacrament or observed their practices." The inquisitors pointed out that the statement was hardly credible, since by non-compliance he would make enemies. Bruno replied: "Wherein I have transgressed I have told the truth. Herein I did not sin, and it shall never be found of me. Moreover, in these heretical lands Catholics are always to be met with who do not observe their usages." [1] And the Parisian diarist writes: "John Vincent says that Jordanus paid penalty on his knees at Geneva for calumniating M. de la Faye, a doctor of medicine of Padua, and printing a sheet containing 100 (sic) blunders committed by La Faye in a single lesson. Then Jordanus said he would have attached himself to their religion had they not so dishonoured him. The said de la Faye is preaching at the present time." [2]

Bruno had been kindly received by the Italian reformers at Geneva; he had been ill-treated by his own Church; he had achieved by this time his own esoteric interpretation of Christianity, and he would gladly have united himself with a truly liberal Church. Indeed one could hardly get daily bread on any other terms than that of joining the dominant Church of a place, Roman or Protestant. As to the sacrament, that would present no insuperable difficulty were he once sure of the sincerity and liberal wisdom of the religious community administering it. He did not dabble in theological niceties. Peter and Paul, he said, had no

---

[1] *Doc. xij.*

[2] Auvray, L; *op. cit., sub Mar. 20th* 1586. De la Faye became Rector of the Academy in 1580 and, later, held the chair of Philosophy. Prof. McIntyre says of Bruno's antagonist that "his one title to fame is that he was the biographer of Beza."

knowledge of subtleties; they only knew that "this is my body"; and, while he accepted the Catholic doctrine of transubstantiation, he gave it an interpretation of his own: the whole universe, in his philosophy, is an eternal trans-mutation of the World-Soul, the Divine Word, the ever-present Absolute. He laughed at the fuss that men made about "mysteries of Ceres and Bacchus."[1] Bruno was not the man to submit to the narrow yoke of acrid Calvinism. But the ecclesiastical despotism of Geneva had prohibited the sacrament, and he was sent away remonstrating, not against the formal sentence, but against what it implied. He had to request that it should be withdrawn, probably because there would otherwise be no sustenance for him forthcoming either from the printers or from the incensed Italian Community. Henceforward he had no leanings towards Calvinism.

Once, on the occasion of some meticulous theologic tiff, Calvin himself was exiled with the polite intimation that "the gates of the city were open." They were still un-closed to dissentients. "Having been told," says Bruno, "that I could not stay if I did not bring my mind to accept the religion of that city, and, besides, having received no aid from them, I determined to leave, and I journeyed to Lyons, where I stayed a month; but not finding the where-withal for my daily bread and necessities, I went on to Toulouse."[2]

There was an Italian colony at Lyons, chiefly of emigrants from Lucca. There were also several famous printing-presses, which turned out more books every year than Paris could boast of. Such men as Doletus, Henricus Stephanus

---

[1] Cfr. Doc. xij.—Tocco, F; Nuova Antologia, 4° ser., CI, Sept. 1902.—Archives of the Inquisition, vol. 1482–1600 A.D., fol. 1379, 80, 81.—Sigillus Sigillorum, "de Cerere et Baccho crudelitates"; De Immenso, I, i; Spaccio, III, i.   [2] Doc. ix.

D

and Servetus had earned their living there by reading proofs.[1] So Bruno had good reason to hope for the success he failed to obtain there.

Toulouse was a bulwark of orthodoxy and one of the most intolerant cities in France. The university boasted its 10,000 students, most of them following the law-courses, for which Toulouse had acquired particular fame. Petrarch had studied law there, and there Lully had taught.

The Dominicans had a monastery in the city, wherein lay the bones of Aquinas; but we may be sure that Bruno did not seek hospitality at a place which, for the memories it aroused, presented so much of interest to him. That easy charm of the children of the south, so attractive and ingratiating, must have been his, for here, as in every new place throughout his life, he speedily made acquaintances. He began to enjoy brighter days than had fallen to his lot during the past three years. He was asked to "read the Sphere with certain students,"[2] and continued to do this and teach philosophy for about six months.

His sympathies were with the concrete organic life of Catholicism, and not at all with the atomic individualism of the Protestants and that tendency towards social and moral disruption which was already apparent among them. Geneva had cured him of all illusion on that score. Until he was seized by the officers of the Inquisition, he could never understand that the belief of the Roman Church was expressed in other than "language of accommodation," and that truly instructed and wise Catholics would prefer rigid and incomprehensible dogma to his own esoteric and rationalized explanation. Bruno felt as might an ancient Greek exile, a homeless wanderer from his own city, which meant more than home to him, and deprived of the civic

[1] Bartholmèss, C ; *J. B., t. I, p.* 68 ; Berti ; *op. cit., p.* 106.
[2] *Doc. ix.*

rights he held so dear. Religion and religious functions were, in the sixteenth century, an integral part of the moral and social organization of each civil state. He was an outlaw, an object of suspicion and reprobation. Moreover, it is hard to break with ancient habit, and there is nothing which appeals, even to a rationalizing Catholic, so persistently as does the Mass; nothing which he feels so acutely as exclusion from unity with his fellows and with God, which, even if taken symbolically, is emphasized in receiving the sacrament. Honourable scruple kept him from participation: "I always abstained from that, knowing that I was excommunicated for abandoning my order and casting its habit aside."[1] And, to be sure of bread, not to speak of the comforts of life, it was necessary in a foreign and catholic city that he should reconcile himself with the Church. The Jesuits were learned men; they mixed with the world and bore themselves as men of the world; they possessed great influence in the most powerful quarters; on the surface they were sympathetic, even lax. He trusted to priestly honour or to the secrecy of the Confessional, an office, however, of which, as excommunicated, he had no right to avail himself. He went to a Jesuit father;[2] but got no help.

An "ordinary" chair in the University fell vacant. The University here did not require attendance on Mass, as did that of Paris, from its ordinary lecturers; so, although under charge of heresy, there was not this particular stumbling-block before him. He was peculiarly qualified for the post; for it was to teach philosophy. As a first step, he says: "I procured my doctorate through the Dean of Arts."[3] The Parisian diarist tells us that "Bruno is a doctor of theology, passed at Rome."[4] This is a mistake of course,

[1] *Doc. ix.*   [2] *Doc. xij.*   [3] *Doc. ix.*
[4] Auvray, L; *op. cit., sub Dec.* 7, 1585.

and it is easy to see how it arose. The diarist gives clear evidence that he did not catch or remember everything Bruno told him, and it was Bruno's habit to call himself a "doctor in Roman theology."[1] "The theses for his doctorate," the diarist continues, "were 'Whatever St Thomas says in his summary against the Gentiles is true' and 'Whatever the Master of Sentences' (St Peter Lombard) 'says is true.' He ranks St Thomas above all in his 'Summa' and 'Disputed Questions.'"[2]

Armed with his degree, Bruno entered into the contest for the chair. In those days, as still for the Rectorship of our Scottish Universities, the election lay with the students: it had done so from the first beginnings of Universities. He must have got a considerable reputation through his private lessons, for the choice fell on him. "I presented myself to the meeting and was appointed and approved, and gave instruction on Aristotle's *De Anima* and other philosophical subjects."[3] This text-book would give him an opportunity of treating a popular subject in his own original way. The nature and destiny of the soul had been eagerly debated for a century, with all the inevitable rancour and vituperation which attend on disputation without real knowledge. Probably the new professor, whose zeal and courage, in the end, always got the better of his modicum of tact, contrived to arouse bitter opposition. He could hardly have avoided expounding the germs of the philosophy which was shaping itself in his mind; and there was plenty to offend therein. In the MS. of his evidence at the Venetian trial, a passage which runs: "But in certain disputable points which I gave forth, and proposed

---

[1] He inscribed himself in the roll of students of the Protestant university of Marburg, July 25, 1586, as "Jordanus Nolanus Neapolitanus Theologiæ Doctor Romanensis."

[2] Auvray, L ; *loc. cit.*   [3] *Doc. ix.*

conclusions . . . " is cancelled.[1] This points to some opposition ; and elsewhere Bruno wrote of the rowdy bearing of students towards him at Toulouse, Paris and Oxford.[2] At the two last named universities, we know that his attacks on Aristotle aroused violent resentment. Little freedom of thought was allowed at Toulouse in days when France was distracted by faction and Catholics and Huguenots were at each other's throats. During the year which saw Bruno's arrival in the city and the first complete year of his stay there (1579–80) the Huguenots made more than forty attacks on neighbouring towns.

The passage referring to disputes in the school having been cancelled, Bruno continues : " I left on account of the civil wars, and went on to Paris."[3] A very excellent reason ; but did it stand alone ?

He would seem to have employed his time at Toulouse, when he was not teaching, in writing a big book on Lullian method and artificial memory which he entitled " Clavis Magna " " The Great Key." He conceived that he had included and systematized in it all the theories and practical devices of previous writers on these subjects and this in a complete philosophic form. The work was never published, although Bruno frequently refers to it in his earlier writings ; but there is little doubt that parts of it were the bases of his " Seal of Seals "[4] and " Combinatory Lamp."[5]

---

[1] Doc. ix. [2] J. Bruni Oratio Valedictoria.
[3] Doc. ix. [4] McIntyre; op. cit., p. 17.
[5] De Lampade combinatoria Lulliana. Est et UNICA CLAVIS ad omnium Lullianorum etc.

CHAPTER VI

FIRST STAY IN PARIS

THERE was relative peace in France. The seventh of a series of monstrous wars had been ended by a patched-up agreement. Wrecked cities and unpeopled villages, burnt farms and fields laid waste bore witness everywhere to the fury of faction and the malevolent rancour of opponents who disguised personal hatred under the convenient mask of religion. From the disappearance of tolerant classic paganism, the unformulated aspirations or discontent of races and classes found in this or that religious creed a suitable rallying cry; and now the opposed forces which made for liberty on the one hand and for the compact state on the other set up their separate religious banners. All the scoundrels in France gathered round the one or the other of these; they dubbed themselves Catholic or Huguenot; all that was atavistic in human nature was aroused, and all the vilest and most primitive passions were set loose. "Pick me out," wrote Montaigne, "pick me out from the Catholic army all the men who are actuated either by a pure zeal for religion or by loyalty to their country and you will not find enough to form one single company." Everywhere poverty, hunger, suffering and disease were the result of these wars. Bruno journeyed to Paris through provinces marked by scath and bale. All the way, to use the words of Castelnau, was "one long bleeding wound." Bruno crystallizes his experience in three significant phrases: "the French uproar," "the French fury" and "the bloody

Seine."[1] The best of the sons of France, men of broad mind and dignified character, brilliant scholars and original thinkers had, for the most part, been slaughtered or exiled. Montaigne retired to the remote home of his ancestors; he speaks of it as the only château in France " which had no guard or sentinel but the stars."

The Gallic fury, which had been let loose on Italy and brought ruin there, was now expending itself at home. Yet the invaders brought back a novel appreciation of letters and refinement, coupled with a far greater appreciation of luxury. When the descendant of Florentine pawn-brokers became the mother of French kings, fashion aped the superior civilization of Italy; and in this way Italy came to exercise an enduring influence on the quick aptitude of France. The slaughter of St Bartholomew's day had not wholly extinguished the torch of the Renaissance which French hands had snatched up: it still burned brightly in literature and art; and Frenchmen shewed their innate genius for history, memoirs and the essay. Montaigne had just published the first two books of his immortal work. A group of French humanists, although unpossessed by passion and unendowed with originality, had aimed at a rich vocabulary and a splendid style. They took the later Italian literature as their example, and although stricken in years, most of them were still living. French artists and architects still imitated Italian models, breathing into their copies a grace and refinement which is peculiarly Gallic. At Court, the Queen Mother and her Italian followers were copied with such absurd detail as changed permanently the very pronunciation of the language; the French o was flattened by fashion into a. In spite of the terrible and protracted strife throughout the land, all manner of Italians from each little State came pouring over

[1] *Lamp. Comb., Dedic; Spaccio, Dial. II, iij; Causa, Dial. I.*

the mountains to find their El Dorado at the French Court or in French cities; and, for the most part, they were cordially welcomed.

Paris was chiefly a mass of miserable hovels. The luxury of the Court contrasted strangely with the squalor of the streets; the ignorant noble, caring for nothing but warfare, horsemanship and sport,[1] was a figure which implied the famished beggar. Even the priests besought alms as they paraded the streets with open missal.[2] Yet Italian traders did well. Italian astrologers and actors, teachers of horsemanship and fencing-masters, doctors and scholars found a temporary or permanent home in France. The pulpits were filled by Italian preachers and eager ears drank in draughts of eloquence in Italianised French. Italian professors were appointed to vacant chairs at the seats of learning. Small wonder that Bruno cast his eyes on Paris!

Moreover, the University, although she was no longer mistress of theologic thought and arbitress in Philosophy, and her schools were now badly attended, maintained some measure of her ancient prestige.

Furnished with his degree, Bruno, whom we find calling himself by his monkish name Giordano again, arrived in Paris towards the end of 1581. It was a common thing for scholars to wander from place to place and fight their way into office by securing popularity or influence. He says: "When I went to Paris, in order to get me known and my measure taken, I gave thirty expositions of the Thirty Divine Attributes, taken from the first part of [the Summa Theologia of] St Thomas [Aquinas]."[3] "I have always admired Catholic theologians, particularly St Thomas, whose works I have always kept at hand, perused and

---

[1] Castiglione, B; Il Cortigiano; Tasso, T; Lettere.
[2] Doc. xij.   [3] Doc. ix.

praised. I have them still and hold them dear."[1] The
Angelic Doctor, as the accepted exponent of Catholic
philosophy, was no less highly rated by the professors and
students of Paris. Humanism had never taken deep root
in the University, and, after the massacre of 1572, true
scholarship languished and Catholic studies triumphed.
What choice of subject could have been a happier one?
Bruno's disquisitions were so successful that he remained
in Paris, lecturing on mnemonics and the art of Lully as
improved by himself, throwing into it the germs of his own
philosophic views. He was a stimulating teacher, full of
fire and originality. He would dictate with great rapidity,
standing on one leg as he did so. He could be persuasive
and convincing: often he became provocative and tactless.
His pupils say that he was marvellously ready of thought
and speech; he could deal with any subject that turned
up; he often employed a barbarous Latin jargon, but
became truly eloquent at times; he would carry his hearers
away with him and his lecture room was packed.[2]

His desire " to get known and his measure taken " was
achieved; he was offered a chair at the University.[3] Unable to accept an ordinary professoriate, since, unlike the
University of Toulouse, that of Paris made attendance at
Mass obligatory, " which," says Bruno, " I always avoided
doing, having left my order and cast off my habit. . . . I
continued my teaching." His reputation reached the Court.
" I got me such a name that King Henry III summoned
me one day to discover from me if the memory which I
possessed was natural or acquired by magic art. I satisfied
him that it did not come from sorcery but from organised

---

[1] *Doc. xij.*

[2] Nostitz, J; *Artificium Aristotelico—Lullio—Rameum, Bregæ,*
1615.—Eglin, R ; J. B. *Summa terminorum, præfatio.*

[3] *Doc. ix.*—Toland, J ; *Schoppius' letter to Rittershaus, in Miscell.
Works,* 1747, *vol. i.*

knowledge ; and, following this, I got a book on memory printed, entitled ' The Shadows of Ideas,' which I dedicated to His Majesty. Forthwith he gave me an Extraordinary Lectureship with a salary." [1] Bruno invented an enigma and paradigm whereby the King might remember the Book of Genesis, and " a fruitful figure of letters, signs and numbers." [2] Among other subjects he probably lectured on the Physics of Aristotle. [3]

Giordano's royal patron was of a singular and difficult disposition. He had received the fatal inheritance of a neurotic and unstable temperament; he was quick to imitate and quick to change. His susceptible mind had received some cultivation ; but his nurture was even more unfortunate for one of such unbalanced disposition than is usual with the ordinary prince : he was brought up in a sty of luxury and encouraged to let himself go to each momentary impulse. Tasso believed that Henry's character was injured in critical years by the dissipations which were forced on him during his sojourn in Italy. [4] His contemporaries maintained that he was sound at heart, but vacillating, a man of whims, subject to the allurements of the moment and the seductions of his companions. One day he would parade in the street as a penitent ; another day he would don female garb and enact the painted harlot at a banquet, graced by the sanctioning presence of the Queen-Mother. He filled his Court with loose women and scandalous youths. Often well-intentioned, his favour could not be depended on, for he frequently became irresolute, incapable and indolent. He left affairs of state to others in order to fondle lap-dogs. So nervous that a thunderstorm would frighten him into the cellars of his palace, he

---

[1] *Doc. ix.*   [2] *De Umbris : Ars Memoriæ, near the end.*

[3] Tocco, F ; *Op. inedite de G. B. Nap.*, 1891, *p.* 100.

[4] Tasso, Torquato ; *Prose Diverse, Firenze*, 1875, *vol. ij., p.* 286.

could be rash and bold at times, welcoming adventure and playing the man. He was skilful among statesmen in setting traps for his foes. A seeker after forbidden things, he was nevertheless devout, ordering prayers for the success of a projected murder and attending mass during its accomplishment. A fribble, he preserved some interest in things of the mind, and he had learned in Italy that to patronize learning and art adds to the prestige of a prince. While, as Tasso tells us, the nobility of France abandoned letters to the vulgar, Henry III favoured Italian scholars, founded some professorial chairs and augmented the endowment of others.[1] De Thou thought that, with all his vices he would have made a good prince in a better age, and D'Aubigny admitted that he was a man of good parts who, as Tacitus said of Galba, would have been judged worthy of the royal power if he had never reigned.

Henry was but little in Paris; he spent most of his time at Blois; when Bruno saw him he saw his better side. In consequence of this and of the favour shown him—favour of which he got so little in life—Bruno thought more highly of Henry than he deserved. He calls him the "admirable light of nations" and speaks of his "first-rate mind, most like a mirror."[2] Such praise sounds extravagant to modern ears, and, as addressed to a reigning monarch, is suggestive of insincerity. But the adulation of great folk was a formal necessity then. The age was one of hyperbole "triple-piled," and it was Bruno's nature to bespangle his friends and bespatter his foes with reckless superlative. And we should not forget that, in the 16th century, the throne was

[1] *Archives curieuses*, 1834-40, *vols. x, xi.*—De Thou, J. A; *Historia sui temp.*, 1620.—Duplex, Scipion; *Histoire de Henri III*, 1633.— D'Aubigny, T, Agrippa; *Les Tragiques*, 1616.—L'Estoile, P de; *Journal de Henri III*, 1620 (?).—Bartholmèss, C; *Op. cit., vol. i, p.* 81.

[2] *De Umbris.*

regarded as a sacred temple of protection and liberality, a sanctuary for learning and a source of honour and power; the Court, too, was the school of manners, the patron of scholarship, science and the arts; all hope of the advancement of letters rested on princes and nobles; the very means of livelihood might depend on their favour; the Court was the avenue to success. And, even in our own simple-minded and undesigning days, it is not every one who shall be so downright as was the Ettrick shepherd and address an antagonist as "damned sir" or subscribe himself "yours disgusted."

But Bruno, although he fell in with the courtly fashion of the time, felt real gratitude to Henry, and there is nothing servile in his tone; he lauds the King, but he is also conscious of his own worth and asserts it. In the sentence wherein Henry is addressed as "famous and magnanimous" he is informed that the work presented to him is "among the greatest; noble as to its subject and remarkable in its concoction." And Bruno's gratitude was exceptional in being no mere passing flush of feeling. When away in England, he extolled Henry,[1] and later, in Southern Germany, when Henry had incurred the reproach of all Europe, Bruno had a work printed in which he allowed a laudatory preface, written in Paris, to stand.[2]

It has been considered uncertain whether the "Extraordinary Lectureship with a salary," which the King gave Bruno, was at the Sorbonne or at the *Collège de Cambrai*, an institution which bore several names and is generally known as the *Collège de France*.[3] I have, however, little doubt that he was appointed to the latter college, and think

[1] *Cena, Proemiale epistola ; Spaccio, Dial. III, iij.*

[2] *Acrotismus, Vitebergæ, apud Zachariam Cratonem, anno* 1588. Compare *Centum et viginti articuli. Impressum Parisiis* 1586.

[3] Crévier, J. B. L ; *Hist. de l' Univ. de Paris,* 1761, *II,* 407-8. It was also known as the College of the Three Bishops.

so because, first, although founded in 1348, it was remodelled and endowed by Francis II and remained fostered and protected by the Throne. Secondly, it was a modern school, opposed to the teaching of the " ignorant Sorbonne," which had pronounced " Greek, Hebrew and elegant Latin to be the language of heretics " and directed its attention to more Catholic studies. As more liberal than the Sorbonne, the College of Cambrai was less unsuited to the highly unconventional teaching of Bruno, and, although both establishments now slavishly followed Aristotle, not long before, it was at the Cambrai that the would be subverter of his logic, Pierre de la Ramée (Ramus) delivered his lectures.[1] Thirdly, Besler, who acted as one of Bruno's copyists, wrote after the title of one of his works : " a treatise by Giordano Bruno, verily the living sap of the Cambrai," [2] and Bruno himself calls a work, published in 1588, the " Acrotismus of Jordanus Brunus of the Cambrai." [3] Fourthly, two of his works, that dedicated to the King and one dedicated to the Venetian Ambassador at Paris, were printed in the immediate neighbourhood of the College of Cambrai, as is set forth on their title-pages.[4] Again, on his second visit to Paris (1585) Bruno was partly supported by friends and dwelt with them,[5] and the diarist already quoted notes that

---

[1] Lefranc, A ; *Hist. du Collège de France*, 1893, *pp.* 240 *sqq.*—
Crévier ; *op. cit, t. vj, pp.* 384-86.

[2] *Tractatus succus immo G. B. Nolani camoeracensis, Erlangen Codex* 1279. Vide Tocco, F ; *Opere inedite di G. B., Nap.*, 1891, *pp.* 98 *sqq.*

[3] J. B. Nolani *Camoeracensis Acrotismus.* "Camoera" is bad Latin for "căměra" or "cămăra," an arched roof or chamber = French "chambre," taken as = Cambrai.

[4] *De Umbris Idearum* . . . . . *Parisiis apud Ægid. Gorbinum, sub insigne Spei, e regione gymnasii Cameracensis,* 1582, *cum privilegio regis.—De compendiosa Architectura* . . . . . *Parisiis apud Ægidium Gorbinum, sub insigne Spei prope collegium Cameracense,* 1582.

[5] *Doc. ix.*

"he lodges near the College of Cambrai."[1] It is unlikely that he then held any chair, or he would not have required such aid, and the fact that his friends lived close to the College points to that as the one where he had held a post. Moreover, the famous disputation, to which we shall come in due course, was held at the College and not at the Sorbonne.[2] It is true that the College of Cambrai was opposed to the Jesuits, and Bruno consulted a Jesuit. But Prof. McIntyre is mistaken in supposing that he did so during his first visit to Paris.[3] He did so during his second stay, at the instigation of the Spanish Ambassador.[4]

Bruno was kindly received by his fellow-professors. At first, at least, his lectures were popular,[5] and he speaks of the attendance of learned persons both at his public and private teaching.[6] He made the acquaintance of Regnault, secretary to Henry of Angoulême, Grand Prior of France. Angoulême was the bastard son of Henry II by a Scots lady named Leviston, and, therefore, was half-brother to the King. Manuscript copies of Bruno's second book "The Chant of Circe"[7] were in circulation, and Regnault wished his friend to get the work printed. Since Bruno was "occupied by weightier matters," i.e. the instruction of the King, Regnault undertook its production, dedicating it to D'Angoulême. It appeared, bound up with the "Shadow of Ideas," (1582). Among other influential persons whom he got to know was Giovanni Moro, the accomplished ambassador of Venice. Moro had just replaced Lorenzo Priuli, who was destined to preside over Bruno's trial at Venice; so Priuli may have known Bruno at Paris or heard of his reputation for heresy, which, as we shall see, was afloat.

---

[1] Auvray, L ; *op. cit., sub 6th Dec.* 1585.
[2] *Ibid., sub* 28*th* and 29*th May.*   [3] McIntyre ; *op. cit., p.* 20.
[4] *Docs. xij, xvij.*   [5] Nostitz ; *loc. cit.*
[6] *Centum et viginti articuli ; Acrotismus Camoeracensis (Epist. ad Filesac).*   [7] *Cantus Circæus.*

He inscribed to Moro his " Substance And Completion Of The Art Of Lully," [1] (1582). Lecturing and correcting proofs make heavy work in themselves; but Bruno's energy was unbounded and expended itself in close and continuous application. The same year which witnessed the publication of three Latin books saw that of a fourth, this time a comedy in Italian called " The Chandler." [2]

He was in the royal favour, held a royal appointment and was not unfriended at Court. Yet all was not so well with him as it seemed. How could it be with a man who might say with his English contemporary, " My thoughts are stitched to the stars " ? [3]

He sat apart, a solitary thinker, a somewhat disappointed man. Excommunication debarred him from his due. We learn how he was regarded, or regarded himself, from the title-page of his play: he is " il fastidito," " the man with his stomach turned." But he has learned to accept life as it comes, with serene outlook and even temper; he declares that he is " cheery when sad and sad in cheer; " [4] yet surely there is a sub-acid flavour in the announcement that he is " an academician of no academy "—he is that strong, sad man who thinks for himself, and, therefore, stands alone.

It behoved him to walk warily; and Bruno was not a wary person. The Catholic Reaction was triumphant in Paris, and his printed books contained dubious doctrine. It

[1] *De Compendiosa Architectura et Complimento Artis Lulli. Ad illustrissimum D. D. Joannem Morum pro serenissima Venetorum Rep. apud christianiss. Gall. et Polon. regem Henricum III legatum.*
[2] *Il Candelajo.*
[3] John Lyly; *Endimion, Act I, sc. i.* The phrase seems to have been Americanized by Emerson who talks about hitching one's waggon to the stars.
[4] " In tristitia hilaris, in hilaritate tristis," Title-page of *Il Candelajo.*

is hardly likely that his lectures were free from all offence.
There had been a time when Ramus and Postel attacked
Aristotle before crowded benches ; and it was still possible
to introduce new ideas under cover of the Stagirite's mantle ;
but former attacks had not been made on the Aristotelian
Cosmology. Bruno had once held with Aristotle, but
Copernicus had obliged him to change his mind.[1] Aristotle,
as accepted and expounded by the schoolmen, was held to
be a pillar of Christian philosophy; the new science over-
threw more than one foundation-stone in the teaching of the
Church, and Bruno never missed an opportunity of assailing
Aristotle on a side which was generally unquestioned.
Pundits, too, like poets, are an irritable folk. Scholars, in
the sixteenth century, were not invariably endowed with
breadth of vision, and they were apt to grow waspish.
Students at the universities were undisciplined in manners,
and the natural genius of the student calls on him to seize
every opportunity of converting the lecture-room into a
bear-garden. Moreover, in social intercourse, Bruno was
far from cautious ; [2] what fermented in his brain must out
on his tongue. In a somewhat confused manuscript record
wherein he runs, or was reported as running, two separate
stays in Paris together, he told the Inquisitors that he left
France for England on account of tumults which were
brewing.[3] But, from the peace of Fleix in 1580 to the
outbreak of the " war of the three Henrys " in 1585, there
was an almost complete lull in religious and political strife.
Bruno must have been conscious that personal trouble
loomed ahead. His scandalous doctrines got talked about.
Opinions so unhallowed shocked every kind of Christian.
Sir H. Cobham, the English Ambassador in Paris, was in

[1] *Infinito, Dial. I.*
[2] Cfr. *Cena; Eroici furori, Argomento del Nolano.*
[3] *Doc. ix.*

correspondence with Sir Henry Walsingham, the Queen's Secretary. Walsingham was a master-organizer of espial, and it was Cobham's business to find out everything that was going on and send the news home. The Ambassador told the Secretary, in a letter dated March 28th 1583 : " Il Sr Doctor Jordano Bruno Nolano, a professor in philosophy, intendeth to pass into England; whose religion I cannot commend."[1] Whatever may have happened, Bruno departed from France bearing a letter of recommendation from the King to Michel de Castelnau, Lord of Mauvissière, who was his Ambassador at the Court of Elizabeth. It is evident that Henry could be broad-minded on occasion, and had some respect for intellectual pluck and power : it softens one's judgement of that egregious monarch.

[1] Elton, O ; *Modern Studies, Arnold, London,* 1907, *p.* 334, *addendum to note* 9.

E

CHAPTER VII

THE EARLY WORKS

I. THE SHADOWS OF IDEAS

IN 1582, Gorbin, whose shop was under the sign of "Hope," produced the second of Bruno's printed works, but the first which has been preserved down to our own time. "De Umbris Idearum" "The Shadows of Ideas" was dedicated to Henry and issued "with his privilege." Now Chicus Æsculanus asserted in his commentary "In Spheram" that Solomon wrote a work on the shadows of ideas, and perhaps this statement suggested the title to Bruno; for more than once he refers to Solomon and his Song in this book.[1] The work aimed at setting before the King, men of cultured mind, scholars and students an improved art of remembering; but, since the mnemonic system displayed is loosely associated with metaphysical bases, the latter are treated of in the first part of the book as "Shadows of Ideas," while the second part is entitled the "Art of Memory." The first part is frankly Neo-Platonic. Bruno had absorbed much Neo-Platonism; it was a popular doctrine in his time. It is true that he despised its Italian exponent, Pico della Mirandola;[2] but the symbolic doctrine of the One True Light approached so near to the conceptions

---

[1] Bartholmèss, C; *J. Bruno, Paris*, 1846, *II, p.* 190. Tocco, F; *Opere Latine di G. B, Firenze*, 1889, *p.* 44. The Canticles were supposed to be symbolic. "I sat down under his shadow with great delight," *Canticles II*, 3; "Until the day break and shadows flee away," *ibid.*, 17; also *IV*, 6.

[2] Auvray, L; *op. cit., sub Dec. 7th.*

he was forming, or had already formed as to the immanence of God that he had no scruple in using it. He accepts, too, the doctrine of universal animism, which was held by the ancient world and generally received by thinkers of his own age. The "Art of Memory," following the philosophic treatise, is in three divisions which contain some rudimentary psychology and an attempt at mental analysis. The notions which Lully conceived to be irreducible are replaced by an increased number of concepts, chosen for their convenience in illustrating mnemonic method.[1] Bruno retains Lully's mechanical arrangements, the various compartments bearing symbolic labels for economy and concentration of thought. There is, however, little serious attempt at systematic treatment. Severe orderly arrangement would seem to have been repellent to all the men of the Renaissance, and it was by no means conformable with the swoop and circlings of Bruno on the wing. The book was intended to be generally acceptable; and therefore its author reserved much which must have been maturing in his brain. His thought was to be quickened and strengthened by the clarifying stimulus of opposition and contumely; his bold and penetrative insight to be sharpened by the obtuse folly of his foes. His present object was to arouse the mind of his reader without incensing him unduly.

Eastern ideas reached Plato, and he endeavoured to formulate them; but Neo-Platonism retranslated thought into imagery.[2] Bruno never entirely departed from the Neo-Platonic method. He often associates his concepts with a mystic symbolism which is not always a mere aid to memory, but implies some subtle and profound cosmic sympathy. Words, nay alphabets, he holds are the shades

---

[1] Tocco; *loc. cit.*

[2] Zimmermann, R; *Gesch. d. Aesthetik als philosoph. Wissenschaft, Wien*, 1858.

of things, and things are the vestiges of the Being of beings. Throughout, he presupposes an ultimate identity of thought and thing; of memory and nature; of what is knowable and the unknown; of fact and power. This opinion has been pretty generally held by the profounder thinkers. The age was so convinced of the reality of a single principle that it sought eagerly for the Elixir of Life and the Philosopher's stone.

It had been shown by the later Greeks that sense-perception was not to be depended on for the discovery of truth. The Neo-Platonists therefore relied on the directness of intuition concerning high matters; they regarded intuition as having the force of perception on a higher plane. This was also characteristic of the mystics and it greatly influenced Bruno. But he held man to be incapable of achieving the very truth.[1] We are but shadows of the Ineffable One;[2] for the light which reaches us is confused and contradictory and mixed with darkness; we perceive good and evil together and in contrast, the beautiful associated with the ugly to which it is in opposition.[3] Looked at from the eternal point of view, all, even the worst evils are perfection; everything descends from the perfect and everything strives to wing a homeward flight.[4] The human soul is to the human body as is a pilot to the ship: it is in it, but not of it,[5] and, being associated with body, the soul perceives truth confusedly and as in flux. But the Idea draws us on; and, in itself, it is not abstract but concrete and articulated.[7] Our ideas, we must remember, are as an admixture of light and shadow and not that absolute truth which they can never reach;[8] but none-

---

[1] *De Umbr, Int. I.*   [2] *Ibid., Int. II.*   [3] *Ibid., Int. XXI.*
[4] *Ibid., Int. VII.   Cfr.* Plot.; *Enn., iv,* 4, 36; *v,* 5, 12; *vj,* 5, 12.
[5] *Ibid., Conc, IV, V.   Cfr.* Plot.; *Enn., iv,* 3, 21; *iv,* 7, 1.
[6] *Ibid., Conc. V, VI.*   [7] *Ibid., Conc. XV.*   [8] *Ibid., Int. II.*

theless the mind can rise above the things of sense, perceiving unity in plurality.[1] Mystic union with the Divinity was experienced by Plotinus and others.[2] From the acceptance of this mystical experience thus avowed in this early work, Bruno never departed. But in his later works, wherein he reproduces far less Neo-Platonism and becomes vastly more original, he proclaims that by the exercise of reason also we can attain comprehensive contact with the Absolute, Who is at once the source and object of our search.[3]

God is immanent as well as transcendent; for does not man share a measure of the Ineffable Light?[4] The interconnection of ideas naturally corresponds with that of things.[5] But memory is apt to break down, and, where it does so, we may mend it by working on the lines of its natural operation.[6] He feels the significance of the principle of the Association of Ideas, which Aristotle was the first to indicate, and uses it. He also culls the best from all writers of his time on mnemonics, as he told us in the preface he intended to do. Our ideas being shadows of truth,[7] we use shadows of these shadows in mnemonics. We can economize thought by means of signs the nature of which is that they are shadows or traces.

To fix attention, maintain interest and arouse emotional force, he introduces mythological subjects.[8]

Imagine what a good "draw" a really useful tool for unearthing the buried treasures of the mind would be to men who found books so hard to come at! But Bruno was endowed with a prodigious memory, and he falsely attributed his natural power to the artifices he employed. Probably the expectations he excited were not fulfilled. There is no

---

[1] *Ibid., Conc. V.*   [2] *Conc. xvij–xix. Cfr.* Porph. ; *v, Plot.* 23.
[3] This forms the subject-matter of the *Eroici Furori.*
[4] *De Umbris, Int. VII.*   [5] *Ibid., Int. VII.*
[6] *Ibid., Int. XIII.*   [7] *Cfr.* Plato; *Repub. vij.* 515.
[8] *De Umb: Ars Memoriae, Pars II, De Subj.* §§ 2–5.

great novelty in his mnemonics ; he was one of the " celestial thieves " of his generation.   There are, in *De Umbris*, fore-shadowings of his philosophic syncretism ; but he has not yet welded the conclusions of others into a vital whole or made them live anew in his own completer thought ; the work is tentative and contains only the germ of the Bruno that was presently to appear ; but such remarks as the one that religious mysteries are mere institutions to train human eyes¦for the perception of " the steep passage from darkness to light " are truly Brunian.

He introduces symbolic verse of his own composition and gives us brisk dialogue between Hermes, Philotimus and Logifer, with thrusts, less severe than those which were to follow, at the doctors and masters of the schools.

Scholars had travelled a far road from the elegant Latin of Cicero.   Bruno's Latin is full of neologisms ; his syntax is bad ; his prosody, abominable.   In a later work he acknow-ledges that his Latin is coarse and rough.   But it is alive. One finds the elements of Bruno's manner in this early work and they may be conveniently examined here.

He delights in brisk and varied dialogue which knows no curb.   Sometimes the thread of mystical symbolism which runs through it finds a natural expression in metre ; every here and there he breaks into verse, which, no less than prose, he writes with impetuous fury.   At its worst, one is reminded that he came from the land of *improvvisa-tori*.   He is far too much in a hurry to be over careful as to style, and never dreams of polish ; for the thing he has to declare is infinitely more important than the manner of declaring it.   Later, he hinted at being too diffuse,[1] but failed to amend his ways.   In his verses, there is little of craftsman-like skill.   His pen flows as rapidly as his thought ; his mind is full to bursting point ; he indulges

[1] *Spaccio, III, ij.*

in wide circlings and side-long sweeps. He casts about for the most unlikely allegory; for to him, as to Dante and Swedenborg and Emerson, all nature and all the products of the human mind are symbolic of higher truth; and in this he fell into line with the conviction of his century, perceiving deep analogies in fact and fable, whether sacred or profane. Hence, in an age of respect for authority, he supports an argument by drawing on his own vast lore; he lugs in learning by the ears, not for display but to reinforce his meaning. He does this quite impartially: the Bible, the Pre-Socratic philosophers, the Cabala and classic myth are introduced as of equal weight. There is real unity underlying each of his works; but all give the impression of disorder. For, each trivial occasion, each intruding half-thought is as a spark which he allows to burst into vivid and vagrant flame: his imagination plays riotously round his immediate theme, and then suddenly leaps aside. Sometimes this is a trick, done of set purpose. If the men of the Renaissance rejoiced in life, towards the close of the period they expressed their vigour in violence. Hence Bruno lost no opportunity of keeping his readers awake by the oddness of his antics; he surprises them by bombardments and unexpected raking fires. He thinks to throw each noble design, each lofty thought into relief by the dodge (not wholly unknown to modern authors) of smart paradox. Prolixity and the grossly grotesque entertained his age: they bore ours. All is overdone: there is not a thought of repose. Penetrative insight, soaring imagination, novel wisdom, severe thought have a setting of jest and jeer, clumsy buffoonery and sheer indecency. He was justified in being sure of himself; but his bombastic self-assertion repels the modern reader. He delights in contrast and invective. His polemic is implacable and often unjust, but less so than that of his contemporaries and immediate successors ; and he flies less readily than they to the final argument of abuse. As Tocco remarks,[1] his motive is always noble; he "made no thought of life"[2] and proved it by sacrifice and suffering and sealing his faith in death.

II. THE INCANTATION OF CIRCE

Books of the period bore odd titles to catch the eye. Bruno called his next work the "Cantus Circæus" "The Incantation Of Circe." The Homeric sorceress, who transforms men into beasts, discusses with her handmaiden the human vice which each kind of beast represents, and each beast and its vice are memorised under initial letters. Now the nature of memory is occult, and the recalling of ideas may be regarded as a sort of magical process. So the art of memory may be regarded as a fascinating incantation. The dialogue is full of bitter satire on human depravity. A second dialogue follows with different interlocutors. It treats more directly and precisely than the previous "Art of Memory" of that subject. There is an attempt to localise the functions of the brain as the physical conditions of mental process.[3] The principle of the association of ideas is more closely followed than in *De Umbris* and copious illustrations of method are given. The work abounds in obscurities, which were as attractive to superior minds in that age as in our own. Later on Bruno found it convenient to be occasionally obscure where it was wiser to suggest merely to those few who had the capacity really to understand perilous doctrine. But Bruno never erred on the side of over-caution!

[1] Tocco, F ; *Conferenza, Firenze,* 1886.
[2] Bruno ; *Eroici, Dial. III, beginning.*
[3] *Cantus Circæus, Dial. II., Prima pars Th., Cap I.,* § 1.

III. THE LULLIAN ARCHITECTURE

In the same year appeared a third book, the " Brief Architecture Of The Art of Lully With Its Completion."[1] It was published by Gorbin and was little more than a reproduction of Lully's " Great Art." But Bruno thought that art a key to the structure of the universe and the ready way to a complete philosophy, proceeding from foundations of all knowledge; he conceived of it as a demonstration of unity, the shortest of roads for thought and memory, and a useful symbolic logic. Of the value of Inference in extending knowledge, Bruno had little more notion than had Lully. For, although Lully worked outside scholasticism and exhibited much of that spontaneous originality which we find in Scotus Erigena before scholasticism began, mediaeval thought was harnessed in the syllogism and employed itself in ceaseless rotation, like a donkey round a grinding mill, but mostly grinding philosophic chaff. In Bruno's time Lully captured many able minds and had a great vogue. Before Kant, it was not possible to work from other than dogmatic premises; certain concepts were posited as fundamental and ultimate; there was no notion of submitting them to criticism. For Bruno, the art of Lully was alive; for us, it has become dead and valueless.

Lully tried to prove the dogmas of the Church by human reason.[2] Bruno, in this work, denies that they are reasonable: any attempt to prove their truth is a blunder; for Christianity is irrational, contrary to philosophy and in disagreement with other religions. We only accept it by faith and through revelation. As a Neo-Platonist and syncretist he relies on and quotes pagan authority as freely as Christian.

[1] *De Compendiosa Architectura et Complemento Artis Lulii.*
[2] Lully, R ; *De Articulis Fidei.*

Berti thinks that at some time before Bruno left France he wrote a book, never published, of which all we know is that, two years later, he promised to send his English friend Smith his "'Purgatory of Hell,' wherein you shall see the fruit of redemption."[1] One judges from the context that the redemption was from scientific and philosophic error.

IV. THE CHANDLER

The same year (1582) saw another work from Bruno's rapid pen. This time he wrote in Italian, and the book was printed by an Italian who had settled in Paris, Guglielmo Giuliano by name. Bruno tells us it was the fruit of "a few burning days."[2] It differs wholly from his other writings, for it is a stage-play, full of rattling, roaring fun and furnished with a satiric probe for credulity, pedantry and pretence. Its world is full of the pursuers and hucksters of illusions; rogues abound, and fools are duped by miracle-mongers, alchemists and pretenders to magic arts. This comedy is entitled "Il Candelajo," which may be translated as "The Chandler." In Bruno's time the person who supplied candles also made them. Now the manufacture of tallow-dips is a noisome and undignified trade. Bruno, like Dante, loved to load words with more than their surface-meaning.[3] "Behold," he says in the dedication, "behold in the candle borne by this Chandler, to whom I gave birth, that which shall clarify certain shadows of ideas." This product of imagination which shall set forth truth is dedicated with a letter to the lady Morgana, a name very suggestive of *Fata Morgana*—the mirage—which is illusion. In this dedication a multitude of ideas surge pell-

---

[1] *Cena de le Ceneri, Dial IV.*

[2] *Il Candelajo, a la signora Morgana.*

[3] Bacelli, A ; *Il Candelajo, Soc. Dante Al.,* 1901, *p.* 86 *sq.*

mell; they only get themselves out as obscure half-hints; the language is tortuous and the syntax involved. Priests and pedants may banish his body and make chaos of his life, but they shall not shackle his soul or obscure its vision. Here he presents some shifting shadows, but all the moving shadows of the Universe are really the expression of One Reality. "I need not instruct you of my belief: Time gives all and takes all away; everything changes but nothing perishes; One only is immutable, eternal and ever endures, one and the same with itself. With this philosophy my spirit grows, my mind expands. Whereof, however obscure the night may be, I await daybreak, and they who dwell in day look for night. . . . . Rejoice therefore, and keep whole, if you can, and return love for love." [1]

The characters of the play, being vicious, are inversions of virtue, integrals in the scheme of things, fulfilling an office to higher ends, as does the one who gives the play its title, our provider of gross matter which shall furnish shining flame. The title of the play is repeated in three of its scenes. In the two first of these our protagonist, who aims at writing amorous poetry, is told, to his great perplexity, that he is trying to change himself from chandler to goldsmith. [2] In the last, it is related how all the folk with a bee in the bonnet, who hanker after miracle-mongering priests and their "water of St Peter the Martyr, seed of St John, heaven-sent food of St Andrew and marrow from the bones of St Piantorio" are wont to consult an ancient dame who poses as a wise-woman. An intended bride, doubtful as to her marriage, goes to this old lady. The dialogue, though only recorded by one of the characters, may be translated as fairly illustrative of Bruno's brisk and vigorous dramatic manner. It reminds us of that of Plautus and Molière. "Mother mine, they want me to marry Bonifacio Trucco.

---

[1] *Il Cand., A La Sigᵃ Morgana.*   [2] *Ibid., Act I, sc. VIII, IX.*

He is well off." "Have him!" "Yes, but he is too old."
" My daughter, don't have him!" " But my parents advise
me to." " Have him!" " But he don't please me too well."
" Then don't have him!" " I know he comes of good blood."
" Have him!" " But I hear he has not teeth enough to
bite a bean." " Don't have him!" " They tell me he has a
pure-bred greyhound." " Have him!" " But, oh dear
me, I hear he is only a chandler." " Don't have him!"
" Everybody thinks him mad." " Take him! Take him!
seven times over! His being a chandler doesn't count; it's
no concern of yours if he can't eat; if he doesn't please
you, no matter; what if he be old; but he is mad, so take
him." [1] Herein are furtive thrusts all round.

The play begins with a few verses. Then comes the
mock-dedication. By a convention dating from classic
times every play required a prologue. Bruno will none of
this. A love of buffoonery pervaded his age, so our author
next gives us a synopsis of the characters and of the three
closely interwoven but distinct plots of his comedy for
prologue and follows this up with an anti-prologue, then
with a pro-prologue and finally, before the curtain rises,
there is a speech from the beadle; all this, excepting the
synopsis, being done in that spirit of humorous provocation
so characteristic of Rabelais.

The play has five acts and eighteen characters, whereof
Bonifacio, an elderly, amorous miser; Bartolomeo, an
avaricious seeker after the philosopher's stone, and Manfurio, pedant and fool, are chief.

The pedant is of poor but pretentious intelligence;
naturally a vessel of mean capacity, which bursts into
absurdities when crammed with more than it was designed
to hold. His ineptitude overflows in affectation and self-
conceit, and he speaks in inappropriate Latin or latinized

[1] *Ibid., Act V, Sc. XXIV.*

Italian. He is a man of words and phrases, of subtle distinctions with no value in them, and of painstaking accuracy about trumpery matters. He lugs in classical lore at every breath. He is unmarried and is specially attached to his pupil Pollula: it is significant that a female name is given to the boy.[1] Manfurio has a hand in everything that is going on and understands nothing of it; he is fooled and laughed at, eventually falls into the clutch of a sham watch, and is soundly thrashed, as are the other protagonists.

Bonifacio, married to the youthful Carubina, is in love with Vittoria, a lady no better than she should be, who only pretends to return his affection in order to bleed his purse. He commits endless absurdities in order to keep her to himself, and goes to a professor of magic to help him. This gentleman drains him dry; whereupon Vittoria manages to substitute Carubina for herself. Bonifacio, in the dress of Bernardo, a painter, who is also in love with Carubina, is thus confronted by his own wife dressed in Vittoria's clothes. The pretended watch appear and force Bonifacio to give a bribe to their captain; meanwhile Carubina is tête-à-tête with the painter. Finally the deceived husband has to entreat his wife to pardon him, and sails into more tranquil waters " by the grace of the Lord and the Madonna."

The third protagonist, Bartolomeo, trusts himself to the direction of a designing alchemist who well-nigh exhausts his lean purse. A mixture, which contains a fictitious " powder of Christ " fails to work ; and after amusing scenes of roguery, the false watch appear and, by threatening prison, make their profit.

The play is a series of pictures of the seamy side of

[1] For the morals of schoolmasters, see Garzoni, T.; *La piazza Universale di tutte le professioni del mondo, Venezia,* 1617.

Neapolitan life and repeats the coarse talk which Bruno
would have heard as a boy. He may have written the
work when he was in the monastery: certain references
and its fresh and vigorous touches smack of the direct
transcript of recent impressions. But a reference to a
recent event shows that it received at least finishing
strokes in France, if not in Paris. In his castigation of
vice, the very unpleasant is unduly prominent; but the
play is not so foul as those of Machiavelli, Bibbiena and
Aretino. It must be admitted that this comedy exhibits a
great knowledge of the seamy side of life and is a queer
product of monastic discipline. But not so many years
before a Prince of the Church had officiated at the altar of
the Cyprian as well as at that of Christ, and his comedy
brought a blush to the face of that by no means severe
prude, Isabella D'Este, while Erasmus tells us of a priest
who took a part in a Latin play. Even in Bruno's stricter
days of Catholic Reform the full effect of the Council of
Trent was not felt, and no great blame attached to such
lapses. We must not press too heavily on the fault. The
Renaissance found frank indecency attractive; we have
become more "delicately indelicate." Natural instincts
held in leash are apt to manifest themselves in this vicarious
and disagreeable way, and a "virile" young man, in a
"virile" century at least, will roll in the obscene with the
unconstrained gratification of a puppy dog. Moreover,
many young men indulge in obscene speculation for precisely the same reason that lunatic maidens are said to
utter foul oaths: there is fascination in the repellent and
it is apt to produce an undue impression on the mind.

The plot is unduly complicated and reminds the reader
of the Spanish stage. The characters are abstract types,
like those of Ben Jonson and dramatists of the second
rank; but they are drawn with rare felicity. The dialogue

is quite as vivacious and clever as any by Aretino. "The Chandler" is quite *sui generis*—a new development in comedy. It is easy, spontaneous, the overflow of an ardent and imaginative temperament. Both the obscenity and buffoonery of the play are half intended to keep the audience amused; buffoonery and indelicacy are also introduced with this purpose in Bruno's more serious writings.

The rediscovery of the classics led, in time, to degenerate humanists : Bruno is less tender to these pedants than to knaves—probably because he had suffered more at their hands.[1] Philosophical theory peeps out in the play here and there.[2]

He believes that his enemies rejoice at his exile; but he is convinced he will obtain his due, "if not under one hood, then under another; if not in one life yet in another";[3] a remark which some have thought to show that he believed in an immortality not guaranteed by the mere pantheistic Neo-Platonism he had so far expounded.

In a somewhat earlier and more liberal age, Machiavelli expressed his contempt for the miraculous. Guicciardini thought those wonders which were best attested to be examples of natural phenomena not yet understood.[4] This was Bruno's attitude, as is clear from many passages in his books. In "The Chandler" he pours his scorn on the trickery of the priesthood. He hints at the miseries of monastic discipline.

He is aware of his own originality and declares it; he does not disguise his Horatian contempt for the herd.

There is no evidence that the play was ever performed;

[1] *Cfr.* Baccelli, A; *op. cit., p.* 74.
[2] *Cfr.* Telli, Carlo; *Il Cand., Prefaz., Biblioteca Rara, Dælli,* 1862.
[3] *Il Cand., A La Sigᵃ Morgana.*
[4] Guicciardini, F ; *Opere Ined., I,* 129.

but, influenced by prior productions, it left its mark in its
turn on those which followed.[1] The comedies of that many-
sided genius, Giambattista della Porta (who was a Neapolitan
and a contemporary of Bruno), which were published more
than twenty years later than the *Candelajo*, show a singular
resemblance to it.[2] Within two generations, a French adapta-
tion, entitled *Boniface et le Pédant*, was staged, and this was
followed by Cyrano de Bergerac's *Le Pédant joué*. Cyrano
concentrated Bruno's trifold plot to the advantage of the
play; but he missed much of the vivacity of the original
dialogue. He indirectly admits this, for he vows that
" Italian twins would joke in their mother's womb." These
adaptations influenced Molière; he extracted what suited
him from Cyrano's version, saying that he had a right to
it: "On reprend son bien partout on le trouve."[3] Prof.
Adamson suggested that Manfurio was the prototype of
Holofernes in Shakespeare's " Love's Labour's Lost."

[1] Spampanato, P ; *Alcuni antec. e imitaz. fr. del Candelajo, Portici,
Della Torre*, 1905.
[2] Spampanato, P ; *Somiglianze tra due commediografi Napoletani,
Napoli*, 1906.
[3] Bartholmèss ; *op. cit., I, p.* 262, *n. iv.*

CHAPTER VIII

AT OXFORD

HAVING made the disagreeable passage from Calais to Dover (Bruno's first experience of a journey by sea) he would not find that almost distinctive character of English scenery which obtains to-day. It was more like that of Northern France. For the most part, corn-land and pasturage were unenclosed, and there was a vast amount of uncultivated or poorly cultivated land, in spite of enclosures made under the Tudors. He presented his credentials to the French Ambassador and went on to Oxford to try his fortunes there.

Opposition, disappointment and defeat always incited Bruno to some fresh attack on the "parrots"[1] who foolishly repeated ancient and defective teaching or, at best, "tried to excuse the defects of their divinity, Aristotle."[2] Barbarians who dwelt at the ends of the earth must assuredly be only too glad to welcome so highly qualified a teacher as he. So he began by beating the big drum. He sent a foreword to the Vice-Chancellor and dons of the University which began thus: "Jordanus Bruno of Nola, lover of God, doctor in a more perfect divinity, professor of a purer and more harmless wisdom, a philosopher known, esteemed and honourably entreated by the foremost Academies of Europe, a stranger to none but churls and barbarians, the awakener of souls from slumber, the queller of presumptuous and recalcitrant ignorance, one

---

[1] *C. de le Ceneri, Dial. IV.*   [2] *De la Causa, Dial. III.*

who sheweth in all his actions the love he beareth to all men, whether Briton or Italian, female or male, whether bearing the mitre or the crown, the gown or the sword, wearing a cowl or without one; but who chiefly yearns for the man whose converse is peaceful, human, true and profitable; he who seeks not for an anointed head or a crossed brow, for the washed hand or him that is circumcised, but for those true lineaments of man which be his soul and trained understanding; one who is abhorred of them that spread foolishness and are but petty dissemblers, but whom men proven and in earnest love, and who is applauded by the nobler sort . . ."[1] This is the prelude to a request for permission to lecture.[2] Was anything more calculated to

> "Cleave the general ear,
>   Make mad the guilty and appal the free,
>   Confound the ignorant and amaze indeed"?

But, after all, the epistle only follows the pomposity of the age with Brunian emphasis. Even the most courtly and polished gentleman of his time, Sir Philip Sidney, when travelling to the Court of Rudolf II, had his arms emblazoned on whatever house he lodged at, with the announcement in

---

[1] *Philothei* Jordani Bruni Nolani *Triginta Sigillorum Explicatio : Ad excellentissimum oxoniensis Academiae Procancellarium, clarissimos doctores atque celeberimos magistros.*

[2] The letter, the dedication to Castelnau and a few leaves are not in all those copies of the "Thirty Seals" which have been preserved. Moreover they are printed on different paper, a different type was employed, and certain additions, of the nature of improvements, are present, which leads to the conclusion that the extra leaves were inserted as an afterthought. *Cfr.* Tocco, F ; *Le Opere Latine di G. B.*, *pp.* 63–66. May not Bruno have inserted these leaves after his quarrel with the University, as an act of defiance, and conjoined with this a mark, in the form of a dedication to Castelnau, of his appreciation of the service he rendered him after that event? It would, I think, be just like Bruno to do this.

Latin that they were those of "the most illustrious and well-born gentleman, Philip Sidney, son of the Viceroy of Ireland, nephew of the Earls of Warwick and Leicester, Ambassador from the Most Serene Queen of England to the Emperor."[1]

What reply Bruno received we do not know. The University could hardly have acquired "the fine Oxford manner" so early; but, surely, inflated speech and self-assertion were "bad form" and "unEnglish" even then, and this letter may be referred to by a certain N. W, who remarks in the preface to a translation of Paulus Jovius by Samuel Daniel, the poet, at that time an undergraduate at Magdalen. He writes: "you cannot forget that which Nolanus (*that man of infinite titles* amongst other phantastical toys) truly noted by chance in our schools, that by the help of translations all sciences had their offspring."[2]

Oxford, like other Universities, was throttled by the dead hand of Aristotle. In 1574 one Barebones, a follower of Ramus, was ejected from the University for daring to attack the thinker whom a strangely ironical fate had made one of the chief props of the Christian Church.[3] Bruno was prepared to challenge Oxford or any other seat of learning. He had begun the fight, and he continued it through England, France and Germany, seeking and giving no quarter, undeterred by authority, undismayed by poverty, superbly contemptuous of censure, immeasurably confident in his own strength and superiority.[4]

This is the only notice of Bruno at Oxford which has been discovered so far: all else that we know he tells us himself. He set up a class somewhere in the city, and found the University sadly in need of an "awakener"; he

---

[1] Symonds, J. A; *Sir P. Sidney*, 1889, *p.* 38.
[2] Elton, O ; *Modern Studies*, 1907, *pp.* 7, 8.
[3] McIntyre, J. L ; *G. Bruno*, 1903, *p.* 22.
[4] *Cfr. De Monade, Cap. I, v.* 38 *sq; Cap. VII, v.* 128 *sq.*

calls her " the widow of true knowledge so far as philosophy and mathematics are concerned." He laughed at her pretensions to Greek scholarship. Yet, less than a century before, the Oxford Hellenists, although but a small band, were distinguished by the presence of such scholars as Grocyn, Linacre and Croke, and Erasmus found Greek better taught in England than in Italy.[1]

Indeed, the English Universities had fallen from their high estate. Sport had always more attraction for the bulk of English gentry than learning, which was almost confined to the priesthood. The French wars and still more the Wars of the Roses were a hindrance to learning. Even before the Reformation John Barclay wrote of men—

> " Lesynge their tyme at the unyversyte,
> Yet count they themselfe of great auctoryte
> With their proude hodes on their neckes hangynge,
> They haue the lawde ; but others haue the cunnynge.
>
> They thynke that they haue all scyence perfytely,
> Within theyr hertes bostynge them of the same,
> Though they thereto theyr mynde dyd neuer apply ;
> Without the thynge, they joy them of the name."[2]

When the Reformation was effected, Erasmus's warning of the menace it would be to learning proved well-founded. The dissolution of the monasteries impoverished that scholarly class which opened a career to the clever lad of the people and gave him university instruction. But, to employ the words of Descartes, the Universities had not yet begun "to make merchandise of science for the bettering of their fortunes."

Theology was the main interest. The dons were, for the most part, absentees. Appointed by the Court, they

---

[1] Erasmus, Desiderius; *Opera Omnia, Lugd. Batav.*, 1703, *Tom. Tert., Epist. ccclxiii.*

[2] Barclay, John ; *Shyppe of Fooles.*

followed the Court, clad in velvet. Bruno describes two of these graduates. "One wore two resplendent gold chains on his neck; another twelve rings on two of his fingers: he looked like a rich jeweller."[1] A doctorate was easily obtained; it was purchasable; to become a doctor in medicine only needed a fee and that the candidate should have been in the habit of perusing medical books during ten years. The dons "knew much more about beer than about Greek," says Bruno.[2] Most of the students were quite young lads. The statutes provided that any master or doctor diverging one jot from the teaching of Aristotle should be fined five shillings[3] for each offence.[4] No one could be admitted to the degree of Master or Doctor unless he had quaffed of the Aristotelian fountain; but there were three fountains in the city, respectively called Aristotle, Pythagoras and Plato; the waters thereof were used to qualify cider and beer; "so that," Bruno maliciously observes, "by three or four days' stay in a college or elsewhere one could imbibe from all three."[5]

He seems to have found some favour with Matthew, the Dean of Christchurch, and with Culpepper, the Warden of New. He speaks respectfully of both these clergymen.[6] He would make the acquaintance of Italian teachers at the University, and he probably met Alberico Gentile there at festivals or elsewhere. Gentile came to England in 1580 and was appointed professor of Civil Law at Oxford four years later. Bruno certainly knew him in England[7] and met him again at Wittenberg.

After he had taught between two and three months,

---

[1] *C. de le Ceneri, Dial. I.*   [2] *Ibid.*
[3] Equivalent to at least two pounds sterling of to-day's money.
[4] McIntyre; *op. cit., pp.* 21, 22.
[5] *Causa, Dial. I.*
[6] *Ibid.* Concerning these worthies, consult Lagarde, *Op. ital. di G. B., p.* 220, *Gottingen,* 1888.   [7] *Doc. ix.*

there came to Oxford (in June) Adalbart Laski,[1] Palatine of Siradia, a Pole, who was in England on a mission to prevent the exportation of arms to Muscovy. The visit of a prince from regions so remote, one, moreover, who was credited with great bravery as a soldier and with much linguistic learning, created a great stir in England, and Oxford welcomed him with heavy feeding, erudite disputations, spectacular displays and all that ebullience in which the surcharged vitality of the Renaissance found vent. It must have heightened Bruno's acute perception of that "vicissitude" to which he constantly refers that Laski, who had shown his greed of gold by taking the bribes of France at the election of Henry III to the Polish crown,[2] soon had to steal away from his English creditors, with all precautions of silence and secrecy, accompanied by the occultist Dr John Dee and one Kelly, who was another professor of the art of transmuting base metal into gold.

Among the entertainers of Laski was Mathew Gwinne of St. John's, a young Welshman who became one of Bruno's English friends and, later on, helped Florio in his incomparable translation of Montaigne. Gwinne was an all-round man ; he added the accomplishment of music to a knowledge of French and Italian. He became a dramatic author (in Latin) and possessed of a smattering of physic.[3] When Laski was at Oxford, Gwinne held forth with others on such problems as whether males or females are longer lived, and whether events can be foretold from the stars.

These disputations, held in honour of the Prince, gave Bruno his chance. He shall tell his own tale. "Search where you will in England to-day you shall find everybody

---

[1] Camden, W ; *Annales*, *tr.* R. Norton, *sub anno* 1583.—Wood, Anthony à ; *Athenae Oxonienses c. Fasti*, *sub* Alaskie.

[2] Bain, R. N ; *Camb. Mod. Hist.*, 1904, *III, p.* 85.

[3] *Nat. Dict. Biog.*, 1890, *xxiij*, 399–400.

a Doctor in Grammar ; so that the happy country is ruled by a constellation of pedants who exhibit obstinacy, ignorance and presumption, mixed up with such boorish rudeness that it might provoke the patience of Job. Should you doubt, go to Oxford and get them to tell you about what happened to the Nolan when he disputed publicly with these Doctors of theology before the Prince Laski the Pole and certain English nobles. Learn how they replied to his argument and how, on that great occasion, a wretched doctor got stuck, like a chicken in stubble, fifteen times in the fifteen syllogisms he propounded as Coryphæus of the University. Hear tell how vulgar and violent the pig was, and how patient and forbearing was the other, who shewed his Neapolitan breeding and rearing under a kindly sky. Ask how they put a stop to his public lectures, both on the Immortality of the Soul and on the Quintuple Sphere."[1]

Brave, tactless, self-assertive missionary of truth! Like Mr F's aunt, Bruno hated a fool. Nevertheless, to call one's opponent a " pig " merely, was an exhibition of self-restraint in days when scholars, theologians above all, were not content with scurrilous epithets which a bargee might envy and which are now expunged from our dictionaries, but were wont to traduce the whole house and ancestry of an adversary, including the chastity of its female members.[2]

Bruno, then, aroused the Aristotelian lion from his slumbers in a favourite lair. Oxford rejected him, doubtless with many an insular sneer at the excitable, gesticulating foreigner, hairy as Pan.[3]

Later on, when the feeling of resentment had somewhat subdued, while still continuing to pass some satiric strictures on the University he gave a more balanced judgement and

[1] *C. de le Ceneri, Dial. IV.*
[2] As evidence, see e.g., Bayle's Dictionary ; article, Schoppius.
[3] Bruno, G ; *De innum. immenso et infigur. l. viij.*

even tried to make amends. He admitted that she had been " founded on an excellent basis and was marked by such decorum, dignified ceremonies and many other adjuncts as to place her, in these respects, first in Europe, while in polish and quickness of mind she can hold her own."[1] But —she was Aristotelian to the core. Three generations later Sir Thomas Browne wrote of the Copernican theory as being still a subject for debate among the learned.[2]

[1] *De la Causa, Dial. I.*
[2] Browne, Sir T ; *Pseudodoxia Epidemica, l. vj, c.* 5.

CHAPTER IX

IN LONDON

BRUNO was in sad plight: stranded in a strange country, unable to speak its language and with a lank purse at his girdle. He found a saviour in the French Ambassador. Castelnau, he tells us, rescued him "from these doctors and from hunger"; he proved a "firm and effective defender . . . a solid, secure and enduring rock."[1] The Ambassador was himself in pecuniary straits: his salary was irregularly paid and he was obliged to borrow money,[2] but he gave the wandering Italian scholar a home. "You did not maintain a man in your household of whom you had need, but one who stood in need of you in many ways," Bruno wrote him.[3] "I remained in his house as his gentleman— merely that."[4] Doubtless Castelnau found him of service; Bruno frequently accompanied him to the Court of Elizabeth, and the French Ambassador, in want of money, might have been glad of the aid of an unofficial secretary at no great cost.

Michel de Castelnau, Lord of Mauvissière, was sixty-three years old, a man of considerable learning and experience of life. He was one of the very earliest men north of the Alps to become a professional diplomatist. He had travelled in Italy and had served in campaigns there and elsewhere; he had been ambassador at the Court of Mary Stewart and also in Germany, and had represented France

---

[1] *Causa, Proem. Epist.*   [2] McIntyre, *op. cit., p.* 27.
[3] *De l'Infinito, Proem. Epist.*   [4] *Doc. ix.*

at Elizabeth's court during the past ten years. He had
literary tastes and had translated Ramus' book on the
Gauls. His memory was excellent, and he shows himself,
in the memoirs which he wrote for the instruction of his
two sons, a searcher after causes, truthful, and a man of
impartial judgement.[1]   Unhappily he tells us nothing about
Bruno, for the memoirs end with the year 1574.   He seems
to have been reticent and firm ; but too scrupulous to obtain
great success in diplomacy.   It is a testimony to his high
character that while he defended the interests of Mary
Stewart he retained the warm regard of Elizabeth Tudor.
His great antagonist was the Spanish Ambassador, Bernardino de Mendoza, for whom he was a poor match in guile.
Indeed, Castelnau was a broad-minded generous gentleman,
sincerely religious, but so tolerant that he excused Bruno
from attending mass and the other religious offices held at
his house ; nay more, in permitting the dedication to himself
of four of Bruno's works Castelnau accepted three of the
most daring he ever wrote.[2]

Bruno found the embassy a peaceful haven, where, for
more than two years, he was sheltered from the blasts
which had whirled him hither and thither for seven years
past and were to swoop on him again.   The embassy was
known as Beaumont House ; it was in Butcher's Row,[3] a
narrow lane which led into the Strand, close by St Clement
Danes, not far from the boundary line of the City—a
"timber-framed house, with projecting upper stories and
barge-boarded gables, the front decorated with *fleur-de-lis*
and coronets."[4]

[1] Castelnau, M de; *Mémoires, Paris,* 1621.
[2] "Exposition of the Thirty Seals" in Latin ; "The Ash Wednesday Supper," "On Cause Principle and Unity," and "The Infinity
of the Universe and its Worlds," in Italian.
[3] Pulled down 1813.
[4] Wheatley, H. B ; *Story of London,* 1904, *p.* 392.

We have a word or two about the lady of the house from Bruno. It occurs in one of those innumerable and protracted digressions which seem to have served the double purpose of entertaining the reader and discharging the surging back-waters of his own mind. For a century there had been in Italy a stupid and interminable discussion which is not obsolete even now—a battle of books between the extravagant eulogists of woman as a prodigy of impossible perfection and equally absurd detractors[1] who debased her even below the more recent depreciations of Weininger and Strindberg. Bruno satirises the "oratoric art" that was employed by making one of his interlocutors almost exhaust the language of vituperation; he loads the female sex with no fewer than nine and thirty consecutive epithets, all equally abusive.[2] Yet one retains a lurking suspicion that, behind the obvious satiric intention, there lay a secret satisfaction in the diatribe; an acquittal of the inherent obligations of masculinity and of coarse monkish prejudice. And he had suffered recently from the active ill will of some woman of whom he complains bitterly to Castelnau. She is mad and malicious, he says, with an evil tongue, and trusts to squeezed-out tears to back up her evil designs.[3] Anyhow, Bruno succeeds in keeping his reader thoroughly awake after his long diatribe by one of his swift turns. In the worst possible taste all these objurgations of Madame de Castelnau's sex are made to serve as a foil to her own excellences! She is an exception to the general depravity of woman. By a clumsy literary artifice another interlocutor is made to say that all men are not unfortunate in their experience of the sex: Castelnau is happy in a wife "of no mean beauty, which

---

[1] These works make curious reading. Sometimes, as in Bruno's case, opposite opinions fall from the same mouth.

[2] *Causa, Dial. IV.*, Polinnio *loq.*   [3] *Ibid., Proem. Epist.*

indeed is a fit clothing to her soul ; she is a lady of judgement, prudence, modesty and polite dignity,"[1] whence we
may conclude that the noble lady, who was in failing health at
the time, had still some traces of good looks and was fairly
gracious and kind to Bruno.

But the heart of the monk, pathetically debarred from
fatherhood, went out to the younger of the two girls of the
house, to whom, perhaps, he gave lessons. One can discover real tenderness in his description of how "hardly yet
six years of age, she speaks Italian, French and English so
equally well that no one can tell her nationality ; she plays
various instruments so that one wonders whether she be
flesh or spirit, and from her already ripe and noble bearing,
whether she be of earth or have come down from the skies.
Both her parents reappear alike in her body and in her
mind."[2] In a year or two both mother and little daughter
were among the dead.

However filled with the music of the starry heavens and
with immortal thoughts, genius is peculiarly " gey ill to live
wi'." We can credit Bruno with being very thin-skinned
and not a little trying at the fire-side. He honestly believed
himself to be a model of politeness and self-restraint. He
thought that every one was against him. " No one ever
blamed me for discourtesy "—so he assures Castelnau—
" no one can justly complain of me." He plunges us into
a cataract of contrasts in order that we may know how
the worthy love and the unworthy maltreat him.[3] Small
worries tortured the nerves of a man whom the cruelest
death could not dismay. Like the rest of us, his was a
strangely compounded clay. Full of noble gratitude, lofty
conception, serene wisdom and an heroic passion to know
truth and proclaim it, he was yet a trifle prejudiced, a trifle

[1] *Causa, Dial. IV, Gervasio loq.*   [2] *Ibid., loc. cit.*
[3] *Cena, Dial. V.*

irritable and vain, very impulsive and restless, a little snappy, somewhat resentful, wholly indiscreet and given to singular crotchets and ill-timed bursts of strange, if generous, enthusiasms—probably such would be a contemporary's judgement of Bruno. But our wonder at this man of high and continued purpose is not lessened by his human weaknesses; our respect for the unfailing patience and kindness of the Castelnaus towards their somewhat difficult guest is increased.

The passionate Southern Italian, knowing about three words of the English tongue and, since he deems it fit for dogs, not wishing to learn more,[1] may have got into trouble in the London streets; if so, possibly the lady whose "malicious feminine rage and false tears, which can be more powerful than any volume of swollen billows"[2] had something to do with it. Sensini thinks he got into a row, was imprisoned, released by the good offices of Mauvissière and kept at home for a time.[3] Certainly Bruno rehearses to Castelnau how "not only did you receive and sustain me, but defended me, set me free, held me safe, kept me in harbour."[4] We certainly learn that, on account of his severe strictures on the English people,[5] he dared not appear in the streets and remained shut up at home,[6] and possibly the lady in question had some hand in this.

Very soon after taking up his abode at Beaumont House, Bruno must have accompanied his host to the Court, for he knew the Spanish Ambassador there,[7] and Mendoza was expelled from England in January 1584 after the detection of his complicity in the plots against Elizabeth's life. "The Queen knew me," says Bruno, "for I accompanied the

---

[1] *Cena, Dial. III.* [2] *Causa, Proem. Epist.*
[3] Sensini, T ; *Sul pensiero filosofico di G. B.*, 1907.
[4] *Causa, Proem. Epist.* [5] *Cena de le Ceneri.*
[6] *Causa, I*, where Armesso speaks for the first time. [7] *Doc. xvij.*

Ambassador to Court habitually."[1] Italian gentlemen were welcome at Elizabeth's Court. She prided herself on her knowledge of their language; most of her courtiers had visited Italy; many of them were well-versed in Italian literature, and all formed their manners on the Italian model. It was to the incalculable advantage of our behaviour and of our literature that so many gentlemen were "tried and tutored in the world"; but the less stable spirits came back from their travels to exhibit "strange antic tricks," the absurdity of which Bruno did not catch. But Shakespeare did. "Look you lisp, . . ." says Rosalind, "and wear strange suits and disable all the benefits of your own country and be out of love with your nativity, and almost chide God for making you of that countenance you are, or I will scarcely think you have swam in a gondola." It was the prevalent passion for Italy and deep respect for the Italian language and literature which gave Bruno an opportunity of publishing, through a London press, his noblest works in his own tongue. There was no university in London, or its scholars would have despised any thought, however profound, which was not expressed in the language of the learned.

Bruno admired Elizabeth and wrote of her as superlatively as custom demanded.[2] He called her—a Protestant ruler—"*diva*" "sacred" or "divine," just as he did His Most Christian Majesty and the Head of the Holy Roman Empire: it was treasured against him and brought up at his trial.[3]

Of Elizabeth's courtiers, he neither knew nor expected to know Leicester, at least in the earliest part of 1584;[4] but he would certainly be known to Walsingham. He was noticed by Fulke Greville, a scholarly young courtier, about two years younger than himself. Greville stood high in

[1] *Doc. xij.*
[2] *Cena, Dial. II ; Causa, Dial. I.*
[3] *Doc. xiij.*
[4] *Cena, Dial. II.*

Elizabeth's favour and was fortunate in enjoying "the longest lease and the smoothest time . . . . of any of her favourites."[1] To know Master Greville was to know Sir Philip Sidney, his close friend from their school-days at Shrewsbury. The two friends were, at this time, busy translating the Frenchman, Philippe de Mornay, lord of Plessis-Marly. Sidney, whom Spenser calls "the president of nobless and courtesie" was the cynosure of his time— polished courtier, poet, scholar, patron of letters and the stage and a passionate admirer of Italian literature.[2] Bruno was not exempt from the fascination he exercised.[3] Sidney, Greville and Dyer were devoted to each other, but of Dyer he does not speak.

The courtiers probably regarded Bruno as an interesting oddity, an eccentric foreigner, and accepted him as the London society of to-day accepts a philosopher from Thibet.[4] The more sympathetic Sidney expressed willing- ness to do him some service, and Greville followed with the same offer. Greville might have proved quite as munificent a patron as Sidney, for he held more than one post with light duties and enormous salaries attached—about £2000 a year—but he spent a great deal in furnishing the Court with tournaments and amusements.[5] Bruno contrived to displease him; perhaps by the strictures he passed on English life in the "Ash Wednesday Supper" and by associating them so closely with the banquet supposed to be given by Greville. He tells us that "the arsenic of vile, ill-conditioned and unworthy folk" caused their relations to

---

[1] Naunton, Sir R ; *Fragmenta Regalia, ed. A. Arber,* 1870, *p.* 50.

[2] Cfr. Bourne, H. R. Fox ; *Sir P. Sidney, N.Y,* 1891.

[3] *Spaccio, Epist. Esplic ; Eroici, Argomento del Nolano.*

[4] Symonds, J. A ; *Renaissance in Italy : Catholic Reaction, II,* *p.* 55.

[5] Edmondson, J ; *An Historical and Geographical Account of the Family of Greville,* 1766, *p.* 79.

be strained: he proposed to dedicate a book to Greville,[1] but never did so. To Sidney he dedicated his two important works on moral subjects.[2]

Sidney was the English representative of Petrarchism, though he was far from copying the current ignoble and degenerate affectation of love which now prevailed in Italy. He tumbled head over ears in love with Penelope Devereux when she was still a child. The only satisfaction he ever obtained was a kiss stolen from her when she was asleep; but sexual fascination remained so divorced from matrimony in the sixteenth century that he continued to address verses of passionate devotion to her after she became Lady Rich (1581), with the full knowledge and consent of both his sister and the lady who was now his wife. He identified "Stella" with Beauty;[3] and it is the opinion of the best judges of the age that the representations of Spenser [4] as to the sincerity and depth of the passion are "calm and deliberate facts."[5] Now Sidney's verses were not published until after his death; but they were widely circulated in manuscript and were already famous; his love for Stella was generally known. Bruno writes to him as a distinguished poet;[6] he had been in London and attending the Court at least considerably more than a year, if not over two years, when he did so, and would know therefore of this passion, and of how, repelled by Stella, Sidney had turned his love to nobler issues than personal gratification, though he nursed it still. Bruno wished to put before Sidney and the world a higher form of adoration; he would substitute devotion to the imperishable beauty of wisdom for the courtly

[1] *Spaccio, Epist. Esplic.*
[2] *Spaccio de la Bestia Trionfante ; Gli Eroici Furori.*
[3] Sidney, Sir P ; *Astrophel and Stella,* 1598, *xlv, lxxxvj.*
[4] Spenser Ed ; *Astrophel.*
[5] Arber, P ; *Eng. Garner,* 1897, *vol. I, p.* 469.
[6] *Eroici, Argomento del Nolano.*

service of mere perishable charms, whether of body or mind ; so, with characteristic zeal and directness of attack and equally characteristic absence of prudence and tact, he sneers at "that Tuscan poet who displayed such spasms on the banks of the Sorgue for a lady of Vaucluse—though I do not desire to say he was mad."[1] No one who was not entirely insensitive to what might be passing in the mind of another could write thus. But Bruno was singularly defective in this regard and, ultimately, it brought him to his end.

In the same dedicatory letter there occurs a pæan of virility. It has been remarked that "his tone is that of Walt Whitman ; he is strenuous and invincible and male."[2] Falstaff might be addressing Prince Hal in the Eastcheap tavern when Bruno asks : "What do I hold? Am I perchance a foe to generation? Do I hate the sun? Do I regret having come into the world? Shall I keep men from the delicious fruit of our earthly paradise? Is it for me to bar the holy law of nature? Shall I try to set myself or others free from the sweet-bitter yoke which God, in His providence, hath placed on our neck? Am I to persuade myself and others that we are not born to carry on the life we have received? Methinks I am not cold. I doubt if the snows of Caucasus would put out my fires. . . . What do I conclude? Eminent Knight, that we should render unto Cæsar the things that are Cæsar's and to God the things which are God's. That women, being women, should be honoured and loved as such."[3] We should not forget that, like Mercutio, Bruno is "a gentleman that loves to hear himself talk. He will say more in a minute than he will stand to in a month." Nevertheless, here was strange matter for Sidney's "wit, high, pure, divine"[4] to digest,

---

[1] *Eroici, Argomento del Nolano,* The work bears the date 1585.
[2] Elton, O ; *op. cit., p.* 22.   [3] *Eroici, Argomento.*
[4] Spenser, Ed ; *Epitaph upon the Rt. Hon. Sir P. Sidney.*

G

unless there was a side to his character which disappeared from our view in his apotheosis after Zutphen. And he is favoured, a little farther on, with the unromantic avowal, "made without blushing, that a woman is worthy of being loved in the flower of her beauty and ability to produce children of Nature and God." [1] Still farther on, "the Nolan" contrasts the sexual instinct with intellectual ardour. A strange address from a poet to a poet! but at least it shews that Bruno knew his patron to be broad-minded and tolerant. Sidney would perceive that Bruno was wholly incapable of covering up a single one of the many sides to his character and that he trusted to candour as the best possible title to consideration. It is evidence of the merit of both men—the sincerity of the suitor is matched by the tolerance of "a spotless friend, a matchles man, whose vertue ever shinde."

Here in London, Bruno seems to have renewed his acquaintance with Gwynne, and he became friendly with John Florio, an Oxford man, but an Italian by birth, being the son of a refugee who was a protestant preacher in this country. Florio introduces Bruno and an unidentified adversary at Oxford as Nolano and Torquato [2] in "Second Fruites," published six years after Bruno's departure from England. A follower and friend of Bruno's was Alexander Dickson, who published "The Shadow of Reason" [3] in the year of Bruno's arrival in England. It is in Latin and is a mnemonic and Neo-Platonic work of little value, being but a poor imitation of Bruno's "Shadows of Ideas." Bruno says Dickson was as "dear to him as his own eye." [4] Among other adherents of "the Nolan" was one Smith, who be-

---

[1] *Eroici, Argomento.*

[2] Called Torquato by Bruno himself in the *Cena.*

[3] *De Umbra Rationis. Cfr.* McIntyre, *op. cit., p.* 36, for Dickson and Watson, who mentions Bruno.

[4] *Causa, Dial. I.*

comes an interlocutor in the "Ash Wednesday Supper."
The difficulty of identifying this particular bearer of the
patronymic is enhanced by the absence of his Christian
name. He may have been John Smith, to whom Claudius
Hollyband dedicated the "Italian Schoolmaster" in 1575,[1]
or Joseph Smith, who was at some time, not yet ascertained,
consul at Venice,[2] or William Smith, the author of " Chloris
or the Complaint of the Passionate Despised Shepherd."[3]
There are other folks introduced into the dialogues who
also remain unidentified.

[1] Einstein, L ; *The Italian Renaissance in England*, N.Y., 1902,
p. 101.

[2] Sicardi ; *Il Candelajo, Prefaz. e note*, 1889, p. 39. *Cfr.* Gentile,
G ; *G. B. nella Storia della cultura*, 1907.

[3] McIntyre ; *op. cit., pp.* 35, 36.

CHAPTER X

IMPRESSIONS OF ELIZABETH'S ENGLAND

BRUNO produced seven books while in England. The first of these, a treatise on the Lullian art, Mnemonics and Metaphysics in Latin,[1] appeared in 1583. The second, entitled "The Ash-Wednesday Supper,"[2] the main object of which was to refute Aristotelian Physics and Astronomy and extend the Copernican conception; the third "On Cause, Principle and The One,"[3] a metaphysical work, and the fourth, "The Infinite Universe And Its Worlds"[4] were in Italian, dedicated to Castelnau, and appeared in 1584. The "Supper" professes to have been printed in Paris; the "Cause" and "Infinite Universe" at Venice; but experts declare that all were issued from some unidentified London press.[5] Bruno told the Inquisitors that "all those which set forth on the title-page that they were printed at Venice were really printed in London. The printer wished it to appear that they were printed in Venice to secure a better sale and get them abroad better; for if it had been indicated that they were printed in England their sale would have been more difficult. They were all printed in England although they bear the mark of Paris and elsewhere."[6] The "Expulsion of the Triumphant Beast,"[7] dedicated to

---

[1] *Explicatio triginta sigillorum. . . . Quibus adjectus est sigillus sigillorum. . . .*

[2] *La cena de le Ceneri.*   [3] *De la causa, principio et uno.*

[4] *De l'infinito, universo et mondi.*

[5] *Cfr.* Elton, O ; *Modern Studies,* 1907, *p.* 322, *n.* 20.—McIntyre, J. L ; *G. Bruno,* 1903, *p.* 358, *n.* 5.

[6] *Doc. xi.*   [7] *Spaccio de la Bestia trionfante.*

Sidney, bears the press-mark " Paris, 1584 "; but, since the work contains a reference to a riot at Naples which occurred in May 1585, it is obvious that it must have been printed after that date.[1] The next work, the " Cabala Of The Steed Like unto Pegasus, With the Addition of the Ass of Cyllene,"[2] bears the press-mark " Paris, 1585," and is dedicated to an imaginary bishop of Casamarciano, a little place in Bruno's native province. Following this, in the same year, came "The Transports Of Intrepid Souls,"[3] purporting, like the Cabala, to have been printed by a fictitious Antonio Baio at Paris. It was dedicated to Sidney.

Several of the Italian books contain remarks on England ; but the " Ash-Wednesday Supper" has pages of satiric observation mingled with half humorous exaggeration, never without a touch of severity. Bruno makes some apology for these in the "Causa" but sticks to his main indictment. He was struck by the pasturage in England, so rich and green, by the splendid flocks of " pretty, excellent, fat, white and nimble lambs " it nourished, and by the Englishman's love of sport;[4] he liked the climate, "the heavens being more temperate than anywhere else beyond and on this side the Equinoctial; snow and heat being banished from the subjacent earth as well as the excessive heat of the sun, which the perpetually green flowery ground witnesses, and so enjoys a perpetual spring."[5] Like Erasmus, he found the Englishwoman charming. She is "graceful, gentle, soft, delicate, youthful, beautiful, slender, with fair hair, rosy cheeks, divine eyes, firm breasts and shining hands ";[6] to select from a string

---

[1] Fiorentino, F ; *Dialoghi Morali di G. B., Giornale Napoletano, N.S.,* 1882, *fasc.* 19, *p.* 42.

[2] *Cabala del Cavallo Pegaseo, con l'aggiunta de l'Asino Cillenico.*

[3] *De Gli Eroici Furori.*   [4] *Spaccio, III, iij.*

[5] *Spaccio, III, ij.*   [6] *Cena, Dial. I.*

of epithets. He "lives long on the almsbasket of words" to express his admiration ! One of the very best stanzas that he wrote in England praises the "gentle nymphs who make a stay on the green banks of the Thames so charming": just before this, he had spoken of "the beautiful and gracious nymphs of Father Thames."[1] He noticed the marking of the royal swans, and the great flocks of crows; how inhuman the game-laws were and how eager was the Englishman to be a landowner.[2] He valued the broad-minded Britons who became his friends, and the educated Italianate gentlemen of the Court. But his disposition was not a specially forbearing one, and he was fastidious as Horace in shrinking from the rude humours of the mob. "I hate the populace" he told Castelnau.[3]

To pass from Italy to France was to go back more than one generation in polish of manner and cultivation of mind; and, compared with France, England was still a semi-barbarous country. Poetry, after nearly two centuries of almost complete silence, was indeed chirping the first imperfect notes of a new morning-song, and Spenser trilled a fresh, delightful music in his "Shepheard's Calender"; Lyly in "Euphues," a rural romance, attempted to give finish and elegance to British prose; but "Marlowe's mighty line" did not yet resound in the rude play-houses of the metropolis, and "Gordobuc," "Ralph Royster Doyster" and a few masque-like productions of Lyly represented the best that had as yet been done for British drama.

---

[1] *Eroici, P. II, Dial. V.*

[2] *Spaccio, Dial. III, ij, iij.*—"What must we do with the swan, demanded Juno. Said Jupiter, I order that it be marked on the bill with my seal and put into the Thames; because there it will be more safe than in any other part. And thus none will be able to rob me, for fear of capital punishment." *Ibid. II, iij.*

[3] *De l'infinito, Proem. Epist. Cfr.* Horace ; *Odes, III, i.*

After a year's residence in England, he could not contain his disgust for the British commonalty. He expresses it with wonted ebullience, hurling epithet after epithet and piling metaphor on metaphor. "England can boast a common people which will yield to none other in disrespect, outlandishness, boorishness, savagery and bad bringing up." "When they see a foreigner they become so many wolves and bears, by the Lord ; they put on the malevolent look of a pig when you take away his trough." English courtiers " who sit near the sun" [Elizabeth] are well bred, but the natural proclivities of the masses, or at least of some of them, are only comparable with those of "Arabs, Tartars and Cannibals." He describes the swaggering bully who, " if you don't make way for him, will give you a shove with his shoulder and spin you round. Should you be a foreigner you shall be made as well acquainted with space as if you had encountered a bull." [1]

He speaks of two great classes in the English plebs : there are traders and serving-men. The former, " smelling out somehow that you come from abroad, twist their faces at you, jeer, snigger, make disgusting noises, and call you dog, traitor and foreigner, which last is the vilest epithet they can bestow and implies that you are fair game for the worst treatment conceivable ; [2] it matters not whether you be young or old, a noble or gentleman, wearing a robe or bearing arms. Should you, finding yourself in a fix, repel one of them or put your hand on your sword, you shall straightway see them come surging out of their shops and filling

[1] *Cena, Dial. II.*

[2] Three generations later, an Englishman, returning from the continent, would, if he were incautious enough to wear foreign dress or foreign manners, be pelted with garbage by the London rabble, who would shout " French dogs ! French dogs ! A Mounseer ! A Mounseer !" *A character of England, as it was lately presented to a Noble Man of France, London,* 1659.

the whole street, and you find yourself surrounded by an excrementitious mob of rowdies who have sprung up more quickly than did the warriors, fabled by the poets, when Jason sowed the dragons' teeth. It would seem as if earth disgorged them; but, in fact, they come from the shops, and present a highly dignified and civilized array of long-staves, halberds, partizans and rusty forks which, for whatever worthy purpose the Sovereign may have granted them, are always held in readiness for this and the like opportunities. They shall fall on you with outlandish fury, not reflecting on whom, why, wherefore or how; there is no deliberation; each discharges himself of his natural contempt for the stranger; and, if he be not impeded by the very press of folk, all bent on the same purpose, you shall have the measure of your doublet taken by fist or rod, and, if you be not wary, you shall have your hat staved in. All this even if you be accompanied by some person of means or quality—let him be count or duke, it shall be to his damage and not to your profit—for, in a herd, these folk are no respecters of rank, and, however he may disapprove, he must stand aside, look on and await the finish." [1]

The serving men, he says, are of various grades: needy gentlemen, bankrupt merchants, broken-down students, runaway soldiers and sailors as well as gaol-birds and wastrels who are wont to hang about the Exchange and St. Paul's for hire. [2]

Even in refined circles, the loving cup was passed round, much to Bruno's disgust: he draws a nauseating picture of this and of some other scenes.

These are not the only strictures he makes on English social life. The work entitled "The Ash Wednesday Supper" is an attack on Aristotelian Physics and Cosmology, but this is led up to by a row on the Thames and a

[1] *Cena, Dial. II.*   [2] *Ibid.*

walk through London to Fulke Greville's abode, where a
supper has been prepared for Bruno and his antagonists.
A hot disputation follows the repast. Everyone seems to
have taken this as a veridical account of real happenings.
I cannot do so.   I do not dispute that, at some time, Greville
may have heard Bruno debating the point, perhaps in his
own apartment, and certainly it would be a very frequent
subject of discussion between Bruno and his friends or
visitors at Beaumont House, and he admits that this was
the case at supper on an Ash Wednesday. When asked
by the Inquisitors whether he had written concerning an
Ash Wednesday Supper and what was his purpose therein,
he replied: " I have written a book in five dialogues so
entitled, which dealt with the earth's movement, and, because
I debated the matter in England at an Ash Wednesday
supper with certain doctors of medicine *at the house of the
French Ambassador at which I dwelt*, I called the dialogues
the Ash Wednesday Supper. It may be that there are
certain errors in the book which I cannot now recall precisely.[1] The book was intended to ridicule these doctors
and their opinions concerning these matters." [2] The Inquisitors did not pursue the subject. It has been suggested
that Bruno deliberately made a false statement as to where
the supper took place in order to minimize his offence, and
located it, therefore, at the house of an orthodox Catholic.
That would not be like Bruno : like other men he sometimes
evades an inconvenient question or puts the best face he
can on the answer he is obliged to give, but, to direct
unescapable questioning, he invariably gives perilously
straightforward replies. The Inquisitors knew about the
book ; they may have had it before them ; taken *au pied de
la lettre* it refutes Bruno's reply so far as the place is con-

---

[1] There were errors in his exposition of Copernicanism which he
corrected in *De Immenso.*   [2] *Doc. xiij.*

cerned. And he could not have forgotten where the supper was held after he had written a whole book around it. A careful examination of the work convinces me that, while the supper and disputation are based on facts, these have been altered, rearranged and played upon by Bruno's lively imagination and worked up into literary form. He wants to make discussion go down by furnishing attractive dishes; he wants at the same time to open the safety-valve of his indignation at British obtuseness and British manners. If he and a few friends discussed Natural Philosophy and fish together on Ash Wednesday, it would be quite in his manner to turn the Aristotelian physics and cosmology into a " Supper of Ashes."

He more than hints that he has invested everything with such literary merit in his prefatory letter to Castelnau. " You will ask me, ' What symposium, what banquet is this ? ' ' It is a supper.' ' What supper ? ' ' Ash Wednesday's.' ' Who talks about a supper on Ash Wednesday ? The repast must have taken place before then. Would you say " I have eaten ashes like bread "? '[1] ' No, it is a banquet *after sunset*[2] on the first day of Lent, which our priests call the day of Ashes and Remembrance.' ' What is the banquet for ? ' Not to consider the mind and possessions of the very noble and worthy Master Fulke Greville, at whose honoured abode it takes place; nor the fine manners of the very courteous gentlemen who were there as lookers-on and listeners; but who will may see what nature is capable of in producing two fantastic fooleries,[3]

[1] *Psalm cii*, 9.

[2] We must always bear in mind the possibility of symbolic allusion in an age passionate for allegory and at the hands of a past-master of the art. The Aristotelian sun had set for the wise. I do not wish to push this, however, after the manner of Shakespeare-Baconians.

[3] *I.e.*, the journey and the display of ignorant prejudice at the discussion.

two dreams, two shadows [1] and two quartan agues, of which as one goes on, *criticizing the historical meaning* and then tasting and chewing, one comes on apposite topographical, geographical, moral enquiries, and yet others of a metaphysical, mathematical and natural character." [2]

Bruno must have gone often enough to Court by water (the usual and pleasanter route), and he says that on this occasion he was accompanied by Florio and Gwynne, the former, at least, being very well acquainted with London ; yet (although it is late, the company await them at Westminster and they are in a hurry) he makes his party go eastward in order to get westward to Westminster; they ignore the nearest stage—the Temple Stairs—and take their boat from Dorset Stairs, [3] as if to indicate more clearly that this long introduction to the main subject of the work, with the "topographical and geographical enquiries" and absurdities it includes, is a literary invention.

Nor is this all. Although England had thrown off the yoke of Rome the Anglican Church did not violently repudiate venerable religious habits, nor has it ever ceased to observe Ash Wednesday as a Fast-day. The Courtiers were not Puritans. But it might be urged that there would be no court-festivities on that day, and it would be a convenient season for a quiet supper and discussion. This may be so. Yet the town-house of the Grevilles was close by Holborn ; and one did not go from St. Clements Dane to Holborn by water. Prof. Elton suggests that Greville was lodging " in or near Whitehall." [4] Assuredly he was not lodging near Whitehall. The crowd of people

---

[1] Query, the dream of the supper and journey to it and the dream of the Peripatetic physicists?

[2] *Cena, Proem. Epist.*   [3] Elton, O ; *op. cit., p.* 12.

[4] Elton, O ; *loc. cit.*

and servants whom the guests find in the hall is suggestive
of the palace itself, and Bruno, who gibes at their rudeness,[1]
may have directed his sarcasm at Elizabeth's servitors
because he had experienced small courtesy at their hands.

If my view be correct, Bruno has run together a multitude of experiences, one of which may have been at
Greville's table, and adorned them, not merely to "ridicule these doctors," but also to satirize English manners.
Let us look at Elizabeth's London through Bruno's eyes.

Two messengers come to him from a certain esquire at
the Court, asking him to give his views concerning the
Copernican theory. He replies that he does not see
through Copernicus' eyes, but with his own.[2] We next
find Bruno in conversation with Fulke Greville, whom
we must infer is the esquire in question. Greville asks
Bruno why he believes in the rotation of the earth. Bruno
replies that he has not the measure of Greville's capacity
for grasping it; he (Bruno) may be as one of those
who talk to images and address the dead; if Greville will
furnish the reason for *his* belief he will reply to it.
Greville is very pleased at this answer, and invites Bruno
to meet and discuss the problem with a company of gentlemen and learned folk on Ash-Wednesday. Bruno accepts,
but begs that opponents may be chosen who are not
"ignoble people, miscreate and of small understanding in
these matters. Master Fulke replies that Bruno need have
no fear, for the men he has in mind are of the best learning
and behaviour."[3] The "learning and behaviour" thus skilfully introduced is by no means exhibited to their advantage
in the sequel. Bruno hears no more of the matter, and when
the day appointed comes round he waits and waits; dinner
time passes over, so he gives the whole thing up and goes

---

[1] *Cena, Dial. II, end.*   [2] *Ibid., Dial. I.*

[3] *Ibid., Dial. II.*

out to call on some Italian friends. He does not return to Beaumont House till after sunset and, behold, John Florio and Matthew Gwynne are kicking their heels at the doorway while they impatiently await his return. They tell him he must hurry on with them; for a company of knights, gentlemen and doctors have assembled at Greville's and expect him. Bruno is aggrieved and shows it: he supposed he should be asked to dinner and discuss the matter with a long day ahead. Gwynne says certain knights desired to be present, but they were unable to come to dinner and have come to the later meal. Reading between the lines, Bruno, while always ready to praise those English gentry who have travelled in Italy and learned manners there, has received a slight or so from them and resents it. It is conceivable that Greville may have found in this some side-hit at himself.

Our author then works up his London experiences, placing the narrative in the mouth of Teofilo, who serves as his own mask.

The little party who, although in such a hurry, have taken anything but the shortest cut, reach the great watery highway—the safest, speediest and pleasantest route to Westminster. "Yelling 'oars' we wasted as much time as it would have taken to go by land and do a trifle of business on the way. At length two boatmen answered from afar and slowly, slowly drew in. After much question and reply as to whence, where, why, how and when, they brought the prow to the foot of the stairs. And lo! one of them, who might have been old Charon, held out his hand to the Nolan, and another, who was his son I think—a fellow of about 65—took us in." The boat looked like a cork—it was so ancient and worm-eaten—but it went like lead, so palsied were the arms of the rowers. Its creakings and gratings, mingling with the splash, splash of the feeble oarsmen, were

the burlesque of a musical accompaniment and incited Florio
to break out with a love-ditty, and Bruno followed on with
another song. "It took us a long time to make little way
and, before we had covered a third of our journey, just past
a place called the Temple, our old fathers, instead of hurry-
ing on, turned the prow shorewards. The Nolan asked,
'What are you doing? Do you want to take breath?'
Their answer was interpreted to him: they were not going
farther; their station was at this spot. Entreaty after
entreaty proved worse than useless . . . Having paid and
thanked them (what else could be done to such scoundrels
in such a place?) they showed us the way to the street. . . .
The footpath commenced in mud which, nilly willy, must be
gone through." Here comes a sly laugh at himself, in the
satiric spirit which pervades the whole composition: "The
Nolan, who had studied and taught in the schools more
than we, said, 'I observe a filthy way out: follow me.'
But while he was yet speaking, he got so firmly stuck
in the mud that he could not stir a limb; and we had to
help one another, hoping that this purgatory would soon
come to an end. But by malicious luck, he and we found
ourselves engulfed in a slimy passage, which was surrounded by strong walls, as if it had been a veritable
enclosure of jealousy or a garden of delights. And, there
being no light to guide us, we could not tell the way back
or on; so, hoping every step would be the last, we waded
on up to the knees through that deep and gloomy hell."
Bruno must have sighed for his Italian cities, their side-
streets, even, paved with stone!

At last the adventurers came to a mud-cake with a stony
margin where they could walk dry-foot, but in some danger
of tumbling and breaking head or limb. "Finally, we
arrived at what seemed to us to be the Elysian fields—
the main street . . . . and behold! there we were about

twenty paces from the spot which we had set out from to look for a boat—close to the Nolan's abode! . . . . We had so effectively annexed Masters Filth and Slime that we could hardly move our limbs."

They now debate what shall be done. Shall they venture on through dangerous streets in black night? Civility urges that they must not disappoint the expectant supper-party. After much hesitation Bruno musters up courage to keep his word. Soon they are descried and mobbed, and matters grow very bad "at the pyramid near the mansion where three streets meet" (Charing Cross). Bruno musters up enough of the "dog's language" to say "Thank ye, Master" to a man of higher rank than the rest who is content with giving him a mere shove or two, "and not a reminder from the boss of his buckler or the crest of his helmet. There be gentlemen who are such in nothing but descent; and it is to their advantage and ours to have nothing to do with them."

Arrived at last, "we enter and find many sorts of people and many servants in the hall. They neither made way nor inclined the head nor gave any sign of reverence, but disdainfully did us so much favour as to point to the way upstairs." The guests had wearied themselves out with waiting and were sat down to supper. There is a little polite dispute as to seats of honour; finally, Florio takes the foot of the table, with Greville on his right and Bruno on his left, and the meal is resumed.[1]

After supper comes the discussion. "Your Englishmen of quality," says Bruno, "know that their own tongue is confined to their own island, and would deem themselves savages could they not speak Latin, French, Spanish and Italian."[2] But English doctors who are called Nundinio and Torquato were present, and they were not travelled

---

[1] *Cena, Dial. II.*   [2] *Ibid., Dial. III.*

men.   Even small tradesmen educated at the grammar
schools could write to one another in Latin, so, in deference
to the doctors, the debate was conducted in that language,
since Bruno spoke no English.

The portraits of Bruno's opponents were engraved for
all time by a scornful, pitiless burin : there they stand, self-
important pompous pedants.   One "has an emphasis on
his face such as the Father of the Gods wore when he sat
at the celestial council to fulminate an awful sentence
against impious Lycaon."[1]   He "admired the gold chain
round his neck and then glanced at the Nolan's breast,
where the loss of a button were more likely to be found."
"Then he sat bolt upright, took his elbows off the table,
shook himself a little, gave a short snort, adjusted his velvet
cap, twirled his moustache, made his scented face assume a
due expression, arched his eyebrows, distended his nostrils,
cast a glance backward, set himself in order, struck an
attitude—left hand to left side, as if he were opening a
fencing-match—held up three fingers of his right hand and
began, with a few preliminary flourishes."[2]

But the longer Bruno stayed in England the more reconciled he became to its ways.   He even finds it "a beautiful,
fortunate and chivalrous country."   When in Germany he
forgot the petty annoyances and disappointments he had
experienced and expressed his admiration at the aggressive
achievements of our sea-dogs.[3]   After all, he had spent the
most peaceful days he ever knew during his exile in England.
A French contemporary wrote of "blessed England, the
abode of quiet and humanity."[4]   Yet even here "the Nolan"
was far from feeling settled ; for Castelnau's recall had been
issued and he had long awaited it to be put into effect.   And
even the most distinguished among Elizabeth's courtiers were

---

[1] Ovid ; *Metamorph., I*, 170 *sqq.*   [2] *Cena, Dial. IV.*
[3] *De Immenso, Lib. I.*   [4] Languetus, H ; *Epistolæ, xciv.*

far from recognizing the genius of the most distinguished Italian they had ever received among them. The "footfall of his thought" raised little echo here;[1] contemporary Englishmen seem to have had small inkling of the profound originality of his speculations ; his Neo-Platonism they could easily grasp and found it all too familiar ; his subject-matter was, in truth, not cared for, and his Italian style, by no means easily read, even by his own countrymen, was very unpleasing to a generation that delighted in Tasso.

At last, late in October, 1585, the Castelnau family went back to France, Bruno with them. Black clouds were already gathered round the Ambassador ; still more evil days awaited that generous gentleman. During the journey he was robbed of everything he had, down to his shirt. He landed at Calais in a state bordering on destitution.[2] A recently discovered manuscript informs us that Bruno, who, even less than Castelnau, could afford the loss of worldly goods, was also plundered. A diarist enters, under Dec 27, 1585, " Jordanus has told me that his man-servant either has robbed him or suffered him to be robbed."[3]

Bruno had spent two and a half of the years when a man's powers are at their fullest flow in England, and these years had witnessed the writing and actual production of great books. Not content with these labours he was busy at an astronomical work, to be called the " Purgatory of Hell," which he promised to lend to Smith "that he might see the fruit of redemption."[4] We hear no more of

---

[1] Bacon groups him with Patrizzi, Telesio, Campanella and others as neither excellent nor successful (*Hist. Nat. et Exper., Londini,* 1622). He is just mentioned by the author of *Antidicsonus* and by Thomas Watson in the dedication of *Compendium Memoriae Localis ;* the former ranking him with Dickson and others as a self-advertising writer on mnemonics ; the latter speaking of his mystical and profound *Sigilli.*

[2] McIntyre ; *op. cit., p.* 47.

[3] Auvray, L ; *op. cit.*

[4] *Cena, Dial. V.*

H

this.   Was it ever printed?   He may have altered the title,
and we may possess the work in the Latin poem *De Immenso;* for he would seem to have been labouring on this
during the hours of waiting to embark at Dover,[1] although
it was not finally finished and published until six years
later.

[1] *De Immenso, I, iv, schol.*

CHAPTER XI

I

THE THIRTY SEALS AND SEAL OF SEALS

SOON after Bruno's arrival in England appeared " The
Explanation of Thirty Seals [1] For Finding Out, Arranging
And Memorising All Sciences And Arts. To which Is
Added A Seal Of Seals For Comparing All Mental Opera-
tions, And Is Conducive In The Highest Degree To Em-
bracing Their Reasons," etc. etc.[2] Some copies, as already
stated, do not contain a preliminary poem, a letter to
Castelnau, the famous letter to the Vice Chancellor of
Oxford and an Introduction.[3] The second part of the
" Incantation of Circe " is reprinted under the title of " The
Art of Recollection."[4] Then follows " The Explanation of
Thirty Seals," and then more important pages, " The Seal
of Seals." The " Thirty Seals " is but one more exposition
of Mnemonics. The " Seal of Seals,"[5] in two parts, is
Neo-Platonic and is very artificially arranged. But it is an
important work. Bruno wishes it to be understood that his
views must not be taken as absolutely true, but as more
conformable with sense and an understanding of the world
than is the generally received opinion to which they may
seem to be in opposition.

[1] Or Impressions or Images.
[2] *Triginta Sigillorum Explicatio, etc.*
[3] Tocco, F ; *Opere Latine di G. B., pp.* 63–66.
[4] *Ars Reminiscendi.*   [5] *Sigillus Sigillorum.*

He makes an advance on the Neo-Platonists in declaring intellect to be always with us, whether we are aware of the fact or not;[1] there is an evolution from sense upwards, more complex and more perfect as it ascends.[2] One Principle alone unfolds itself in all its manifestations, whether these be high or low ; for Essence, Power, Activity, Actuality and Possibility are all one in the last resort, as Parmenides saw.[3] The guides of the Intellect are Love, the producer of all things ; Art, which is highest when nearest Nature (for in Nature the Soul of the World [4] operates) ; Mathematics and True Magic, which reveals the inner nature of things.[5] Form and Matter do not exhaust themselves in any particular thing; they are endless *continua*.[6]

Here and there acute observations are to be found ; such as that Alchemists will never arrive at the secret of the Philosopher's Stone, but will make many valuable discoveries in their attempt, and that Logic is a sharp spur, but emotion is its driving force. And he expresses his abhorrence of the enthronement of suffering by religion. He is at one with the less cautious of the Psychical Researchers of our own time; he accepts the levitation of St Thomas Aquinas, second sight, the migration of the soul, and trances, wherein a wise " control " unites with the spirit of the psychic ;[7] while he scoffs at vulgar pretenders to magic arts.

---

[1] *Sig. Sigill., Pars II*, § 31.   [2] *Ibid., Pars I*, §§ 31–34.
[3] *Ibid.*, §§ 33, 34.
[4] The Middle Ages found in Plato the notion of the world and stars being " animals," and of a Soul of the Universe proceeding from the Creator and enjoying " a never ceasing and rational life." Cfr. Plato, *Timæus ;* 30–37. This philosophical doctrine was generally current in Bruno's time.
[5] *Sig. Sigil., P. II*, §§ 2–5.
[6] *Ibid., P. II*, § 7.   [7] *Ibid., I*, §§ 45, 46.

II

THE ASH WEDNESDAY SUPPER

In the next work, so full of those English experiences with which we have already dealt, Bruno for the first time gave his great original genius free scope in a novel direction. At a time when the old Greek questioning of experience had been well nigh abandoned for centuries, and before the advent of methods of induction, he provided, to borrow Bacon's phrase, "anticipations of Nature rather than reasoned interpretations." [1] These were brilliant, and, if somewhat rash, they have usually turned out to be true. He perceived that to get at truth you must extract it from Nature, wherein it lies imbedded like her own gold. Nature is the one solid ground on which to "build for aye." He was one of the first to break away from the worship of antiquity and the retention of time-mouldered opinion and to open a new era.

The "Cena De Le Ceneri" "The Ash-Wednesday Supper" has five brisk, entertaining dialogues between four interlocutors. Teofilo, who is Bruno under another name, recounts those famous episodes we know of and defends the Nolan's views to Bruno's friend Smith, Trulla and Prudentio, the last named being a representative of narrow-minded, ignorant and obstructive pedantry in general and, in particular, of those Peripatetics who "get heated over what they don't understand—not even the titles of Aristotle's books." [2] As we know, the talk is enlivened with caustic observations on the Aristotelians and social England, for "these animals have no such tender skins that they would mind a trifle of blows yet heavier." [3] Now,

---

[1] Bacon; *Nov. Org., xxvj.*　　　　[2] *Cena, Dial. I.*
[3] *Ibid., Proem. Epist.*

as always, he scoffs without reserve at men who object to changing their opinion simply because they detest novelty, and he seizes each congenial opportunity of displaying a patrician and scholarly prejudice against the common herd, those

> " souls of geese
> That bear the shape of men."

Bruno took his opportunity of being among " Italianised Englishmen " to write in his own tongue; in this, as in much else, being a pioneer; for he was one of the first to treat of such high matters as philosophy and science in a modern language; nor was the dignified and once convenient habit of addressing the cultured classes in Latin quite abandoned until two centuries later.

He will give full expression in his native Neapolitan to his fulness of thought and feeling. His style, he determines, shall imitate the painter, " who does not content himself with depicting his main subject, but, in order to fill his canvas and to make art conformable with nature, puts in rocks, mountains, trees, fountains, streams and hillocks. Here, you may find a royal palace, there, a wood; here a strip of sky with the half of a rising sun, and, scattered about, a bird, a pig, a stag, a donkey, a horse; but these merely indicated by head, horn or limb; or ears, even, may suffice; but at another spot is the whole shape of a beast; some characteristic movement or expression is given; so that one discerns everything with enhanced interest; one criticises and, finally, centres one's attention on the main subject." [1]   Again, he tells us he will achieve " a full and mighty prose, taking its own time; coming, not as of clerkly art, but flowing and strong as are the waters of a mighty current." [2]

With what success does he pursue this aim ?   He records

---

[1] *Cena, Proem. Epist.*   [2] *Ibid., Dial. I.*

a feast and compares his work to a banquet.[1] Each dish is designed at once to gratify and stimulate the palate for the next. But the courses are served in tumultuous profusion, and his table groans with " miscellaneous feeding." Nor is this all ; the repast is accompanied by a wild, resounding orchestra, which stuns a delicate ear and makes the brain spin round. For not wind and brass and strings only are employed ; big drum, marrow-bones, cleaver, every conceivable instrument is used in turn, and sometimes, which is worse, together. We pass rapidly from key to key without modulation ; we are swept along in a Bacchic rout. Sometimes boisterous gaiety drops into coarseness ; but the age was unwilling to omit the zest of obscenity ; it appealed to every reader and, throughout time, wit has flourished on the dung-heap. Bruno alights but he does not dwell there. For him even the Earth is no abiding place ; when he can, he escapes, soars aloft and bursts into rapturous song. The characteristics of " The Supper " are to be found in even richer measure in almost every other work. All are filled with the wealth of a full and impetuous personality.

Aristotle conceived of space as being " the limit of the surrounding body in respect to that which it surrounds." [2] His universe is split into a celestial region above and a terrestrial below — a doctrine very convenient for the localization of Heaven, especially as his upper region is filled with ether and is removed from the strife of the four elements. Above the solid sphere of earth, which lies in the centre of the universe, are those of water, air, fire and ether. On earth the elements are mixed and therefore impure,[3] and, since everything passes from opposite to opposite, one passes into another. But everything tends

[1] Cena, Proem. Epist.
[2] Zeller, E ; Arist., tr. Costelloe and Muirhead, 1897, I, p. 432.
[3] Aristotle ; Gen. et Corr. II, 3, 330, b, 21.

to move to its own proper place; hence there can be only one world. Like Plato, Aristotle conceived of the stars as being souls of a god-like nature,[1] the causes of physical change.[2] Such was the accepted faith. Bruno conceived it to be his mission to destroy every article of it which pertained to physical theory. He carried it on with zeal. Not of him as of Aristotle can it be said that he was "moderate to excess."

In the "Supper" Bruno's bent towards natural science bursts forth with all the sudden vigour of an Italian spring. Henceforward the secrets of Nature claim the greater part of his attention. He did not accept the Copernican theory in his youth;[3] but when he became convinced of its truth he was the first to see beyond it. Liberated from the fetters of the past by the genius of one solitary thinker, he sent a search-light through the heavens and applied Copernicus' theory to the fixed stars. If Nature repeats her operations in planets all of which revolve round the sun, each showing but a variation of one single plan, shall she cease to repeat herself through an unending universe of stars and planets? The universe is all of a piece; the principles which obtain on earth are observed throughout space. Here lies his indisputable merit. He was the first to extend the Copernican theory to all the hosts of heaven. He did so with characteristic boldness. It was a marvellous sweep of the scientific imagination, for we must remember that Galileo and Newton had not yet come to supply their confirmatory evidence. He went further: he was soon to declare that the physical universe occupies infinity—a magnificent conception which the hardihood of the science of to-day would perhaps hesitate to affirm.

[1] Aristotle; *De Cœlo, II*, 12, 292, *a*, 18; *Eth. Nic., VI*, 2, 269, *a;* 30, *b*, 14.

[2] Aristotle; *Meteor, I*, 2, 339, *a*, 21.   [3] *Cena, Dial. IV.*

He accepts the animation of the universe ; some creatures are vastly higher, others vastly lower than we are ; but the earth, the planets, the stars, are "celestial animals, more intellectual than we."[1] In a universe which is infinite and eternal " the flaming bodies of space are the messengers of God, declaring his excellent glory and majesty. Thus our vision is enlarged to behold the infinite effect of the infinite Cause, and we are taught to seek the divinity not far off but closer to us than we are to ourselves."[2] He perceived that if the discovery of Copernicus had diminished the importance of man in the Universe, it had exalted him as a being capable of grasping so large a view. The Aristotelian view of the universe was based, like the plain man's, on sensible appearance ; but it is the function of the intellect to pass beyond the mere appearances of sense to truth.[3] Yet, to do this we must observe Nature and, quitting the Aristotelian definitions of Essence and Attribute and the like, we should examine natural phenomena and enquire for the conditions under which events do or do not happen.

Existence and its Cause are alike Infinite, and nothing perishes though everything changes. "This entire globe, this star, not being subject to death, and dissolution and annihilation being impossible anywhere in Nature, from time to time renews itself by changing and altering all its parts."[4] There is no absolute up or down, as Aristotle taught ; no absolute position in space ; but the position of a body is relative to that of other bodies. Everywhere there is incessant relative change in position throughout the universe, and the observer is always at the centre of things. All celestial bodies are no less secure than is the

---

[1] *Cena, Dial. III, 4a Prop. di Nundinio ; cfr.* Aristotle ; *Eth. Nic., vj,* 7, 1141, *a,* 34 ; *De Cœlo,* 1, 2.

[2] *Ibid., Dial. I.*   [3] *Ibid.*   [4] *Ibid., Dial. V.*

Earth; they require nothing to support them.[1] There is
no absolute lightness or weight in things, as Aristotle
taught, but (here he almost foreshadows the great discovery of Newton) they have a certain impetus towards or
away from each other.[2] He accepts an ancient scientific
conception: there is certainly an ether; for movement can
only take place by direct contact; but, since the ether is
too light to move the heavenly bodies, they must be pro-
pelled by the energy of their souls.[3] The sun moves on its
axis; but this is not all: it varies its position among the
stars, of which it is one. He tells us of the discovery of
Cusanus that there are spots in the sun,[4] and he attributes
the scintillation of the stars to their being suns which give
out their own light; Venus does not twinkle, because hers
is a reflected light.[5] He observes that the Earth's atmosphere rotates with her. Much shrewder is the geologic
discernment that natural forces are in constant operation
and produce very slow but vast changes in land and sea.[6]

Bacteriologists may choose to find a remarkable anti-
cipation of modern discovery in the passage: "It seems
to me more than likely, since everything shares in life,
that a countless multitude of creatures live not only in
us but in all composite things."[7] He goes on to say:
"when we observe anything to die as we call it we should
not so much believe it to be death as change; the mere
accidental composition and harmony ceasing, but the things
to which they happen remaining immortal whether they be
spiritual or material, as we shall show on another occasion."[8]

[1] *Cena, Dial. V.*   [2] *Ibid., Dial. V.*
[3] *Ibid., Dial. III, 4a Prop. di Nundinio.*
[4] *Ibid., 3a Prop. di Nundinio.*   [5] *Ibid., 2a Prop. di Nundinio.*
[6] *Ibid., Dial. V.*   [7] *Ibid., Dial. III, 4a Prop. di Nundinio.*
[8] *Ibid. Cfr.* Ovid; *Metam. xv.* "In this vast universe nothing
perishes; but it varies and changes its appearance; and to begin to
be something different from what it was before is called birth, and to

Instinct is not mechanical activity induced from without, but is due " to a sixth sense or reason or pure intellect, working within the creature who manifests it." [1]

Bruno was keenly alive to the evils which attend commercial greed, especially those which follow the conquest and occupation of alien lands. [2]

In Science, then, he shows himself the precursor of Galileo, Newton and Lyell, and points to paths which recent investigators have pursued.

He could not but recognize in Aristotle one of the most inquiring minds of Antiquity. Passages are to be found in his works wherein he accepts the teaching of the Stagirite and follows him very closely. He felt the force of a thinker who, even in the mutilated form in which he came to the Middle Ages, exercised despotic sway over many generations of highly disciplined minds. But he regarded the Aristotelian Cosmology as wholly reactionary : it had put an end to the advancing speculation commenced by the early Greeks ; and the dead weight of Aristotle's authority kept the world in bondage. The Christian followers of Aristotle were far more obscurantist than he. So Bruno determined to smite and spare not. In the Cena he commences a battle which occupied most of his energies through the years when he was still at liberty. " Ever a fighter," he attacked the defenders of Aristotle wherever he could find them with whole-hearted zeal. In the Cena he opens up new channels for mental energy and substitutes genuine thought for the paralysis which had come of making everything conform with Aristotle and the Bible. What he finds worst in his opponents is their

cease to be the same thing death. Whereas, perhaps, those things are transferred hither, and these things thither ; yet in the whole all things continue to be."

[1] *Cena, Dial. I.*   [2] *Ibid.*

pretentiousness born of their ignorance. It were better
to be frank about one's ignorance than to pretend to false
knowledge.[1]

From a perusal of Algazel, the Arabian theologian, he
has learned that religions have a practical object: their
ordinances are designed for good conduct, general welfare,
social needs, peace and the progress of the State.[2] Their
authority must be recognised; but there are as many
interpretations of the abstract and metaphoric as there
are faiths.[3]

Now such early Fathers of the Christian Church as
Tertullian and Augustine had taught that much of Scripture must be regarded as purely allegorical;[4] Aquinas had
emphasized their doctrine,[5] and Dante had expounded in
the vernacular that " such speech must accommodate itself
to your mind. Scripture condescends to your faculty of
comprehension."[6] But it was a great advance to declare
that religions embody a merely practical attitude, and have
nothing to do with theoretic truth—an advance on the
compromise of William of Ockham and Duns Scotus, who
excused the results of their dialectic by asserting that,
however much the results of reason may contradict the
teachings of the Church, both are equally true. Bruno
will have but one final truth and one final reality, and
the approach thereto is by the free exercise of intellect.[7]
He foresaw the quarrel between science and religion, but
thought, if the Scriptures were interpreted in the light of
science, this might be avoided.[8] Nay, he is persuaded that
lofty minds will find support in religion more than in any

---

[1] *Cena, Dial. I.*   [2] *Ibid., Dial. IV.*   [3] *Ibid.*
[4] Tertull.; *Adv. Marc. II,* 16.—S. Aug.; *In Gen. xvij.*
[5] Aquinas; *Sum. Theol. I, i,* 10; *xix,* 11; *I², iv,* 7.
[6] Dante; *Par., IV,* 40–48.   [7] *Cfr. Sigillus, I,* § 33.
[8] *Cena, Dial. IV.*

other philosophy.[1] And, quite ingenuously, he adopts a
time-honoured device: he quotes everything from the
Scriptures which may suit his purpose and artlessly inter-
prets them to his own end.

He forgot that in filling the stars and planets with
inhabitants, some better and some worse than ourselves,[1]
he dealt a blow to the central Christian doctrines of the
Fall and Redemption.

He is fully aware that the thinker and the investigator
of nature have no easy road to traverse in their aim to
overcome contradictions and arrive at the unity which
underlies them. "O difficulties to be endured, cries the
coward, the feather-head, the shuttlecock, the faint-heart. . . .
The task is not impossible though hard. The craven must
stand aside. Ordinary, easy tasks are for the commonplace and the herd. Rare, heroic and divine men overcome
the difficulties of the way and force an immortal palm from
necessity. You may fail to reach your goal. Run the
race nevertheless. Put forth your strength in so high
a business. Strive on with your last breath."[2]

He is always conscious of the importance of his own
labours. "The Nolan has given freedom to the human
spirit and made its knowledge free. It was suffocating in
the close air of a narrow prison-house, whence, but only
through chinks, it gazed at the far-off stars. Its wings
were clipped, so that it was unable to cleave the veiling
cloud and reach the reality beyond."[3] These are big
words; but in sooth Bruno had pierced the stubborn vault
of old heaven and enlarged the boundaries of the Universe.

[1] *Cena, Dial. IV.*   [2] *Ibid., Dial. II.*   [3] *Ibid.*

III

On Cause, Principle, And The One

This is a brilliantly original treatise on Metaphysics. The new view of the Universe carried with it a perception of the inadequacy of scholasticism and the need of a new departure in Philosophy.[1] The work consists of five dialogues.[2] The first of these has three interlocutors and is intended to excuse and vindicate the strictures on England which had proved distasteful. In the four following dialogues, Teofilo expounds the Nolan's philosophy to Gervis, Dickson and a humanist called Polinnio. The dialogues are prefaced by a letter to Castelnau and five short poems, of which three are in Latin and two in Italian. These verses strike that note of lofty thought and feeling which finds fuller expression later on in the work. Bruno springs from the ground and wings skyward like the lark, soaring in ever widening circles, floating his throbbing song into the infinite, but interrupting it now and again by a sudden drop for rest to the homely earth.

Throughout Bruno's life-work we find Plato's doctrine of Ideas and the Neo-Platonic imagery of Emanation becoming less and less operant. In the " Cause " he takes up Aristotelian conceptions and works by means of these philosophic distinctions, as well as through certain theologic distinctions, to an independent view. But, while he is obliged to use current terminology and the categories of Aristotle and the schoolmen, he feels that they hamper him in getting his thought out clearly and unmistakably. " Aristotle never tires of distinguishing by reason what

---

[1] Cfr. Cena, Dial. I.

[2] The second dialogue has been translated by I. & K. Royce in Rand's Modern Classical Philosophies, London, 1908.

is indivisible in Nature and Truth."[1] For Aristotle had reduced Actuality into two principles, Matter and Form, and neither can be deduced from the other. Further, he set bounds to the Universe, and, which is worse, perceiving thought to be non-corporeal, he assumed an unmoved mover beyond the ether, at the circumference of the world and unconditioned by it.[2] Bruno finds such abstractions as matter, form, potency etc. incapable of yielding a true interpretation of the world.[3] He must rise above these logical distinctions, unshackle the mind and give it free play in order that it may grasp the unity to which they point and wherein they must coincide.[4] He opens up a new path; but, as is always the case, in doing so, to some extent, he confuses methods and boundaries.

Human knowledge is limited; it is no easy matter to discover the immediate cause and principle of dependent things. And things which are knowable by us are but traces, the universal effect, of the First Principle and Cause. To use an illustration, in contemplating statues which are the works of a sculptor we do not behold the real being of him from whom they proceed, but only its effects.[5] "No eye can draw near Him who is at once absolute light and deepest obscurity."[6] Bruno will therefore leave the Absolute, as transcendent, to revelation and theology and turn himself to the interpretation of Nature, where he shall find the Absolute as immanent. There is a "Soul of the Universe."[7]

---

[1] *Causa, Dial. II.*

[2] Aristotle ; *Met, vj,* 1, 1026, *a,* 13 ; *xij,* 1, 1096, *a,* 30 ; *De Anim.,* I, 1, 403, *b,* 7 *sqq* ; *Phys., viij,* 10, 267, *b,* 6 ; *De Cœlo, I,* 9, 279, *a,* 16 *sqq.*

[3] *Causa, Dial. III.*   [4] *Ibid., Dial. III, V.*

[5] *Ibid., Dial. II.*   [6] *Ibid., Dial. III.*

[7] *Ibid., Dial. II.* The germ of the notion is to be found in the *Timæus,* 34.

He has worked himself through the trammels of scholastic terminology and subtle but inadequate distinctions; but they are mental currency and there is no other way than to employ them. So he begins by distinguishing between Principle and Cause. A Principle is that which lies within the constitution of a thing and is necessary to its being, while the cause of a thing is external to it, yet "concurs" with it as necessary to its production. Now the Schoolmen, following Aristotle, employed certain useful distinctions in Causality. Bruno deals, therefore, with Cause as Efficient, the source of change; Formal, that which makes a thing what it is, and Final, purpose to be attained. In the Efficient cause of the Universe he discovers the "Universal Mind, which is the inmost, most real and characteristic faculty and potential aspect of the Universal Soul." It is not fully expressed in any particular thing, and, so far, is extrinsic; yet it also operates within the thing, and is therefore also intrinsic. The Formal Cause is that "ideal reason" without which the agent could not operate any more than an artist can work without the idea of his work in his mind. The Final Cause of the Universe is its "perfection, wherein, in different parts of matter, all the forms actually exist. This end so delights and satisfies the universal intellect that it never wearies in giving birth to all kinds of forms in matter."[1] But while the "ideal reason," as presupposed in the actual, is a Cause, as actualized, it is a Principle. We find that, in this regard, Principle and Cause coincide. So far we have been dealing with Forms (another ancient distinction):[2] we have also to deal with the Matter in which they are realized, using

[1] *Causa, Dial. II.* Aristotle asserted the ultimate cause of movement to be a final cause. (*Met. xij,* 7, 1072, a, 25.)

[2] μορφή, ἔιδος, ἰδέα, figure, species, appearance, are almost synonyms. For Bruno, Form is an "impression" of the Ineffable, whether idea or material configuration.

the term as that out of which anything may come to be formed.

Of course there is not to be found in Bruno any sharp distinction between the "thinking thing" and the "extended thing." Until Descartes made that distinction, thinkers were content, with the child and with primitive man, to take body and soul as a unity in action. In less mature years, he had indeed been led away by ancient philosophers and Avicebron, and had regarded Matter as the sole substance of things. "But on deeper thought and taking other facts into consideration, we must distinguish between form and material substance."[1] The Soul of the Universe must be as the individual soul and, to use our old image, may be likened to a pilot guiding a vessel,[2] who is none the less within that which he guides. In our world Matter and Form are never separate. Virgil knew this when he wrote that the world is interpenetrated by Spirit and that Mind moves Mass.[3] Solomon declares the same thing when he says "The Spirit of the Lord filleth the world: and that which containeth all things hath knowledge of the voice."[4] "If Spirit, Soul, Life, is in all things, it is the form of all things, directing and governing matter."[5] Forms are for ever changing; what has been, in the vicissitude of things, becomes nothing; there must be something, then, beyond the varying forms of spirit; there must also be something beyond varying material forms.[6] There must be a Soul of the Universe which gives it unity. We must conclude that this exists wholly in the whole and in every part. To understand how this may be, let us borrow a metaphor from Plotinus: "It is as a voice which is wholly

---

[1] *Dial. III.* For the Scholastics the Soul was a Form.
[2] *Cfr.* Aristotle ; *De Anima, II, j;* Plot. ; *Enn., iv,* 3 ; 7.
[3] Virgil ; *Æn., VI,* 724–7.   [4] *Book of Wisdom, I,* 7.
[5] *Causa, Dial. II.*   [6] *Ibid., Dial. II, III.*

I

throughout the whole of a room and in every part of it;
it is wholly heard by all. . . . Could it fill the whole
universe it would still be all in all."[1]

It became a necessity with the early mediæval thinkers
to posit *substance*. In a nugget of gold, for example, there
is yellowness, hardness, etc.; but these qualities are to be
found elsewhere also. They exist in unity in the nugget,
and the inexplicable fact that they do so may be indica-
cated by the word substance. Later on, in order to support
the doctrine of transubstantiation, they went further and
attributed to substance an underlying, enduring reality
which " supports " its accidents. To substance, unalterable and ever the same with itself, attributes were ascribed.
Bruno usually employs and works through the earlier
notion of substance, the "I know not what" of Locke,
which gives unity.[2]

We allow substantive value to brute matter and also to
spirit. Let us consider material substrate, that invisible
something which gives one-ness to all visible forms.

It exists not merely in actual being, but also as the possibility of being. All that is possible and all that is actual
must be referred to a principle which is both possibility and
substance. Everything that exists is possible, but power
or potency has caused it to be. So matter is more than an
existing substrate; it is potentiality and possibility and
actuality in undistinguished unity. Aristotle held the infinite to be potential only, not actual.

Now in what relation does the substrate of brute matter
stand to Spirit or Form in general? The spiritual and
material worlds can be distinguished; but there can be no
distinction without an underlying identity; so we are

[1] *Causa, Dial. II.—Cfr.* Plotinus ; *Enn., VI, iv.* 12.
[2] *Cfr.* Sensini, T ; *Sul pensiero filosofico di G. B.*, 1907 ; McIntyre,
op. cit., p. 165.

bound to acknowledge that, in the last resort, spirit and brute-matter, Form wherever it occurs and Matter in all its forms, imply one Subject or Substrate or Substance. Nor is this enough: Power, Possibility and Actuality, whether material or spiritual, must also be One.[1] Nature is one and many, sending all forth from her womb in endless flux.[2]

Bruno comes near asking the question: What is left of existent matter when stripped of all sensuous quality? But he never did so. One little step and he had anticipated Berkeley's advance, made a century and a half later. He would have asserted sensuous experience to be the minimum of being. He perceives however that there is no real divorce between the individual mind and that Universe in which it dwells and whereby it is. " That judgment of Heraclitus shall not sound badly which says all things are an unity which, through mutability possesses all things in itself, and since all forms are in it, all definitions come together therein, and all contradictions are enunciations of its truth." " The universe is one, infinite, unalterable. One is absolute possibility, act, thing, being, the greatest and the best, which cannot be comprehended, to which limits and completion cannot be set, which, for that reason, is infinite and unending and consequently established. It does not move its place, for there is no whither to which it can transfer itself, since it is all. It does not come into being, for there is no other to desire or wait for it. It does not decay, for it can change with no other, all things being itself. It cannot increase or grow less, for it is infinite. It adds and takes nothing to itself, for the infinite has no proportional parts."[3]

[1] *Causa, Dial. III.* [2] *Ibid., Dial. IV.*
[3] *Ibid., Dial. V*, beginning. Aristotle had got so far as to assert the eternity of the world ; he claims to have been the first to do so (*De Cœlo, i*, 10, 279, *b*, 12). But he also declared the world to be a complete, finite whole (*Phys. iij*).

Plotinus and the Neo-Platonists, while apprehending the one-ness of the Universe, had divorced unity from reality and unwarrantably asserted the independent being of a mere abstraction. Bruno advanced far beyond this ; nor, although Schelling found in the Nolan's thought a kinship with his own, was Bruno's Absolute a mere *Indifferenz-punkt*, a " blank featureless Identity." " We rejoice " he writes " in the unity of the sensible (*in uno sensibile*) but most of all in that which comprehends in itself all sensibility ; in one knowledge which comprehends all cognitions, in one power of apprehension which embraces all that can possibly be apprehended, in one being which completes everything ; most of all, in the unity which is the whole itself." [1] It is " absolute simplicity "—not because it is abstract, not because no differences exist within its bosom, but because all divisions are healed in the one single comprehensive, harmonious intuition which is God. In other words Bruno arrives at One Reality, which moves and knows itself in its many aspects and is that Whole in and through which the manifold exists. All things in process are nothing apart from the Whole. " The highest good, the highest perfection, the highest blessedness consists in the unity which enmeshes the all." [2]

Bruno's thought reappears in Spinoza, whom he directly influenced ; [3] but Bruno's speculations are less rigid, statical and systematic than Spinoza's. Bruno never loosens his hold on the notion of Living Spirit. He stands by his master, Cusanus ; philosophy points for both thinkers to the union of all distinctions and contraries in that which

---

[1] *Causa, Dial. V, end.*   [2] *Ibid.*

[3] Spinoza, B ; *Tractatus De Deo et Homine ; Œuvres, tr. et annotées par* C. Appuhn, *t.* 1, 1907.—Sigwart, C. von ; *Spinoza's Tractat v. Gott etc., Gotha,* 1866 ; Ibid., *T. v. Gott, Tübingen,* 1870. —Avenarius, R ; *Die Beiden Ersten Phasen d. Sp. Pantheismus, Leipzig,* 1868.

transcends and includes them and which is no mere collection of parts or mere unity of parts.   Both men were on the road towards the Metaphysic of a great English thinker of our own day:[1] they had the root-idea of an all-including Absolute, wherein are all centres of experience and all differences as such, but not *merely* as such: in and for the Whole they are also transmuted and harmonized.

Whatever else the Absolute may be we know that, as transcendent, it unites all contraries in one perfect cognition; as immanent it is the Universal Soul, unfolding the eternal meaning, infinite and without beginning or end. Living out our share of the divine meaning and being actually one with the Infinite and Eternal, we need not fear death. Bruno flatters himself that he has " taken away the dread of Orcus and greedy Charon, which spoils the sweet of life."[2]

Such are the conclusions of Reason, let Theology say what it will.   But " discreet theologians will always admit natural reasoning, whithersoever it may lead, provided it does not dispute divine authority but submits to it."[3]   Indeed, from the early days when Scotus Erigena wrote, there had been thinkers who had no desire to oppose dogma if they were permitted to interpret it by their own metaphysical conclusions ; nor had the Church thought it wise to interfere with them seriously.   As has been said, from the less courageous days of William of Ockham and Duns Scotus, philosophy had evaded the interference of the Church and secured some independence in philosophic thinking by a dodge. Truth was held to be of two kinds, philosophic and theologic, which might be in opposition to one another.   Bruno belonged to the bolder line of Erigena.

[1] Bradley, F. H ; *Appearance and Reality.   Cfr. Book II, chaps. xiij–xv.*

[2] *Causa, Proem. Epist.*   [3] *Ibid., Dial. IV.*

It has been generally supposed that Bruno, following Cusanus, had some dim perception of the possibilities of a dialectic method when he wrote : " Profound magic is it to draw the contrary out after having discovered the point of union." [1] Hegel in his review of Bruno's philosophy found in this "a great word." [2] Schelling, too, discovered in Bruno a spirit akin to his own in his attempt to deduce the Universe logically from the " point of union." [3] But it is very doubtful whether he had first-hand acquaintance with the Causa. Bruno's point of view seems to me to be closer to that of the thinker who is to day in fashion ; for he is of the intuitive rather than of the logical, abstract school. Bergson writes : " Concepts, as we shall show elsewhere, generally go in couples and represent two contraries. There is hardly any concrete reality which cannot be observed from two opposing standpoints, which cannot consequently be subsumed under two antagonistic concepts. Hence a thesis and an antithesis which we endeavour in vain to reconcile logically, for the very simple reason that it is impossible, with concepts and observations taken from outside points of view, to make a thing. But from the object, seized by intuition, we pass easily in many cases to the two contrary concepts ; and, as in that way thesis and antithesis can be seen to spring from reality, we grasp at the same time how it is that the two are opposed and how they are reconciled." [4]

Bruno writes : " It is one and the same series whereby Nature descends to the production of things and the intellect ascends to the cognition of them ; and in both unity

[1] *Causa, Dial. V.*

[2] Hegel, G. W. F ; *Werke, Vorlesungen ü. d. Gesch. d. Phil., B. xv, pp.* 224-44.

[3] Schelling, F. W. J. von ; *Bruno, oder ü. d. gött, u. natural. Prinzip. d. Dinge.*

[4] Bergson, H ; *Introd. to Metaphysics, tr. Hulme*, 1913, *p.* 34.

proceedeth to unity, through the multitude of means "[1]—an emphatic statement of the essential identity of the process of thought with the transformations of Nature.

Bruno's philosophy of the " animation " of the Universe —his view that it was no mere " collection " but " infusion," "interpenetration"—readily lent itself to doctrines of "secret sympathy " or " magical properties "—that is to say undiscovered natural principles.   Hence he thought very highly of that half-quack, half-genius, Aureol Theophrast Paracelsus,[2] who audaciously burned Galen and Avicenna in his lecture-room and commenced a new era by studying Chemical Therapeutics.   That worthy had at least directly questioned Nature and experimented on her, and Bruno was desirous of a Natural Philosophy above all things.   Because Ramus neglected to attack Aristotle from the side of Physics, he regarded him as nothing but a logical trifler.   For the same reason he despised Patrizzi and denied that he had an intimate acquaintance with the philosopher he attacked.   Blind folk cannot open the eyes of the blind.   So Ramus is for him a " French archpedant " and Patrizzi " another filth of an Italian pedant "; but for Telesio he has nothing but praise.[3]

Following the Italian Platonists, he shows a great interest in all kinds of out of the way, unverified or " occult " phenomena.[4]   " I do not contemn those who in the various departments of physic set to work magically by applying roots, hanging stones on, and murmuring incantations, if the rigor of theologians will allow me to speak in a purely

---

[1] *Causa, Dial. V.*

[2] *Ibid., Dial. III.*   In *Sigillus* Bruno calls Paracelsus " chief author among physicians."

[3] *Ibid., Dial. III.   Cfr.* Tocco, F ; *Le fonti piu recenti della f. del B., Acad. dei Lincei, Ser. Rend. V, vol. i, p.* 530.!

[4] *Cfr. Sig. Sigill., II,* § 5.—J. B. N. *Opera, Vol. III, c.* Tocco and Vitelli, 1891, *De Magia etc.*—Troilo, E, *La filos. di G. B, Torino,* 1907.

natural sense. . . . That physician who shall cure me is better than others who kill or torment me." [1]   In fact he was ready to employ those forces which he did not understand, just as we employ electricity.   He accepted much of the miraculous as due to undiscovered natural causes.   He hints at this when he writes: " I am not now considering that not without reason do necromantists hope to do much with the bones of the dead, believing that these retain some vital activity." [2]

The dialogue of the Causa is natural even at its highest flights.   Sometimes Bruno thinks to give his readers breathing time by digressions, which, however, are anything but restful.   Every now and then, to press a point, he calls every auxiliary he can think of into his service; every kind of sacred writing, the lore of strange peoples and of far-distant ages is drawn upon; any utterance, sacred or profane, in which he can detect a resemblance to his own views, is pounced upon and cited as authority.   For is there not a measure of the truth in all things?   Without any discrimination he heaps together Mystics and Magi, the Cabala and the Latin poets.   Wonder-workers and wise men are referred to as of equal value.   The effect on the modern reader is comic.   Goldsmith, one thinks, must have come across him when he put " Sanchoniathon, Manetho, Berosus and Ocellus Lucanus " into the mouth of the vendor of the gross of green spectacles to Moses Primrose.

IV

THE INFINITE UNIVERSE AND ITS WORLDS

This work begins with a dedicatory letter to Castelnau which contains much self-revelation—words which he had not dared to write to one who knew him so well had they

---

[1] *Causa, Dial. III.*   [2] *Ibid.*

been other than strictly sincere. " I wish," he writes, " the world to possess the glorious fruit of my labour, to awaken the soul and open the understanding of those who are deprived of that light which, most assuredly, is not mine own invention. Should I be in error, I do not believe I wilfully go wrong. And in speaking and writing as I do I am not contending through the desire of being victorious ; for I deem every kind of renown and conquest God's foe, vile and without a particle of honour in it, if it be not the truth; but, for love of true wisdom and in the effort to reflect aright, I weary, I rack, I torment myself." [1]

He will give his reasons for holding that the Universe endures, ever one and itself, in eternal flux throughout infinite space. " From which contemplation, if we apply the mind, we shall neither be dismayed by incidence of pain and dread nor exult in pleasure and hope ; we shall pursue the path of right conduct, shall be large-minded observers of puerile thoughts and shall behold greater matters than gods whom the vulgar adore ; we shall secure clear-sighted contemplation of the course of nature, which is written in ourselves, and observe, with even tenor, those divine laws which are graven in our hearts." The same nature is to be found in the skies as here ; so we may quit ourselves " of the vain desire and stupid anxiety and hankering after distant good ; for it is already at hand and with us." " By means of this knowledge we shall surely attain that well-being which we so vainly seek elsewhere." [2]

The consideration of the Universe as the manifestation of God will, he considers, set the human spirit free. " Here is the philosophy which opens the senses, contents the soul, enlarges the mind and brings true blessedness to man. . . . For deeply considering the Being and Substance in which we are fixed, we find there is no such thing as death, not

[1] *Infinito, Proem. Epist.*   [2] *Ibid.*

for us alone, but for the true substance. Substance never diminishes but changes, and this throughout infinite space. Since, in the vicissitudes of particular being, we are all subject to the best Efficient Cause, we ought not to believe, think or hope otherwise than that everything, which is wholly derived from the good, is good, through good and to good. The contrary can only be held by one who understands nothing but what is immediately before him: the beauty of an edifice is not to be judged from its smallest part . . . . . but is most apparent to him who views the whole and the relation of part to part."[1] Good and evil are contraries which are, in fact, eternally reconciled in the eternal core of being—the " That Which intrinsically brings to pass "[2] the whole of reality, "wherein we live in an appointed order." Contraries imply that which transcends and holds them in harmonious unity. God is above Good and Evil, but our highest conception of him is as Good.[3]

" The Divine one extols his own glory and sets forth the greatness of his sway, not in one sun, but in uncountable suns; not in one earth, but in worlds without end."[4]

After the letter to Castelnau come three sonnets, and then all the new intellectual tendencies of the era are brought to a head and the directions which science was to follow are pointed out in five dialogues. Bruno habitually introduces real people into his dialogues as interlocutors, and, in the first four of the *Infinito*, Filoteo expounds the Nolan philosophy to Girolamo Fracastoro, the humanist,[5] and two other persons, one of whom is the indispensable pedant. In the

---

[1] *Infinito, Proem. Epist.*   [2] *Causa, Dial. II.*

[3] Cfr. De Immenso, VIII, vij, ix, x ; Lampas Triginta Statuarum, Op. Lat, iij, pp. 21, 108 ; Eroici, passim. For modern treatment of the conception see Taylor, Prof. A. E ; *Problem of Conduct*, London, 1901, cap. viij.   [4] *Infinito, Proem. Epist.*

[5] For Fracastoro, see Greswell, W. P ; *Memoirs of Politianus etc.*, 1805.

fifth dialogue, Alberico Gentile, the great jurist,[1] whom he
had met here in England, is introduced. The entire work
has an unwonted didactic tone ; yet the dialogues are easy
and spontaneous. I have attempted furnishing some feeble
indication of Bruno as a poet by a free translation of the
third sonnet in the Introduction.

> " Rising on wing secure, with burning heart,
>   What fate may scare me, smiling at the tomb,
>   Bursting all bonds and scorning gates of doom,
>   Whence few are chosen for such lofty part?
> I soar beyond the mortal years, and start
>   For regions where grim irons cast no gloom
>   Nor adamant restrains. Forth from the womb
> Of darkness, free and passionate, I dart.
>   I dread no barrier of banished spheres ;
>   I cleave the sky, and other suns behold ;
>   Celestial worlds innumerable I see ;
>   One left, another company appears ;
>   My pinion fails not, and my heart is bold
>   To journey on through all infinity." [2]

He frequently quotes passages from Lucretius throughout this work. The Latin poet exercised a powerful influence over Bruno, as the upholder of atomism and of the
infinity of space. The notion of a plurality of worlds was
very old, dating from Anaximander, but the paramount and
paralysing authority of Aristotle and the Church put an
end to all such speculations.

Bruno opens his campaign by distinguishing between
certain functions of cognition. " The service done by sensation is to excite the reason into action, to indict, to point
out the way, to impart and to witness." The sensible

---

[1] Author of *De Jure Belli,* not written at this period.

[2] Its author would seem to have approved of this sonnet, for he
paraphrased it in the Latin poem on Immensity (*De immenso, I, i*).
It is an imitation of two sonnets by Tansillo, which open : " Amor
m'impenna l'ale," and " Poi che spiegat'ho."

object "is only a small part of Truth; it is as a mirror"; therein lies no certitude. The reports of sense may be brought into harmony by discursive thought—the "understanding" of Kant—which Bruno calls "reason." Still higher is intellect, which directs principles and draws from them their conclusions. Highest is a fourth faculty, "mind," which is "the proper and living form of truth," and is none other than direct insight or intuition or immediate apprehension, beholding its contents in an immediate comprehensive whole.[1] We shall find in later works that this crown of enquiry is an experience in which we share, in our feeble measure, that of the Godhead, and he allows the rare experiences of Plotinus and the Mystics to be of the same essential nature.[2]

His temerity is unbounded; he strikes out a perilous *a priori* path to his conclusions. God's power, he says, is infinite; therefore his works also must be infinite; for the agent would be imperfect if his works did not fulfil his power; infinite power, then, must have infinite effect. Our imagination, too, which is a shadow of the real, forbids anything but infinity; but we must remember that, in that infinity as it is for itself, all particulars are one: "it is no more an infinite man than it is an infinite ass."[3] "Ass" carries many implications for Bruno, as we shall see later on.

More convincing, perhaps, are other arguments which may be quickly summarized. Our sense - perception is limited and changes with change of position; but we can appeal to reason, which shows all the observations of sense to be entirely relative, as are constructions based on them.

---

[1] *Infinito, Dial. I, beginning.*

[2] *Eroici, P. I, Dial. II, after Canz. xj and xv ; P. II, Dial. I, vj after Canz. vj ; Dial. IV, after Canz. 71.*

[3] *Infinito, Dial. II, end.*

Here is where I stand (my *now* is what I immediately experience). Position and motion in space (and time) must be conceived as relative to any point which we choose to take for the purpose of comparison. " In the Universe there is no centre and no circumference; but the centre is everywhere, and every part is outside some other part." [1] In all this may we not detect some glimmering, primitive perception, some feeble germ of an idea which has been developed by Lorentz and others into the revolutionary "Principle of Relativity"? But Bruno lived too early, science was too little developed for him to pursue his thought; he thinks that, although not the Transcendent Absolute, he can rise above sense and its interpretations and grasp the real conditions in which the World-Soul experiences its vicissitudes. So far as sense goes, it reveals spacial continuity, and so it should be interpreted. All positions and all shapes are contained in space and bounded by space, and if that which contains has no limit, so will it prove with the contained: if space be infinite, so is matter. [2]

Bruno's certitude as to the Infinity of the Universe was by no means accepted by his younger contemporaries Galileo and Kepler. The latter, who refers to him by name, inclined strongly towards the opposite view, perhaps for religious reasons; [3] the judicious Galileo wrote: "Reason and my mental powers do not enable me to conceive of either finitude or infinitude." [4] "No one has proved the world to be finite and determinate or infinite and indeterminate." [5]

---

[1] *Infinito, Dial. V.*   [2] *Ibid., Dial. I.   Cfr. De Immenso, IV, i.*
[3] Kepler, Johann; *Op. Omnia, ed.* C. Frisch, *vj, pp.* 137, 8. Burton writes in his *Anatomy of Melancholy:* "Kepler will by no means admit of Brunus' infinite worlds."
[4] Galileo, G ; *Lettera a F. Ingoli.*
[5] *Ibid., Dial. dei massimi sistemi.—Cfr.* Tocco, *Le Op. Lat. di G. B.,* 1889, *p.* 380.

Bruno grasped the general principle of the relativity of knowledge. In this work he demonstrates the relativity of sense ; in the *Spaccio* he will point out the relativity of morals ; in *De Minimo* he will demonstrate that there is no absolute measure for either time or space. But the assertion of the relativity of knowledge is obviously an assertion which claims to be absolutely true knowledge. Bruno goes further than such a claim, although, while it is an assured, it is by no means a modest one. The contradictions which are involved in conceptual time and space were felt even then. But Bruno unhesitatingly grasped one horn of the dilemma : for him the other horn did not exist. " In infinity, thought out, there is no measure, no proportion, no comprehensible number," he says.[1] Yet he has just argued from mathematical conceptions to physical reality. Space is for him an actually boundless continuity, an endless field for the motion of an actually endless number of solar systems. It is filled with the ether.[2] He writes of the " corporeal infinite . . . the simulacrum of the First Principle "[3] as actual, existent being. He distinguishes between the containing and the contained, between space as room to move in, the condition for motion, and the ether which occupies room ;[4] but, in positing an infinite ether as occupying infinite space, he clearly asserts absolute position in space, or in the language of the generation preceding our own, that space is absolute. This question is under dispute.[5] He perceives that continuity is quite a different thing from

---

[1] *Infinito, Dial. II, III ; De Imm., II, viij.*
[2] *Ibid., Dial. I.*   [3] *Ibid., Cfr. De Imm. IV, i.*
[4] *Ibid., Dial. I. Cfr. De Imm. I, vij, v.* 3, 4 ; 10-13 *and schol.*
[5] *Cfr.* Russell, the Hon. B ; *Position in Time and Space, Mind,* 1901 ; *Foundations of Geometry, chaps. iij A, iv ;* Campbell, N ; *Common Sense of Relativity, Phil. Mag, April* 1911 ; Poincaré, H ; *Dernières Pensées, Chap. II, L'espace et le temps, p.* 35 *sqq. Paris,* 1913. Bruno contradicts himself. See *pp.* 121, 141.

series ;[1] but does not perceive that one cannot think of an
infinite (as opposed to a merely indefinite) series ¡without
thinking of it as a sum, and an infinite sum is self-contradictory.   It is true that of late years Dedekind and others
have defined an Infinite as a systematic whole, the
internal structure of which completely and consistently
expresses a single self-consistent principle ;[2] but Modern
Metaphysics, in trying to apply this analysis of the nature
of Infinity,[3] has fallen into an ancient, hopeless blunder—
that of explaining Metaphysics by Mathematics instead of
confining it to its legitimate task of criticizing the presup-
positions of all the sciences, including Mathematics.   It is a
blunder from which Bruno is not free ; it crops up from
time to time, and is very conspicuous in one of his last
works.[4]   Further, the question does not occur to Bruno,
Are the characters of the members of the series wholly
determined by the principle of endlessness to which they
are referred ?   If not, the answer would be fatal to his
claim.   The grave perplexities which are involved in terms
or qualities and relations, like those already referred to,
were, happily for the Nolan cosmology, reserved to a later
age.

For the present, too, Lorentz's Principle of Relativity
would appear to have banished the ether to the museum of
scientific curiosities.   But it may only be suffering temporary eclipse.[5]

Not content then with merely stating that we can extend
our knowledge by taking Nature to be of one pattern, indefinitely repeated with variations, he asserts and reasserts
that Nature repeats herself infinitely throughout infinite

[1] *Infinito, Dial. I.*
[2] Dedekind ; *Was sind und was sollen die Zahlen.*
[3] *Cfr.* Royce, Josiah ; *The World and the Individual, Ser. II,
Appendix.*   [4] *Cfr. De Monade.*
[5] Campbell, N. *op. cit.;* Poincaré, *op. cit., c. vij.*

space. " There are countless suns and an infinity of planets which circle round their suns as our seven planets circle round our sun." [1] Particles are incessantly shot out through space from each of these worlds to other worlds and from one body to another, bodies being a composition of these. [2]

He tells us that each heavenly body, being animate, moves by its own intimate energy. The moon is an earth, and our earth, seen from the moon, would appear a luminous disc, as the moon does to us. " It is not unreasonable to suppose that there are planets which circle round other suns, not perceived by reason of great distance or small mass or not much (reflecting) water on their surface." He speaks of the World-Soul as an " animal, the all-sustainer of worlds which are souls and contain souls, some of which are higher, some lower than we ; and there must be plants and minerals in the worlds of space like those of our earth or different. We can attribute life to worlds with better reason than we can to our own earth." [3]

He had the merit of perceiving that comets have a regular course and are bodies not altogether different from the planets. [4] Some of his speculations are very remarkable ; they read like intuitive forecasts of modern discovery. Of such are : The sun's heat is produced by similar causes to those which produce heat on earth ; light emanates from the atmosphere immediately surrounding the sun ; [5] the sun has its own motion ; some of the suns may revolve, as planets, round others ; there are suns which cannot be seen by reason of their great distance ; [6] probably the heavenly

---

[1] *Infinito, Dial. III.*　　　　　　　　[2] *Ibid., Dial. II, IV.*
[3] *Ibid., Dial. III, IV.*
[4] *Ibid., Dial. IV.* In fact he thought they revolved round the sun.
[5] He supposes solar heat to radiate outwards only : the sun is a relatively cold, dark body.
[6] *Infinito, Dial. III.*

bodies decay and give place, in time, to new formations;[1] their particles are in constant motion;[2] and the fixed stars are really in motion.[3]

He accounts for the phenomenon of cohesion by the presence of water.[4]

Possibly the difficulty of accounting for the phenomena of light, heat and meteors was one of the reasons which induced Bruno to adopt the theory of indecomposable atoms or "prime bodies" of which all worlds are really made up. These atoms are always in incessant movement, passing from body to body and from world to world; they are for ever entering or leaving some combination of themselves.[5] This reads almost like a dim prophecy of the discovery of radio-activity; and the disappearance of the ether, if not temporary, will necessitate a very serious modification of the undulatory theory of light.

A great part of the *Infinito* is given over to vigorous attack on Aristotle's limited conceptions of the Universe. Bruno's arguments are acute, and many of them are destructive; but they sound strange to-day: the work of Galileo and Newton brushed them aside. Two of them may serve for examples of the remainder. Aristotle had imagined spheres of water, air and fire surrounding the earth.[6] Bruno points out that there is no evidence for the existence of these spheres. On the contrary, the evidence is all the other way; the elements are all mixed up together; there is air in the earth; hot and cold springs prove the presence of water in the rocks; fire leaps forth from the mountains.[7] An argument employed by Aristotle against infinity was

---

[1] *Infinito, Proem. Epist.*   [2] *Ibid., Dial. II.*
[3] *Ibid., Dial. III, V.*   [4] *Ibid., Dial. III.*
[5] *Ibid , Dial. III, IV.*   [6] Aristotle; *De Cœlo.*
[7] The centre of the earth is the hottest part of it, for being an animal, this must be so to sustain its vitality (*De Imm. III,* v.).

that heavy bodies move down; light bodies, up; therefore there would be infinite lightness and infinite heaviness in an infinite universe. Bruno shows that the phenomena of upward and downward motion are determined by relations of situation between bodies; what appears to us as an upward motion towards the moon would, to an inhabitant of the moon, appear a fall towards his own globe.[1] All this is acutely argued, but Bruno's cosmology is less reasoned construction than leaps towards truth, many of them reaching it. The most powerfully logical mind may wander far from truth: by innate disposition or education or habit or prejudice it is apt to incline towards wrong paths. It was Bruno's strength that, in the main, he had an instinct as to the right direction. And it is to such an instinct that success is most likely to fall. He was ahead of his time in emphasizing the need of observation and experiment, abstraction and comparison. " Why turn to vain fancies when there is experience itself to teach us ? "[2]

He retains a lively recollection of the Calvinists of Geneva and other protestants he had come across. He has a word to say on the doctrine of Predestination and its moral effect. In God, since to make is the same as to be made, free-will and necessity are the same; but for man they are partial, yet valid aspects. Theology is right in maintaining that the will is free, for man is not the same as God, though supported in His immanence. Men misconceive of absolute truth. Antecedent determination is not basal truth. Practically to will and to be free are one and the same, and man possesses a measure of freedom.[3] " The rude and ignorant are wholly unable to understand election, dignity and the merits of justice, whence predestination, filling them with assurance or desperation, they become very vile. Whiles,

---

[1] *Infinito, Dial. II.*   [2] *Ibid., Dial. III.*
[3] *Ibid., Dial. I.*

certain corruptors of laws, faith and religion, wishing to appear wise, have infected so many folk by the conclusions they draw from such like premises that they become more barbarous and wicked than they were before, despisers of good works and tightly bound to all vice and wickedness." True theologians condemn such evil teaching, allowing instructed and disciplined minds only " to entertain true propositions, from which we do not infer other than the truth of nature and the excellence of its Author; which we do not set before the populace, but only before the wise who may be able to understand our reasoning. Hence men not less learned than religious have never obstructed philo- sophic freedom, and true, politic and experienced thinkers have supported religions; for both the one and the other know that faith is necessary for the organisation of rude folk, who require government, and that ratiocination is for the thoughtful who can govern themselves and others." [1]

Later on, Bruno set too much of his philosophy before one who was not wise or " able to understand our reason- ing," with the result that he learned what sort of notion Pope and Princes of the Church " not less learned that religious " had of " philosophic freedom." [2]

[1] *Infinito, Dial. I.*

[2] Bruno, whose works had never become popular in England or on the continent and had become scarce in Catholic countries on account of their being on the Index Expurgatorius, impressed John Toland, the English Deist, as being the forerunner of free thinkers, and he translated the Introductory Letter of the Infinito and wrote an account of the book. *Coll. of sev. pieces of T.*, 1726, *v. I.*

V

THE EXPULSION OF THE TRIUMPHANT BEAST, PRO-
POSED BY JOVE, EFFECTED BY THE COUNCIL,
REVEALED BY MERCURY, RELATED BY SOPHIA,
HEARD BY SAULINO, AND SET DOWN BY THE
NOLAN; DIVIDED INTO THREE DIALOGUES, EACH
OF THREE PARTS.

In an "Explanatory Letter" to Sidney, Bruno tells him
that this work is introductory to another, which shall be "a
treatise on moral philosophy according to the inner light,
which the divine intellectual sun has illuminated and illumi-
nates in me." He wishes the present work to be read in
a broad, generous, uncarping spirit: the author must not
be taken "too assertively"; he introduces interlocutors
who "speak for themselves and report the judgements of
many others, equally full of their own convictions, and
expressing them with fervour and zeal, and, emphatically,
in their own character."[1]

The book recalls Lucian's "Parliament of the Gods,"[2]
convened to expel deities introduced by the barbarians;
and probably it was suggested by this classic as well
as by a work of Niccolo Franco.[3] It is crammed with
fragments from Bruno's vast reading and is a proof of
the strength of his memory. He quotes from Ariosto,
Tasso and Tansillo, and it is clear that he knew his
Dante. The Dialogue is mainly between Sophia (wisdom)
and Saulino, some kinsman on his mother's side; but
Mercury makes an appearance also. The general form

---

[1] *Spaccio, Epist. Esplic.*   [2] Θεῶν Ἐκκλησία.

[3] *Dial. nel quale sannio con la suida della virtù va in cielo etc.*,
1539. The author was hanged for a pasquinade by Pius V in 1563.
Cfr. Fiorentino; *op. cit., p.* 44.

is allegorical: It is related how "repentant Jove"[1] "after
having enjoyed youth for so many years, gave himself up
to wild ramblings and took up all his time in the affairs
of arms and love. But now, being tamed, he begins to
decline in his wantonness and vices and to lose the diver-
sions and entertainments of youth and manhood." He
"begins to advance in years and admits none unto his
council but such as have snowy heads and furrowed
brows"; those who have learned to be thoughtful, prudent,
continent, forgetful of affronts, and have acquired general,
practical wisdom.[2] "Jove stands for each one of us:"[3]
for every man is ultimate reality individualised as a
living spirit, which rules over a microcosm; and man
passes through a period of sensual enjoyment and passion
into years that bring the philosophic mind. But Jove
also represents the changes that take place in collective
humanity: he is the *Zeitgeist*. He swears a great oath
that virtue shall reign in heaven. The goddess of love
proposes a ball to celebrate the victory of the Gods over
the Titans; but Jove resolves to hold a grand Council
of the Gods instead. These Olympian deities are our
good and evil qualities personified. Jupiter seats himself
on his throne and announces his determination to purge
the sky of its beastly impurities. The Constellations,
such as the Bear, the Dragon, the Lion, the Hydra, all
represent brutal vices and must be replaced by those
virtues which are their contraries. It should not be forgotten that the revolving heavens were universally believed
to co-operate in determining the character and lives of
men;[4] nor that Bruno had achieved an enlarged conception

---

[1] *Spaccio, Epist. Esplic.*   [2] *Ibid., Dial. I, i.*

[3] *Ibid., Epist. Esplic.*

[4] The belief survived so long as the present century, even if now
extinct. The late learned Richard Garnett wrote in its support.

of the inhabitants of space and believed them, with the men of his time, to be a society of spirits.

The assembled Gods ratify Jove's decision, and the sky is forthwith purged of its " beasts " and ancient signs, one by one. Each is replaced, after much discussion, by the symbol of some quality conducive to good behaviour. By an adroit stroke, Momus, the god of ridicule, is made to act as jester to the Olympian Court, and Bruno is thus able to get out a good deal not to be taken " too asser- tively." Sometimes, too, he attracts attention to novel thought by Momus' over-emphasis or exaggeration. Momus is for ever jesting : he is the spirit that denies ; the critical, earnest spirit speaking through the mask of mockery ; there is something in him of Lucian and Voltaire, of Ibsen and Shaw, even ; he is at once the spirit of humour and of dissatisfaction ; he is an inner illumination, observing what progress is being made in reform and finding relief in bitter jest.[1]

A tumultuous throng of ideas surges to and fro to find expression ; hence the allegory is not systematic or always well sustained. Bruno's real conviction has to be extracted from a hundred odd, fantastic and dispersed imaginations. For his ideas rush forth like the winds escaped from the cave of Æolus. It were interesting could we know how Sidney, whose " wit was the measure of congruitie," took the work dedicated to him.

Allied vices are grouped together in the same constella- tion and are replaced by virtues also more or less related to each other and the contraries of the vices to be expelled ; for " the beginning, middle and end of the birth, growth and perfection of whatever we behold is from contraries, by contraries and to contraries ; and wheresoever con- trariety is, there is action and reaction ; there is motion,

[1] *Spaccio, Epist. Esplic.*

diversity, multitude and order; there are degrees, succession and vicissitude." [1]   Man, in his social relationship and activity may pass from the practice of this or that vice to the pursuit of its opposed virtue.

Bruno formulates no ethical system; he is dependent on no theologic command or sanction; he takes man just as he finds him in social life, and, in the main, he deals with moral qualities from the point of view of the needs of society and active life.   The distinction between active and contemplative life was emphasized by the theologians whom Bruno had studied.[2]   Truth, the divine object, is reserved for later treatment; though the distinction between contemplative and active qualities is by no means strictly observed here.   The Renaissance turned the eye away from heaven and hell to this life on earth; it concentrated its attention on Man.   But, in Bruno's time, natural reason and feeling were deemed to be ethically valueless.[3]   He was the first to ignore Christian tradition and discuss moral conduct as a natural phenomenon, valuing it for its usefulness in binding men together in a social whole.

The relation of the debates of the Gods in reconstructing the heavens is a "grotesque and overpowering farrago" of learning, allegory, metaphor, rhetoric and rollicking, reckless satiric humour,[4] much of the latter being derived, but by no means copied, from Rabelais.   The style is characteristically Brunian: it did not captivate many contemporary readers and is not likely to hold those of our own restless, impatient age.   Those who are by nature Borrowites alone appreciate the flavour of Borrow; chiefly Shavians that of Shaw;

[1] *Spaccio, Dial. I, i.*
[2] *E.g.,* Aquinas, T; *Summa Th., ij,* 2; *Q. clxxix, A,* 2. *Cfr.* Dante; *Purg. xxvij; Conv., iv,* 17.
[3] Spaventa, B: *Saggi di Critica, Napoli,* 1867, *vol. I, p.* 143.
[4] See the excellent remarks in J. Owen's *Skeptics of the It. Renaiss.,* 1893, under *G. B.*

Rabelais would bore most readers but for his indecorum, and no man could ever batter himself into the enjoyment of those peculiar turns of thought and treatment which Bruno takes: he must be born a Brunian. The thinker's torrential rush of ideas and words swerves hither and thither; his metaphors are often fantastic, whimsical, extravagant; he scorns moderation; he knows not the meaning of reserve. Not merely does he play on a thought with all possible variations, but he splashes words about with the rich enjoyment of an urchin in a bath. That he piles words on words, all of similar meaning, is sometimes a trick of emphasis, sometimes because he is aware of the many facets presented by every fact, and desires to deliver himself of a complete meaning. He never learned the lesson of simple directness taught by Boccaccio, or tried to imitate the limpid flow of Tasso's prose. Worse still, he fell into a fashionable vice of his time. Translating the classics directed men's attention to the power lying latent in every word; they discovered the richness of modern speech, and some of them fell into the vulgar view that a sonorous and pompous display of words is impressive, even when they are of almost identical meaning. Bruno marshalled whole battalions of ineffective synonyms and was happy when he had decorated an idea with "verbal ruffles and frills." He would seem to have known that his style was apt to sprawl.[1]

The Gods, after much humorous debate concerning each holder of a constellation, who typifies certain human vices, eject him and seat corresponding virtues in his place. The Little Bear, occupying the fixed centre of the revolving sky, has stood for Falsity, Hypocrisy and allied vices; let Truth, which follows Reality, take his place and preside. "The act of the Divine Knowledge is the substance of the being of all things, and, therefore, all things . . . not like ours,

[1] *Spaccio, III, ij.*

which follows things ; but is before all things and is everything." [1] Since our Knowledge is imperfect, then, we must
be careful how we give liberty to the vulgar to read what
they please and form their own conclusion therefrom.
Certain " books, any more than theological books, should not
be allowed to be read by ignorant men, who would thereby
become wicked, and receive evil instruction from them." [2]

All shams, all that is pernicious to society, all enslaving
dogmas and whatever fetters the mind; the " altar of
superstition," ignorance, violence, conspiracy, cruelty etc.,
are in turn banished, and prudence, courage, law, diligence,
humanity are to reign in their stead. The proper organization and conduct of society being the object of morals, no
laws which have not the perfecting of human intercourse
as their object should be acknowledged.[3] The test of a
supposed virtue is how it works. He would turn chastity,
for example, into a " gallant, humane, affable and hospitable continence ; " " of herself she is neither virtue nor vice,
nor contains any goodness, dignity or merit . . . when she
yields to any urgent reason, she is called continence, and
has the being of virtue, as partaking of such a fortitude and
contempt of pleasure, which is not vain and useless, but
improves human society and the honest satisfaction of
others." [4] Filled with the spirit of the Renaissance, though
possessed by a moral earnestness which scarcely belonged
to it, a " citizen and intimate of the world; son of father
Sol and mother Earth " [5] as he calls himself, quoting
Tasso, he was all for quaffing the deepest draughts of Life.

He perceived that moral practice is not under unalterably
fixed law: it is relative. Like Plato he did not think social
sexual arrangements perfect : perchance Jove may " restore

[1] *Spaccio, I, iii.*
[2] *Ibid., II, ij.*
[3] *Ibid., II, i.*
[4] *Ibid., III, ij.*
[5] *Ibid., Epist. Esplic.*

that natural law by which every man is allowed to have as many wives as he can maintain and impregnate"; and he supports this bold suggestion by the fallacious argument of increasing population.[1] "We call those virtues which by a certain trick and custom are so called and believed, though their effects and fruits are condemned by all sense and natural reason; such as open knavery and folly, the malignity of usurping laws and of possessors of *meum* and *tuum*; the strongest being the most rightful possessor, and he being the most worthy who is most solicitous, most industrious, and the first occupant of those gifts and parts of the earth which Nature, and consequently God, gives to all indifferently."[2] We almost might be reading modern propaganda!

Here and there he drops in a Philosophical sentence. "There is an eternal Principle or Substance which is truly the man and no accident derived from Composition. This is the deity, the hero, the particular God, the intelligence in, from and through whom different Complexes and bodies are formed and form themselves, so that it continually re-appears in different species, names and fortunes."[3]

The Soul, which is the eternal basis and meaning of souls, does not change and cannot become subject to dissolution: but in body and experience there is nothing but vicissitude.[4] "God, considered absolutely, has nothing to do with us, but only as he communicates himself by the effects of Nature, to which he is more nearly allied than Nature itself; so that if he is not Nature itself, certainly he is the Nature of Nature and the Soul of the World, if he is not the very soul itself."[5] Bruno, if he does not go so far as a certain modern philo-

---

[1] *Spaccio, Dial. I, i.*
[2] *Ibid., Dial. III, j.*
[3] *Ibid., Epist. Esplic.*
[4] *Ibid., Epist. Esplic; I, i.*
[5] *Ibid., III, ij.*

sopher, seeks reality not in the Idea, not in static abstractions, but in the ever changing fulness of Life.[1]

Presently Bruno shall "build the soaring spires That sing his soul"; now "of earth he draws Though blind to her, by spelling of her laws His purest fires." He trusts to Nature and all she may reveal; he thinks that, if God is in Nature, man will find himself at home in natural morals. He would have us guide our conduct by common sense. But the world "cannot subsist without law and religion."[2] "All those who are capable of judging will agree that the laws are good inasmuch as they have practice for their scope; and those are always the best that give the best encouragement to the best actions. For all laws have been given to us, or invented by men, chiefly for the convenience of human life: and because some do not see the fruit of their merits in this life, good and evil, rewards and punishments in another life are promised and laid before their eyes according to their deeds."[3]

Unhappily, the success of Theodosius in uniting Christianity and the State resulted in a general conviction that social order was bound up with religious government. This belief, not inoperant even now, although more than fifteen centuries have elapsed, was deeply rooted in the mind of the Middle Ages, was little affected by the Revival of Learning, and strongly influenced Bruno's thought. It was an important factor in those "wars of religion" which he had witnessed; for days when the state had need of strength, unification and organised direction, favoured the very human tendency of pope, protestant prophet or secular monarch towards absolutism, and supported this or the other well-defined form of Christianity within the area

---

[1] *Cfr.* Bergson. *Introduction to Metaphysic, tr. Hulme,* 1913, p. 64.

[2] *Spaccio, II, j.* [3] *Ibid., I, iii.*

of rule, to the forcible suppression of all competing forms of faith. Bruno valued Christianity above all religious systems, because it proclaimed the doctrine of love: it was a "religion, which began, increased and maintained itself with the raising of the dead, the healing of the sick and self-sacrifice for others." Yet, in some respects, he found Paganism superior. It was more tolerant, nearer to Nature and he thought it had a profounder metaphysical basis. "Those wise men knew that God was in things and that the divinity lay hid in Nature, shining and discovering itself differently in different subjects, and made them partakers of itself."[1] "From whence, with magical and divine rites, they mounted by the same ladder of Nature to the very height of the Divinity which descended to the meanest and lowest things by the communication of itself. But what I think most deplorable is that I see some senseless and foolish idolaters, who no more imitate the excellency of the Egyptian worship than the shadow partakes of the nobility of the body, who look for Divinity, without any manner of reason, in the excrements of dead and inanimate things. . . . And what is worse than all this, they triumph for joy to see their own foolish rites in so much reputation, and those of others vanished and annulled."[2] "Divinity hath, is, and will be present in divers subjects, however mortal they may be," and it is a mistake to suppose that the wise Egyptians worshipped "crocodiles, cocks, onions and turnips"; they only adored "the Divinity" therein; "you ought not to count this an evil, for animals and plants are the living effects of Nature, which Nature, you must know, is no other than God in things." The Greeks,[3] too, "did not worship Jupiter as

[1] *Spaccio, III, ij.*   [2] *Ibid., III, ij.*
[3] Sometimes Bruno refers to Christians when he speaks of Greeks. Probably there is a veiled allusion to the nature of the Divinity of Christ in this passage.

if he had been the Divinity, but they worshipped the Divinity as if it had been in Jupiter"; for all the Gods were once really men, and "seeing excellent majesty, justice and magnanimity in a man, they presumed there was a magnanimous just and bountiful God within him . . . or at least the Divinity which communicated itself in such a manner, by the name of Jupiter."[1] Bruno's religion was metaphysical and mystical; he was so strongly imbued with Neo-Platonic thought that he found himself in sympathy with all kinds of faith when philosophically interpreted. But Catholic Christianity, which owed so much to Neo-Platonising theologians in the fifth and sixth centuries and to the systematizing of Alexandrian speculations by the schoolmen, was further endeared to him by early education and habit; the authority of Rome had, until lately, been recognised in the political constitution and laws of the great Western peoples whom it had welded into some sort of union; so it had a strong claim on him as a formal faith; he was always willing to hand over to theology the contemplation of the Divinity as transcending the infinite universe,[2] if he might make an independent study of Nature, and freedom were allowed him to form his own conclusions therefrom. But, as the field of knowledge is enlarged, the demesne of Theology is apt to be encroached on. The incompatibility of systematic knowledge with dogma is progressively discernible in Bruno's writings. Yet he thought adjustment within the Church was possible, if it would give a twist to its doctrines and accept synthetic development. As a Catholic, he pours scorn on irreconcilable Reformers with their new-fangled dogmas and hide-bound forms. Especially does he reprobate those who hold to salvation by faith, despise works, and think "doing good and abstaining from evil

[1] *Spaccio, III, ii.*   [2] *Causa, Dial. IV.*

does not render them acceptable to God; but only hoping and believing according to their catechism." [1] "Among ten kinds of such teachers there is not to be found one who has not formed to himself a Catechism ready to be published to the world, if not published already, approving no other institution but his own, finding in all others something to be considered, disapproved or doubted of; besides that the greater part of them disagree with themselves, blotting out to-day what they had written yesterday." [2] Bruno was all for tolerance, but he perceived a menace to society in every man, however ill-qualified he might be, setting himself up as the sole possessor of truth and endeavouring to coerce his fellows into submission to his own opinion.

But if he despises Protestant sectaries, he is no less severe on the defects of his own Church. He objects to ecclesiastical authority setting up and enforcing rigid dogmas which it either does not in the least understand or which it misinterprets. The practical end of Religion should not be burdened with subtle and valueless theological speculations. Bruno is always as faithful to truth as the needle to the pole; heedless of personal advantage and even of personal safety. He was expecting to go back at once with Castelnau to a country which was suppressing all freedom in religious thought and speech when he put into the mouth of Momus a scoff which is not hard to unriddle: the fate of the centaur Chiron is under debate—a being, he says, "in which one Person is made up of two Natures, and two substances concur in one hypostatical union. 'Momus, Momus,' answered Jupiter, 'the mystery of this thing is great and occult and you cannot comprehend it; and therefore you ought only to believe it as a thing too high and great for you . . . . you should not desire to

[1] *Spaccio, I, iij.*   [2] *Ibid., II, i.*

know more than is necessary to be known; and believe me, 'tis not necessary to know this . . . Chiron being a most just man . . . . healing the sick, teaching the way how to mount up to the stars. I judge him' (says Jove) 'most worthy, because in this heavenly Temple, at the altar where he assists, there is no other priest but himself, whom you see with a beast in his hand ready to be offered up and a libation-bottle hanging at his girdle: and because an altar, a chapel and an oratory are necessary . . . . . therefore let him eternally continue, if Fate has not otherwise decreed.'"[1] Bruno held to life, and never fails to show how he disliked the morbid, pessimistic side of Christianity; its asceticism, self-depreciation and glorification of death and suffering. Saulino exclaims, chiefly hitting at Protestant exaggeration, however: "our professors of a sham religion cry That we ought to glory in I don't know what Cabalistic tragedy."[2] Bruno had already spoken in the *Sigillus* of crude sacramental doctrines, and he returns to the subject here. New evangelists have "found better bread, better flesh and wine than that of the Saone, Candy or Nola."[3] A few years later he declared that he could not discover the Divine splendour in "I know not what kind of material."[4] If the Catholic Church ceased to insist on incomprehensible and self-contradictory dogma, the law of love in its bosom might yet unite the world in common human aspiration and effort.[5] They are hateful persons who cast bones of contention before an ignorant world. Probably, too, he shared the prejudice of Montaigne: "the best and soundest side is that which maintains the ancient religion and government." But it must be purged of superstition and "those

---

[1] *Spaccio, III, iij.* [2] *Ibid., II, j.—Cfr. De Monade, cap. vj.*
[3] *Ibid., III, i.*
[4] *De Immenso, I, i.—Cfr.* Tocco, F; *N. Antologia, S. iv, Sept.,* 1902. [5] *Artic. adv. Math., Dedicatio.*

priests of Diana" should be less ready to exalt their office and mysterious function.[1] Bruno was a "Modernist" of the 16th century; he thought the Catholic position needed revision and re-statement; those qualified to think freely should be free to do so.

He believes neither in a universal deluge nor in the recent creation of man.[2] He cannot credit that the various races of men should have descended from a single pair; if so, it must have been by some miracle like that by which Jonah had a marvellous voyage—"a handsome way of transporting men by some blast of wind or some passage of whales, that have swallowed persons in one country and gone to spue them alive in other parts and upon other continents."[3] Such biblical miracles are absurd, as are those of the saints, and much doctrine taught by the Church. Momus declares that Orion, "who can walk upon the waves of the sea without sinking or wetting his feet; and consequently can likewise do a great many other pretty tricks," shall be sent among men, "and let us order him to teach them everything which he pleases, making them believe black is white and that human understanding, when it thinks it sees best, is mere blindness, and that what appears to Reason good, excellent and choice is base wicked and extremely evil; that Nature is a whorish baggage, that Natural Law is knavery, that Nature and the Divinity cannot concur to the same good end; that the justice of the one is not subordinate to the justice of the other, but are things as contrary to one another as light is to darkness; that the entire Divinity is Mother of the Greeks, and is like a hard stepmother to all other generations, whence none can be acceptable to the Gods but by becoming Greeks. For the greatest Russian or Poltroon who lived in Greece, as being allied to the generation of

---

[1] *Spaccio, III, iij.*　　　　[2] *Ibid., III, ij.*　　　　[3] *Ibid.*

the Gods, is incomparably better than the most just and magnanimous who could come from Rome . . . however preferable in manners, sciences, valour, judgment, beauty and authority; because these are natural gifts, and therefore despised by the Gods, and left to those who are not capable of greater privileges; that is, those supernatural ones which the Divinity gives, such as dancing on the waters, making lobsters sing ballads, cripples cut capers, and moles see without spectacles, and such other fine gallantries without number.[1]   Let them persuade withal, that all philosophy, all contemplation and all magic, which may make them like us, is nothing but bagatelle; that all heroic acts are nothing but knight-errantry; that ignorance is the finest science in the world, because it is acquired without labour and pains, and keeps the mind free from melancholy."[2]   One can hardly wonder, after reading this, that Bruno should request not to be taken "too assertively" and inform his reader that the personages in the book speak sincerely, but in their own proper character.[3]   None the less, he exhibits considerable courage in such free criticism of what was generally held sacrosanct in all Christian countries. That he could do so in England, and especially attack Protestantism in a land which had at least broken away from Rome, testifies to the liberty she enjoyed.

Bruno satirizes the belief in particular interventions of Providence;[4] and holds it "foolish, unworthy, profane and injurious to imagine that the Gods seek reverence, fear, love, worship and respect from men for any other good advantage or end than that of men themselves, being most glorious

---

[1] All these wonders may be found paralleled in those of the *Acta Sanctorum, quas coll.* J. Bollandus, *cont.* 1734-1894.   The Greeks are, of course, narrow Christians, while the Romans stand for the enlightened nations of antiquity and for enlightenment generally.

[2] *Spaccio, III, iij.*

[3] *Ibid., Epist. Esplic.*   [4] *Ibid., I, iij.*

L

in themselves and not capable of receiving any glory from without." [1]

"Give a blow," says Jupiter, "to all prophets, diviners, fortune-tellers and prognosticators, and all such as traverse and run about to spoil my progress." [2]   He expresses contempt for "altars and statues erected to certain persons whom I am ashamed to name, because they are worse than our satyrs, fauns and other half-beasts—viler than even the crocodiles of Egypt." [3]   Bruno has a fling, in turn, at current Christianity, Judaism (for some reason or other he detested Jews),[4] and Mohammedanism: all are useful and valid, but contain distortions of philosophic truth.

He has no belief in a Garden of Eden or "sweet Age of Gold." He foreshadows our modern knowledge of the evolution of humanity: "in the Golden Age men were not more virtuous than the beasts at present are virtuous; and perhaps they were more stupid than many of the beasts." [5] But he derived this view from Lucretius.

Nor was this his sole indebtedness to the great Latin poet. He adopted the theory of "atoms"—imperishable physical identities—which Lucretius drew through Epicurus from Leucippus and Democritus. And the consideration of physical individuals must have led him on to ponder, if he had not done so before, on the problem of individual souls. Is there atomic personality? From his first works to his last, he insists on the One Soul of the World, which is the unfolding of the Absolute to itself. But, in and for the Divine mind, there are centres of experience. "In every man, in each individual a world, a universe regards itself." [6]   Is each centre of experience a permanent, inexhaustible energy? Are souls immortal, even as is

---

[1] *Spaccio, II, i.*
[2] *Ibid., II, iij.*
[3] *Ibid., I, i.*
[4] *Ibid., III, ij, iij; Cabala, Dial. I.*
[5] *Ibid., III, i.*
[6] *Ibid., Epist. Esplic.*

that Absolute, for which they are and which includes them ?

It is not always easy or even possible to get at Bruno's meaning : he often designedly masks it in crooked allegory and veiled allusion. And it is quite in his manner to indulge in " blazing paradox " to excite reflection, or even as cryptic suggestion of his own thought. He writes to Sidney about the possibility of Transmigration, as held by Pythagoras.[1] It may be that he found in that teaching merely a close approximation towards the deepest principle of his own philosophy—the permanence of the One in vicissitude, the Essence animating its different receptacles. Be it understood clearly that Bruno is never wearied of proclaiming, in various ways, the one-ness of the Divine Energy as Sustainer and Embracer of the infinite " communications " of itself to itself, and the one-ness of all experience in the Divine Intuition. But did he also accept the separate immortality of individual souls ?

Seven years later, when asked about Transmigration, he told his judges : " I have held and hold souls to be immortal and that they are *substantiae subsistentiae*, that is intellective souls." He uses a scholastic term which means any special sort of existence taken on by substance. But the statement is vague ; he had not said whether he understood substance in its earlier or in its later meaning ; the phrase might cover the immortality of one single substance which is found differentiated, or it might be taken as an acceptance of the immortality of individual souls. He goes on : " Speaking as a Catholic, they do not pass from body to body, but go to Paradise, Purgatory or Hell. But I have reasoned deeply, and, speaking as a philosopher, since the soul is not found without body and yet is not body, it may be in one body or in another, and pass from body to body. This, if

[1] *Spaccio, Epist. Esplic.*

it be not true, seems at least likely, according to the opinion of Pythagoras." [1]   The answer is a riddle, which may be unravelled in more than one way.   Here, in the " Expul-sion," he suggests that " If not to be believed, it is gravely to be pondered " whether a vile life " be not disposed of by fatal justice, interwoven in a prison-house suited to its failure or crime, with organs and instruments suitable for such a workman or craftsman."   And again : " Let us sup-plicate the Divinity to bestow happy geniuses upon us in our transfusion, passage or metempsychosis ; since, how-ever inexorable he be, we must attend him with wishes, to be either preserved in our present state or to enter into a better, or a like, or one but a little worse . . . he that is favoured by the Gods must obtain this by means of good wishes and good actions." [2]

We may be sure that Bruno did not accept Pythagorean doctrine in a crude and vulgar form.   He employs it, just as he employs Catholic dogma, not by way of dodge, but in the sincere belief that various adumbrations of Truth must be adapted to various grades of illumination.   The result is that his own inner meaning is lost in obscurity.   Pytha-goreanism is far from removing that " dread of Orcus and greedy Charon " which he had promised to take away. [3]   But, co-operating with his Neo-Platonism and belief in hidden " sympathies " in Nature, such facts as the re-appearance of ancestral qualities, vital similarities in widely differing species, and innate tendencies would naturally lead him on to vague speculation in order to explain them. [4]

[1] *Doc. xij.   Cfr. Ovid ; Metam., l. xv.*

[2] *Spaccio, Epist. Esplic.*   Compare page 179.

[3] *Causa, Proem. Epist.*

[4] As pointed out by Bergson, the present is pregnant, as it were, with the past ; is its momentum.   Some scientific men accept Butler's and Hering's suggestions and talk about that contradiction in terms "unconscious memory."   Even to-day we have not quite set ourselves free from vague "explanations" and metaphors.

But so shrewd a thinker as Bruno must have perceived that, if in some way individual centres of experience persist in the Soul of the World, they can hardly be said to do so for themselves. If they endure as centres of energy they do not retain a true memory-synthesis : recurrent habits in life are not equivalent to self-conscious recollection. Individual immortality loses its value if the soul has to pass through the waters of forgetfulness.[1] But that "to be" is "to experience" was not explicitly recognised by Bruno or anyone before Berkeley wrote ; and it is quite possible that he entertained the idea of centres of energy persisting within the Absolute, and that these bear effects, though not precise memories, of past incarnations. The question of immortal souls will recur in connection with the great Latin poems.

The fire, the intemperate vigour of his Southern nature made him rejoice in the "Bacchic rout" of life and nature. He is for ever insisting on the universality and value of vicissitude. The *Spaccio* commences: "If there were no change in bodies, no variety in matter and no vicissitude in beings, there would be nothing agreeable, nothing good or nothing pleasant. . . . We see that pleasure and satisfaction consist in nothing else but a certain passage, progress or motion from one state to another. 'Tis certain that the state of hunger is irksome and unpleasant; and satiety is a state of sadness and dulness : but what is pleasing in any of these is a change from one to another. . . . Labour pleases us only a short time after the state of rest : and we find no pleasure in rest, but only a few minutes after the state of weariness." [2]

Political dissimulation was a prevailing vice in the 16th century. Bruno as an Ambassador's "gentleman" must

[1] *Cfr.* Dante ; *Purg. xxvj*, 106-8 ; *xxxi.*
[2] *Spaccio, Dial. I.*

have had ample opportunity for observing it at work.   He
attacks it with vigour: "You see what a pass the world is
reduced to by a custom which is become a proverb That
Governors are not obliged to keep faith."[1]   Nevertheless,
"even the Gods are forced to use it at times.   For sometimes Prudence hides the truth with her skirts in order to
escape blame and outrage."[2]

He thinks the hunting of game cruel: a sport worthy
only of butchers; "the hunting-dog should be sent to
Corsica or England."[3]   The Cup must be given to the
"chief tippler in Germany, where gluttony is regarded as
heroic virtue and drunkenness as a quality of heaven."
The affected dignity of potentates in their dress and baubles
of rank is satirized, but with a weaker hand than is usual
with our author.[4]

This work, although addressed to Sidney, would, like the
others published in England, seem to have fallen flat.   In
1633, however, a masque, the general idea and details of
which were based on the *Spaccio*, was played before
Charles I and Henrietta Maria;[5] and the *Spaccio* may have
influenced Spenser in writing the "Two Cantoes of Muta-
bilitie."[6]   Interest in Bruno was manifested by a little
group of English deists at the beginning of the eighteenth
century, and one of these, supposed to be W. Morehead,
translated the Dialogues but not the Dedicatory Letter of
the *Spaccio*.   This translation keeps so closely to the
original and renders its involved style and redundant
language so exactly that I have availed myself of it in the

---

[1] *Spaccio, III, ij.*   [2] *Ibid., II, iij.*   [3] *Ibid., III, ij.*
[4] *Ibid., III, iij.*
[5] Carew, Thos; *Cœlum Brittanicum.   Cfr.* Elton, O; *Modern
Studies: G. B. in England,* 1907, *p.* 34.
[6] Whittaker, T; *Essays and Notices,* 1895; Elton, O; *G. B. in
England, Quarterly R., Oct.* 1902.

quotations given. It was a general belief that the Pope was the expelled Beast,[1] an opinion shared by Leibnitz![2]

VI

THE CABALA OF THE STEED LIKE UNTO PEGASUS, WITH THE ADDITION OF THE ASS OF CYLLENE

This work is really a supplement to the *Spaccio*. Both books show what liberty of thought and speech had already established itself in England. Lucian, the inimitable satirist, gave the ancient world the adventures of an ass,[3] and Apuleius wrote that strange romance, " The Golden Ass." [4] After the revival of learning, Machiavelli called one of his poems by the same title, and we have seen that the ass held a distinguished position in a work of Bruno's youth. In the *Spaccio*, the space left by the Great Bear, hard by that occupied by Truth, and also the space left by Eridanus remain vacant. Bruno proceeds to fill the one with Donkeydom in the abstract and the other with Donkeydom in the concrete.

The classical scholar will recall how the winged steed, Pegasus, flew up to heaven,[5] served Zeus with his thunderbolts,[6] and struck forth a fountain with his hoofs.[7] Thereby the Italian poet, Boiardo, connects Pegasus with the home of the Muses. Bruno probably had all this, as well as Balaam's ass, in his mind when he wrote this work ;[8] also

---

[1] Cfr. *Schoppius ad Ritterhaus in* Berti, *op. cit., appendix ;* Bayle, P., *Dictionnaire, sub Bruno.*

[2] Letter to Lacroze, quoted by McIntyre, *op. cit., p.* 346. Bacon, Burton and Budgell just mention Bruno.

[3] Λούκιος ἡ ὄνός.   [4] Done into English, 1566.

[5] Apollodorus ; ed. Heyne, *II, iij.*

[6] Hesiod ; *Theogonia*, 281.

[7] Pausanias, *Græciæ descript., II*, 31 ; *IX*, 31.

[8] Cfr. *Cabala, Dial. II, i.*

Cusanus' "Learned Ignorance," which commends ardent search for truth while encouraging a critical spirit and demonstrating the impossibility of reaching truth as it really is. Cornelius Agrippa's work "On the uncertainty and vanity of all knowledge" was very popular.[1] The lighter touches in the *Cabala Del Cavallo Pegaseo* probably owe something to the perusal of Erasmus' "Praise of Folly"; and part of its title is taken from the Jewish Cabala, a medley, in part, of Jewish, Neo-Platonic and Pythagorean mysticism. The work is gravely dedicated to a mythical personage, the Bishop of Casamarciano, an obscure little place in Italy, and commences with a satiric letter. This is followed by a sonnet in praise of the ass: "Oh, holy donkeydom, holy ignorance, holy foolishness and pious devotion, who alone can so perfect the heart that human capacity and study may not improve it! Thou dost not employ the weary painstaking of any art or discovery, or of study of the skies, where thou has built thy home. Of what worth is study to us, o prying folk, to desire knowledge of the works of Nature, or if the stars are indeed earth, fire and sea? Holy donkeydom does not concern itself with such matters, but with folded hand and on bended knee, awaits what God shall send. Nothing endures, save the fruit of eternal repose, which God only gives when we are buried!" An address to the reader comes next, in the form of a pulpit exhortation: we must strive with all our might to become asses, if we are not yet in that state of grace, and persevere in our asinity if we have reached it: "so shall ye find yourselves written in the Book of Life, obtain grace in the Church Militant and glory in that Church Triumphant wherein God dwells and reigns for ever and ever. So be it!" "A very pious sonnet" follows on "the Ass and its foal."

[1] It was translated into English by James Sanford in 1569.

Bruno has now given the *motif* of the work. The dialogues which follow are filled with bitter irony and merciless satire, interspersed with very serious thought. No one wielded a more incisive lash or knew better how to apply it. Sometimes he becomes unduly violent; but often, when he is girding with sardonic grin, it changes into a laughing smile or takes on noble severity. His object is to destroy the notion that ignorance and superstitious belief and fear are requisite in true religion; he would away with the pretentious simplicity of pietists and the empty mysticism, stupidity, and obstinacy which render religion synonymous with obscurantism. He shows that Scripture has been misused to glorify ignorance; as if the world, that wonderful open book, were not also the work of God. He lashes the hypocrite. But ignorance is by no means confined to the Church. It is to be found among philosophers, whether they be Pyrrhonists or Aristotelians, and also among such as pin their blind faith on authority. In fact, the Ass is to be found everywhere; in the church, the cloister, the law-courts, the schools: Asinity is as widespread as is the Soul of the World. But true religion and true philosophy, must not be confounded with foolish superstition or supine ignorance.

There are three short dialogues. In the first Saulino reappears and holds lively talk with Sebasto and Coribante, a pedant. In the second dialogue, which is in three parts, a fresh interlocutor is introduced, one Onorio, who like the heroes of Lucian and Apuleius, has been an ass and endured much throughout many transformations. Once he was in the service of a gardener and was wont to be loaded with vegetables for Thebes' market; he dragged charcoal after this; then he became a steed of the Pegasus type and served the gods in that happy region where is the fountain which gushed forth when the hoof of the steed struck earth and which Apollo consecrated to the Muses. In the course of his metempsychoses he has occupied the body of Aristotle himself! It is splendid fooling; and all that may impede the progress of human knowledge is treated with withering scorn. The third dialogue has only a few lines. A messenger from Sebasto informs Saulino that his master's wife is dead; he must act as her executor, and, therefore, further discussion is to be postponed; moreover, Coribante has the gout and Onorio has gone away to take the waters.

Bruno recurs again and again to Pythagoreanism.

" SEB. Do you hold that the soul of man is substantially the same as that of beasts and that the only difference is one of form ? ONOR. That of man is the same in its specific and generic essence with that of flies, oysters, plants, and everything which lives, or has a soul: it is not matter, which it possesses in a more or less lively way—there is a thorough permeation of spirit in itself. Now, the aforesaid Spirit, by fate or providence, order or chance, unites itself to this or that kind of body, and, by reason of difference in structure or of members, reaches different grades and perfections of faculty and act. Hence, that spirit or soul, which was in the spider, and possessed its industry, claws and members of a certain number, mass and shape, united with human seed, acquires another intelligence, instruments, postures and deeds." [1] Just before, Onorio has declared that, from experience and memory, he knows the doctrine of Pythagoras and the Druids as to metempsychosis to be most assuredly true.

It will be noticed that, in the quotation given above, Bruno has observed the importance of organs to function. In another interesting digression he points out the important part played by the hand in giving man his position.

[1] *Cabala, Dial. II, i, at the beginning.*

among animals; his domination is due less to intelligence than to that "organ of organs."[1] He is quite confident that mental functioning is dependent on physical structure and physical operations. "Could the form of a snake change; could its head mould itself into human form, its belly swell and grow into the shape of the human breast, its tongue enlarge, shoulders spread out and arms and hands shoot forth from it, and its tail bud into legs, it would understand, breathe, speak, work and walk about like a man, and seem to be so because it would have become no other than a man."[2]

The Cabala repeats the central philosophical theory to be found in nearly all his works: "I say the efficient universal intelligence is one in all; is that which moves and makes intelligence; but there is, moreover, a particular intelligence by which they are moved, illuminated and comprehend, and this is multiplied according to the number of individuals. Even as the power of seeing is multiplied according to the number of eyes, all stimulated and illuminated by fire, light or a sun, so is the intellectual power multiplied according to the number of subjects participating in soul, illuminated by a supreme intellectual sun."[3]

First and foremost Bruno is an idealist; but he is hampered by the notion of spirit operating on something that is not quite spirit. It is his great merit, as Höffding points out, that he is an idealist who is determined to unite his idealism with a scientific conception of the world process.[4]

.   .   .   .

Cyllene is a mountain in simple-minded Arcadia: hence the title of the little adjunct to the Cabala—the "Ass or Cyllene." An ass, wishing to enter a Pythagorean academy,

---

[1] *Cabala, Dial. II, i, at the beginning.*   [2] *Ibid.*
[3] *Ibid., Dial. I, near end.*
[4] Höffding, H; *Hist. Mod. Phil., tr. Meyer,* 1900, *vol. i, p.* 139.

finds that he has to observe the difficult regulation of remaining silent for the space of two years. Mercury takes
pity on the unhappy beast, bestows on him the gift of eloquence and transforms him into a dogmatic pedant. " Be
at home with all, scamper about with all, be the brother of
all, identify yourself with them, rule them, be themselves." [1]
The innocent beast is no such ass as not to want to know
something. " Tell me, sir," he asks, "and help me a little.
Which holds the first rank, a man who has become a
donkey or a donkey transmogrified into a man ? "

Six years later Bruno informed his readers that he had
suppressed the Ass of Cyllene, " for it annoyed the vulgar,
and, on account of its sinister flavour, did not please the
wise." [2] Probably the Cabala was withdrawn as well as the
supplement.

VII

The Transports Of Intrepid Souls

The full significance and subtle associations of the title
Gli Eroici Furori cannot be adequately rendered.[3]

Plato discovered in the passion of Greek friendship an
imperfect image of divine, ideal beauty and goodness, and
taught that it may be converted into a spur to our highest
desire. Through the Alexandrian thinkers, who mingled
Platonic doctrines with Oriental mysticism, this thought
reached the Middle Ages. United with the Provençal sentiment of chivalrous devotion to a chosen lady, it influenced
Dante, and transfigured love occupied the great poet in his
two most important works.[4] Taking a more fleshly form in

---

[1] *Asin. Cellen.*

[2] G. B ; *De imaginum, Signorum et idearum compositione, Frcf.,*
1591

[3] Patrizzi, Bruno's contemporary, wrote " Della diversità de' *furori
poetici.*" [4] *Divina Commedia ; Vita Nuova.*

Petrarch, the sentiment found a lower level, and by the
sixteenth century it had furnished a vast crowd of poetasters
and dilettanti with fashionable affectations. Yet, in the
fifteenth century, Benivieni, Pico and others, and, at the
beginning of the sixteenth, Castiglioni, soared almost as
high as Plato on wing hardly less confident.[1] But the usual
Petrarchistic sonneteer, forced, artificial and absurd, was as
hateful to Bruno as the pedant, and not less foolishly dull.
He makes Tansillo, the Petrarchist, his chief interlocutor,
point out a new and sure way. The intellectual lover may,
by strenuous effort, reach a comprehensive vision of Nature,[2]
which is the very image, nay the presence of God, though
he may not reach that sense of direct union, which is pure
feeling, granted to Plotinus [3] and other mystics.

The work is one long hymn to intellectual beauty, in
prose and verse. One feels the influence of the *Timœus*
and the vision of the Platonic soul " moving about the same
in unchanging thought of the same." Bruno tells us that
he followed lines laid down in the *Symposium* and *Phœdrus*.[4]

In the introductory letter to Sidney, when writing concerning the constant transformation of all things, he
digresses to distinguish between " those who declare according to reason and their own light " and " those who declare
by faith and a higher light." He follows with a frank word
as to his own attitude towards current Christian doctrine.
" As to my faith," he says, " I hold it a most proper thing
to declare and affirm with theologians and those who are
concerned with the laws and institutions of the people in
their interpretation : just as I am not slack to affirm and

---

[1] *Cfr.*, Benivieni, G ; *Commento . . . dello amore et della bellezza
divina, Fir.*, 1500.—Ficino, M ; *Sopra lo amore o ver' convito di
Platone, Fir.*, 1543.—Castiglione, B ; *Il libro del Cortigiano (tr. Sir
J. Hoby*, 1561).   [2] *Eroici, P. II, Dial. II.*
[3] Porph ; *V, Plot.* 23.   [4] Spaventa ; *op. cit., I, p.* 141.

accept the sense of those, among the good and wise, who speak according to reason." [1]   That is to say, The religion of a people, being part of its political constitution and laws, must be followed; but the competent may subject it to judicious criticism.   This is a most important passage, because, when tried by the Inquisition, we find Bruno willing to accept the Church as a practical institution and affirm its dogmas as adumbrations of truth, but resolutely maintaining the freedom of philosophy to interpret them and to pursue an independent course.

He did not write for the crowd however; [2] nor about social ethics as in the *Spaccio;* he will redeem the promise he made therein; [3] that work was but an introduction to this.   The intellectually disposed will discover no abiding home in the transitory world of sense or in ordinary piety; only by the exercise of intellect, which is a divine passion, shall these find anchorage for the soul.   Such as would purify the will sprout " wings to the soul "; [4] they already possess the divine spirit they seek after, and so are at once the lover and the loved; and their love shall enable these undaunted heroes to pass through suffering (which is no other than a golden spur), become spectators of Infinite Power and Act, and be at one, not indeed with the innermost being of God, but with God in the highest manifestations of his mind. [5]   The innermost being of God is not reached, even by the mystic.

Bruno is the first thinker who based the soul's duty to itself on its own nature: not on external authority, but on inner light. [6]   He leaves theology to itself and is not here

---

[1] *Eroici, Argomento del Nolano.*
[2] *Eroici, P. I, Dial. II ; P. II, Dial. II.*
[3] *Spaccio, Epist. Esplic.*   [4] *Eroici, P. II, Dial. II.*
[5] *Ibid., P. I, Dial. II, III ; P. II, Dial. IV.*
[6] Spaventa, B ; *op. cit., p.* 143.

concerned with social duty; still less with vulgar aims, but only with the unwearied ardours of noble desire, and with that hero who shall rise above the tumult of sense and the conflict of contraries. No work of Bruno's is fuller of strange imaginings, or better expresses his inmost soul.[1]

It is in two parts, each of five dialogues. In the first part, Tansillo, the poet, reads his own cryptic stanzas or those of the Nolan or of some other poet; and, sometimes, a symbolic picture is set before Cicada and is described; then, after the manner of Dante's *Vita Nuova*, poem or poem and picture are explained. The same plan is continued in the first two dialogues of the second part between Cesarino and Maricondo; the third dialogue between Liberio and Laodonio contains eight sonnets (two propositions and two replies of the heart to the eyes, and the same number of propositions and replies of the eyes to the heart). In the fourth dialogue Severino and Minutolo discuss, and nine blind men are spoken of, each of whom has disburdened his soul in a sonnet. Finally, in the fifth dialogue, two ladies, Laodomia and Giulia, are introduced. Laodomia describes how the nine blind men, "having overpassed all the seas, crossed all the rivers, surmounted all the hills and traversed all the plains, during a space of ten years, at the end of that time found themselves under the temperate sky of Britain and in the presence of the beauteous and gracious nymphs of Father Thames." The nymphs have passed a sealed vase to one of their number; it opens of itself and sprinkles its contents over the blind wanderers, who, to the amazement of everybody, themselves included, recover their sight.

The allegory is discontinuous, the symbols are far-fetched; there are dubious side-lights of mystic meaning,

[1] Happily, the body of the work is translated: "*The Heroic Enthusiasts*" by L. Williams. *London, Redway*, 1887-89.

and all is intermingled with observations alien to the purpose in hand and even with personal reminiscences. But
obscurity charmed the "intellectuals" of the era; they
found no entertainment more agreeable or more mentally
stimulating than moral conundrums—the more quaint and
singular the better. Bruno certainly succeeds in reviving
any flagging of attention by change of interlocutors, brisk
and natural dialogue, surprise and unexpected digression.

He would have the service of the soul directed to "the
fountain of the Ideas, the ocean of all truth and goodness."
"The Infinite, being infinite, must be infinitely pursued." [1]
The pursuit of Natural Knowledge is a most exquisite means
of endowing the human soul with an heroic temper. For
there are stages in the contemplation of the Divine Love
and Wisdom. But, cast back into the body and bound by
the body, the soul is not always in progress.[2] It must then
arouse itself and make a new intrepid attempt; first through
desire; next, by attention; then by study, and lastly by
being filled with loving enthusiasm.[3] And though we can
never attain the divine infinitude of Power, Love and Knowledge, we can share in its blessedness.

Bruno makes his start then with an impulse of intellectual
passion, and treats of the upward ascent which the intellect
must traverse to reach a right comprehension of God
manifest in Nature. He makes Tansillo utter an *Apologia
pro vita sua*. "That which hath no splendour beyond
bodily charm is worthy only of that form of love which hath
the perpetuation of the race for its object. Methinks it is
piggish to enquire or bother about it. For mine own part,
I was never more infatuate about such matters than I am

[1] *Eroici, P. I, Dial. IV, Tansillo loq., after canz.* 20; *cfr. Spaccio,
III, ii.*
[2] *Ibid., P. I, Dial. IV, Tansillo loq., after canz.* 23.
[3] *Ibid., P. I, Dial. V, vij.*

now about any picture or statue to which I may be indifferent."[1] "The contrary is the reason why its opposite is
hankered after and enjoyed."[2] "But the wise hold all
mutable things as if they were not, and affirm them to be
vanity."[3] Sense would live according to sensible things,
after its own manner; but there are other laws:[4] he who
would aim at the imperishable object must rise, by heroic
effort, above matter and flesh and the transitory things of
earth.[5] The fulness of knowledge must be united with a
burning passion for that which is both love and truth. The
desire to comprehend is the soul's home-sickness which
causes it to soar aloft for true wisdom and joy; it does not
avoid, nay, it voluntarily seeks the path of suffering, the
"Gethsemane of the soul," which shall lead it to true beauty
—the ultimate harmony and conformity of all things.[6]

There are two kinds of ecstasy which may be reached by
the divinely transported: there is the abstraction of passive
mystics, who, usually, are ignorant folk, "into whom the
divine sense enters as it were into an empty room"; and
there are those who are filled with intellectual ardour, which
spurs them to constructive activity, "so that, by rational
process, the spirit becomes godlike in contact with its divine
object." "The first kind *possess* more dignity, power and
efficacy in themselves; the second kind *are* worthier, more
powerful and efficacious and are divine. The first are
worthy as is the ass who bears the sacraments; the second
are as a sacred thing."[7] The experience of the mystic has
empirical value, but philosophy deals with the rational.[8]

To Bruno, philosophy and science were "musical as is

[1] *Eroici, P. I, Dial. II, at end.*
[2] *Ibid., after canz.* 9; *cfr. Spaccio, I, i.*   [3] *Loc. cit.*
[4] *Eroici, P. I, Dial. IV, after sonnet* 22.
[5] *Ibid., P. II, Dial. II.*   [6] *Ibid., P. II, Dial. III, foll. xiij.*
[7] *Ibid., P. I, Dial. III, at beginning.*
[8] *Cfr.* Sensini, T; *op. cit., p.* 19.

M

Apollo's lute." He pursued them with the passion of a lover. He holds that when once intellectual love is aroused nothing else will really satisfy.[1] We are indeed bound to the body, and restricted by our vegetative life; but our proper activity is, in ceaseless strife, to contemplate the divine object, whereby we shall bear even the most terrible of life's evils with unshaken mind.[2] Sensible beauty alters and fades; but there is an intelligible beauty which cannot perish: Love inspires us with love to pursue it. The desire of the soul is an infinite one, and this is of itself an assurance of its own unending fulfilment. The soul which has touched its shining goal holds eternity in a moment. Man "becomes a god through intellectual contact with that transcendent object, and has no thought but of divine things and shows himself insensible and unmoved by that which ordinary men feel most of all; but, through love of the divine, he disdains all other enjoyments and takes no thought of life."[3] These are no mere words. Bruno proved that they were sincere throughout life and in death. "It is neither natural nor expedient that the infinite should be grasped, nor can it render itself as finite, for then it would cease to be infinite; but it is expedient and natural that the infinite, being such, should be infinitely pursued; in which mode of seeking, not by physical desire, but by thought, the imperfect is not to be deemed the perfect, but, circling upwards through the grades of imperfection, strains after that infinite centre which is neither formed nor forms."[4]

Of Bruno, as of Spinoza, it may be said that he was "God-intoxicated." He felt that the Divine Excellence had its abode in the very heart of Nature and within his own body and spirit. Indwelling in every dewdrop as in the

---

[1] *Eroici*, P. II, Dial. I, ix. [2] *Ibid.*, P. I, Dial. IV, V.
[3] *Ibid.*, P. I, Dial. III, *beginning*.
[4] *Ibid.*, P. I, Dial. IV, *after canz.* 20.

innumerable host of heaven, in the humblest flower and in
the mind of man, he found the living spirit of God, setting
forth the Divine glory, making the Divine perfection and
inspiring with the Divine love. The *Eroici* is full of the
pantings of his soul for intellectual enfranchisement and
contact with Truth, the divine object. He breaks out
into many a canzone to express the heroic rapture of the
upsoaring soul. Not all the verses are his own; perhaps
the finest is a sonnet by Tansillo. There is much of the
poetic conceits, so fashionable at the time, and, at his
worst, Bruno has the fatal facility of the improvisatore; at
his best he may be compared with Michel Angelo. A
single example, not of his worst or best verse, may be
translated to give, however poorly, some idea of his poetic
manner in this work:

> " Circles the sun and seeks whence he hath come;
> And wandering lights make ever for their source;
> The child of earth returns to earthly home;
> From sea to sea again, the waters course;
> Divine desire, wherever it may roam,
> Soars ever upward, of its native force.
>   'Tis thus the soul, born of my lady fair,
>   Turns back to find that goddess past compare." [1]

Bruno repeats that his teaching is for the few; for even
the learned of the Universities are soul-less pedants
knowing nothing of the strenuous life and caring less,[2]
and, as for the wholly uninstructed, " the multitude can,
with great difficulty, be kept from vice and urged to virtue
by belief in eternal punishments." [3] This passage suggests
that the permanence of the individual " soul " through the
vicissitudes of the forms it assumes and the retributive
justice which follows it, so pronouncedly brought before

---

[1] *Eroici, P. II, I, viij, Ottava del Nolano.*
[2] *Ibid., P. II, II.*   [3] *Argomento.*

Sidney in the dedicatory letter of the Expulsion, must by no means be taken *au pied de la lettre*.[1]

The heroic soul, says Bruno, shall seek truth and find it. The time had not then come for Pilate's question to be put again. Bruno was happily unvexed by the problem of truth. No germ is to be discovered in any of his writings of any one of the three popular solutions which philosophy has since provided—that Truth is a copy of Reality, or constitutes Reality itself, or is a mere sign for practical life. He takes Truth quite simply and uncritically. But there is a view implicit in the *Eroici* and in all but the earliest of his philosophical writings, and this is that our truth is a progressive, ideal approximation towards that whole Truth which is one with the inmost nature of Being.

Höffding justly remarks that, in this work, complexity of feeling is taken as a criterion for its development.[2] As to the eternal striving of the Infinite, Bruno anticipates Kant and Fichte. The interest he took in physics peeps out even in this ethical rhapsody: he points to the expansive force of steam.[3]

There are excellent remarks on poetry. "Poetry is not born in rules," says Tansillo; "rules are derived from poetry; and there are as many sorts of true rules as there are of true poets." Cicada: "But how are true poets to be recognized?" Tansillo: "By their song."[4]

---

[1] See pages 163 sq. of this work.
[2] Höffding, H ; *Hist. of Mod. Phil.*, *tr.* Meyer, 1900, *vol. I, p.* 147.
[3] *Eroici, P. I, Dial. V.*   [4] *Ibid., Dial. I.*

CHAPTER XII

IN PARIS AGAIN. SOME NEW WORKS

BEHOLD Bruno landed in France in as bad plight as ever, or worse; robbed, homeless, his whilom patron no longer able to help or protect him and with no prospect of better things. Like Dante he was "a wanderer, almost a beggar," and like Dante he might have exclaimed: "Verily have I been as a ship without sail or rudder, drifted hither and thither on different refuges, straits and shores by the bitter blast, the breath of which is wretched poverty."[1]

"I accompanied the Ambassador to Paris, where I stayed another year" (more exactly seven months) "boarding and lodging with the gentlemen I knew there, the greater part of the time at my own expense."[2] We may suppose that he was given food and shelter until he found employment. How he supported himself we do not know; he may have had a little money about him; probably he taught; he may have read proofs. He dwelt near the College of Cambrai.[3]

It may be, as Tocco suggests,[4] that he was weary of persecution and wished to pursue his studies under the protection of some great dignitary. So, he would be able to teach unmolested. But, to this end it was necessary for him to reconcile himself with the Church, which he had never abandoned at heart. He had become an outlaw, a reprobate, a child of darkness. So he went boldly to

---

[1] Dante; *Convito, I,* 3.   [2] *Doc. ix.*
[3] Auvray, L; *op. cit., sub 6th Dec.*
[4] Tocco, F ; *Conferenza, Fir.,* 1888.

Mendoza, who was now Spanish Ambassador at Paris, and who therefore represented the ruler of his native province. He judged ill of Mendoza's character : the Ambassador identified himself wholly with the interests of his Church and country, was mostly indifferent to all else, and was entirely unscrupulous in the pursuit of the ends he set before him.   Bruno said to his judges : " I approached the French Nuncio, Monsignor the Bishop of Bergamo, to whom I was introduced by Don Bernardino de Mendoza, whom I had known at the English Court." [1]   " Whilst I strove by means [of these gentlemen] to return to the Church, I consulted another Jesuit ; and they told me that they could not absolve me of apostasy and that I could not attend the divine offices." [2]   " I prayed the Nuncio and sought again earnestly that he would write to His Beatitude, Sixtus V, at Rome, to obtain his grace and be received into the bosom of the Catholic Church, but that I should not be compelled to return to monkdom.   Wherefore the Nuncio had no hope and would not write unless I were willing to return to my order.   He referred me to the Jesuit father, Alonzo Spagnuolo.   I discussed my case with him, and he shewed me that it was necessary to procure absolution from censure from the Pope, and that nothing could be done unless I went back to my order.   I was further warned by him that, being excommunicate, I could not attend the divine offices, but might very well listen to sermons and say my prayers in Church." [3]

Like Erasmus, like More, he hoped that in the ferment of new thought, in the clash of ancient dogma with the new passion for reason, the real government of the Church would prove sagacious and institute some *modus vivendi* for the genuine thinker ; as if the principle of authority could ever be harmonized with intellectual freedom !   He

[1] *Doc. xvij.*   [2] *Doc. xi.*   [3] *Doc. xvij.*

hoped to reconcile the irreconcilable: no way of mutual toleration was possible.

Bruno got himself talked about on his return to France. Arnold van Buchel, a Dutchman, names him among the eminent folk he spoke to or saw during his visit to Paris, Dec. 1585. Buchel describes him as "a philosopher who is more subtle than is good for his safety, who has taken the pseudonym of 'Lover of God' (Philotheus). He has written a little book *De Arte Reminiscendi* and, in Italian, *Gli Heroici* and *Il Candelajo*, a comedy."[1]

A precious document, already quoted from, gives us a glimpse of Bruno as he appeared to an ingenuous contemporary. Monsieur Auvray discovered in the Bibliothèque Nationale a manuscript diary which he supposes to be that of Guillaume Cotin, Librarian to the Abbey of St. Victor. It contains an account of several visits paid to him by Bruno between Dec. 6th 1585 and Feby. 2nd 1586. The Author discloses himself as very erudite and very sterile; he is immensely interested in foreign missions and pulpit oratory; his statements are bare matters of fact; but matter-of-fact diaries are usually the best revealers of character. He is meticulously precise; so careful that if he has not properly caught a name or a statement he leaves a hiatus; if in doubt as to the perfect accuracy of anything he has written, he erases it. We recognize the kind of man he must have been when we find him enquiring what particular saint the cathedral of Nola was dedicated to. He is overweighted with learning, and, if, as is pretty certain, he was Cotin, so paralysed by his own scrupulosity that he left no books behind him. At this time Cotin was in failing health; indeed he died not very long afterwards.[2] To this pertina-

---

[1] Utrecht Univ. Lib., *M.S. fol.* 189; vide Vidier, M. A; *Mém. de la Societé de l'histoire de Paris etc.*, t. *xxvj*, 1899, *p.* 146.

[2] Auvray, L; *op. cit., p.* 288 *sqq.*

cious, painstaking and somewhat dull person, comes Bruno bursting with self-confidence, naturally vain, conscious of not having received his due, and, therefore, a trifle self-assertive and even boastful. The carelessness, too, which marked the Nolan's style was present in his speech. What he has to say is of so much importance that he must out with it, whether the occasion be opportune and the hearer prepared to receive it or no. Moreover, he is loftily contemptuous of all who have not reached his own large purview. The man "subdued to what he worked in" is obviously interested at first in Bruno, but soon the idiosyncrasies of his visitor begin to irritate him. There is not a word of comment, but a diary always has selected facts, and the facts recounted here are their own comment; we can read between the lines how little inclination two so diverse men discover for one another; they become a little cool; relations are a little strained, and, finally, cease.

At the first meeting we find Bruno telling that he has lectured at Oxford; he is about to print a "Tree of Philosophers,"[1] a work which certainly never appeared from the Press during the author's lifetime, but may be the "Animadversiones"[2] of which the manuscript is at Erlangen. We learn that Bruno's father is still alive at Nola; he is himself lodging near the College of Cambrai. Further conversation turns on an edition of Lucretius.

Bruno comes again the very next day (Dec. 7th), perhaps to consult books, and recounts some passages in his history, of which I have made use. "He says he understands and could explain in an hour artificial memory, like that set forth in the first book *ad Herennium*,[3] which its readers do not comprehend, nor Muret,[4] who admires him as a

---

[1] *Arbor Philosophorum.*

[2] *Animadversiones circa Lampadem Lullianam.*

[3] The work is spoken of on p. 8, n. 2.   [4] Muret died a little before.

Corsican nobleman." The diarist is told about the theses
for the doctorate, and enters in Latin that Bruno told him
he might skip parts of S. Augustine's disputations.[1] This
is a remark very characteristic of the hero of our theme.
The few Latin words may indicate, so precise is our authority, that Bruno dropped from French into Latin. Perchance, like most Italians, he did not speak it too well,
and this may account for certain erasures and hiatuses in
the manuscript. There follows the usual intrepid expression of most intimate opinion, and this to a stranger on the
second day of their intercourse! He " contemns the subtleties of the schoolmen and doctrines concerning the sacraments, even that of the Eucharist, which he says St. Peter
and St. Paul were unacquainted with, only knowing that
' this is my body.' He says that with the removal of these
questions religious turmoil would disappear, and hopes that
will soon be the end of it. But above all he detests the
heretics of France and England because they despise good
works and preach the assurance of their faith and justifica-
tion; for Christianity tends wholly towards life well spent.
He scorns Cajetanus and Pico della Mirandola and the
whole philosophy of the Jesuits outside the subject-matter
and intelligence of Aristotle." (Perhaps his unsatisfactory
interview with Father Alonzo Spagnuolo may have intensi-
fied his intellectual contempt for the Jesuits.) Next comes
a side-light on the interest he took in Natural Science.
" He told me much concerning the geography and cold of
Tartary and Scotland and of the temperature of Ireland."
Concerning this last, he may have " learned the same "
from " consultacions " with some of Elizabeth's " verye wise
Governours and Counsellors whom he had sometimes hearde
treate thereof."

[1] I think the reader will detect an ironical flavour in this and the
other entries which I have italicized.

On Thursday, Dec. 12th, "Jordanus brought me his books on Mnemonic Art; he scorns the whole doctorate, notably Cujas and Passerat, but praises Bossulus for eloquence and delivery; says all the teachers of humane letters in Italy are nobodies and unprofitable, but they make money as private tutors to the children of nobles. Muret got 3000 scudi, out of an income of 5000 scudi in money or its value, for teaching the nephew of Cardinal Colonna.[1] 2000 or 3000 would be bestowed freely on the education of children." Cotin must have led the conversation on to preachers again. Bruno praises some and dispraises others. " Panigarola is without insight and futile; Fiamma has gone off in his old age": he should have given up three years ago. " He strongly disparages Toledo[2] and Jesuit preachers in Italy, for they commence with an overdose of gravity and say that great mysteries are contained in the text, but, at the end, nothing has come out." But Tarcagnota of Gaeta is highly commended; " he has written a Universal History." Bruno talked about the recent severe measures meted out to his turbulent nobles by the New Pope, Sixtus V. He took the side of the nobles.

Bruno calls again on the 21st and tells about his early success in demonstrating artificial memory to the Pope. On the 27th there is another visit. The diarist is told about the robbery. " He cannot get the proofs of his works to order. He has three works in view, 1° the Arbor Philosophorum; 2° the entire Physics of Aristotle, drawn up under a few figures, *which he will teach in half an hour;*[3] 3° an exposition of the Art of Lully,[4] more full than before, with its use, *which its author* (Lully) *did not know.*"

---

[1] He was tutor at Rome to Martin Colonna, nephew of Cardinal Marc Antonio Colonna.   [2] Preacher in ordinary to the Pope.

[3] *Figuratio Aristotelici Physici*, printed by Pierre Chevillot the following year.

[4] *De Lampade Combinatoria Lulliana, Vitebergæ*, 1587.

Bruno is not mentioned again until 2nd Feby, 1586, when he informed the diarist "that Fabricius Saliternus is in Paris." Of whom more anon. Saliternus " is 60 years of age, stands high as a geometer, *surpassing in that all predecessors and contemporaries, knows no Latin.* Jordanus will print his researches in Latin."[1] "Also, the aforesaid Jordanus will read his sentences on Aristotle, containing all the Physics, and he is going to print them." He was already arranging for the famous tournament at the Cambrai. At the end of the entry comes another, dated Feb. 4th. Monsieur Auvray believes it to be an afterthought and refers it to the preceding interview. "Also, Jordanus told me that he knows nothing of the town built by the Duke of Florence where Latin is to be spoken; but he has heard the said Duke wishes to build a City of the Sun, so as to be sure of where the sun is shining every day of the year, seeing that there are many cities celebrated in this way, Rome and Rhodes among them." This is a most audacious " pulling" of the diarist's "leg": Rhodes was famous for the sunshine it enjoyed, but Rome is a misty place for Italy; and doubtless Bruno delighted in a concealed ironic glance at the intellectual resplendence of the Apostolic See. With this parting shot, intercourse between the two men ended. Perhaps Bruno was too busy preparing for the disputation and getting his books out to visit libraries or waste his time in chatter; perhaps, too, both men had got weary of one another.

To prepare the way for the public discussion Bruno wrote that short preliminary exposition of the peripatetic philosophy which the diarist sardonically records, " was to teach it in half an hour." "A Relation In Imagery Of The

---

[1] *Cfr.* J. B. N. *Dialogi duo de Fabbricii Mordentis Salernitani prope divina adinventione ad perfectam Cosmimetriæ praxim. Parisiis* 1586, *Petr. Chevillot.*

Physics Of Aristotle "[1] was printed by Pierre Chevillot, who dwelt under the sign of the Red Rose, in 1586, and was dedicated to Pierre d'Albigny, Abbot of Belleville. He compliments the Abbot on being specially well acquainted with Aristotle and knowing what he talks about, while professed peripatetics do not understand their master. All possible arguments in favour of his views ought to be presented before they are censured. The work is in two parts; the first of these contains a synopsis of the main conceptions of the *Physics* under 15 mnemonic images, such as Apollo, Minerva etc.; the second part is a summary, not invariably correct, of the teaching of the same work and of minor treatises, either by Aristotle or attributed to him at that time.

We saw in the Diary how full Bruno was of Mordente, who came from a place not so far distant from his own beloved Nola. He must have rejoiced at meeting one who was, like himself, a " servant and interpreter of Nature," with a common interest in applied mathematics and possessing the additional attraction of being a Neapolitan. Mordente's mathematics were of no lasting importance; he had invented a new form of compass of no great value, and would seem to have had some worthless ideas on incommensurable quantities at a time when men were feeling their way blindly towards the discovery of new calculi. Bruno got Chevillot to print " Two Dialogues Of Fabrizio Mordente Of Salerno,"[2] with which was united a " Dream."[3] In this work Bruno, to whom moderation was little better than a vice, loads Mordente with extravagant, if generous, praise: " The geometers of the future shall raise him to the heavens and give to his house and the Salernian sky, with its limpid

---

[1] *J. B. Nolani Fig. Arist. Phys. etc.,* 1586.
[2] *Dial. duo de F.M.S. propre divina adinvent. ad perfect. cosimet. praxim.* 1586.　　　　　　　　[3] *J. Bruni Insomnium.*

and majestic horizon, greater renown than befel remarkable
Egypt, laborious Persia or subtle Arabia." Let us believe
that the "god among geometers" [1] had some wider empire
of thought than is indicated by oblivion.[2] Bruno was always
ready enough to break away from the current worship of
antiquity to the admiration of modern men, and it would
seem that he got impressed, through his intercourse with
Mordente,[3] by two facts: that no quantity, however small,
is negligible in calculation ; and that the concept of a minimum is relative in such wise that an instrument used for
taking the altitude of the stars may involve a minimum greater
than the whole diameter of the earth. He also learned
from Mordente that the same kind of reasoning is appli-
cable to fractions as to whole numbers, and that in physical
investigations the indefinite regress must halt at a minimum
—propositions which he was to develop later on. The
dialogues between Mordente and Bottero turn on the Physics
of Aristotle and are condensed, dispersed and dry.

In the " Dream " there is obscurely revealed to Bruno a
triangular instrument for determining degrees of latitude.
He would seem to have had some dim foresight of instruments which were not then invented.

" A Hundred And Twenty Theses Concerning Nature
And The Universe, Directed Against The Peripatetics " was
also printed at the Red Rose " at the solicitation of the
Author." [4] It was apparently issued before the public
wrangle took place in order that the audience might have a

---

[1] Auvray ; *op. cit., sub 2nd Feb.*
[2] *Cfr.* Berti ; *op. cit., Cap. X.*
[3] He renews his eulogies of Mordente in later works.
[4] Discovered by Miss Frith in the British Museum, catalogued
under Hennequin, J ; *Centum et viginti articuli de natura et mundo
adv. peripat. per J. H. Lutetie prop. sub clipeo et moderamine
J. B. N. infra oct. Pentec. Imp. Par. ad authoris instantiam,* 1586.
—Cfr. Frith, I ; *Life of G. B.,* 1887, *pp.* 324-5.

summary of the arguments before them. There are only
twenty pages. First comes a dedicatory address to Henry
III and then an epistle to Filesac, the Rector of the University, in which Bruno expresses, in warm terms, his sense of
the hospitality and kindness he had received at the University. He informs Filesac that he is about to leave Paris.
Theses attacking the Aristotelian Physics and Cosmogony
follow.

Cotin's diary furnishes us with much needed information
concerning the debate. He heard a somewhat coloured
account of Bruno's misadventure at Geneva from one John
Vincent on March 20th, which he carefully sets down, and
the next reference to Bruno is as follows : " 28th and 29th
May, which were the Wednesday and Thursday of Pentecost, Jordanus invited the Royal Lecturers and everyone to
hear him inveigh against seven (*sic*) errors of Aristotle at
Cambrai. At the end of the lesson or oration he bade
defiance, urging anyone who might wish to do so to defend
Aristotle or attack Brunus, and, no one having come forward, he shouted still louder, as having gained the victory.
Then a young advocate, Rodolphus Calerius, rose and, in
a lengthy speech, defended Aristotle against the aspersions
of Brunus, beginning by saying that the professors were
silent because they did not deem Brunus worthy of a reply ;
finally, he called on Brunus to reply and defend himself,
who was silent and left. The students caught hold of
Brunus, saying that they would not let him go unless he
replied or withdrew the calumnies he had cast on Aristotle.
Nevertheless, ultimately, he escaped from their hands, I
know not if on condition that he should return next day to
reply to the advocate. The advocate, having summoned an
assembly for the next day by placards, got into the pulpit
and followed up the defence of Aristotle and the jugglings
of Brunus in fine style, still calling on him to answer. But

Brunus did not appear; and, since then, he would seem to be dwelling in this town no longer.

Jordanus was in a little pulpit, near the garden-door, and in the big pulpit sat John Hennequin, his disciple, sustaining the theses of Jordanus, of which Jordanus claimed to be judge, as it were. The disciple could only reply to the first argument of Calerius. Then Brunus was asked to reply himself, which he would not do, saying that the proper time had gone by; and next day he would not appear, saying that already they had struck him yesterday. Also note that Calerius is a freshman, a Gascon they think, young, who was an advocate but is so no longer, having withdrawn with Monsieur du Perron, the king's orator and chronicler."

It is evident that someone has brought the news to willing ears.

Bruno, in his letter to Filesac,[1] said that many of the professors had attended his lectures; he did not think the University would always hold by the Peripatetic philosophy, for Aristotle owed more to Paris than Paris to Aristotle. He counted on a favourable hearing, since philosophers should be willing to reason philosophically, that is, freely. He hoped, in his new philosophy, to accomplish work worthy of the University.

It was bold to approach Filesac in this matter. The Rector had just been elected to his office (Mar. 24); he was a priest, and renowned for his knowledge of theology and the history of the theological faculty of the Sorbonne. But Filesac's contemporaries gave him no less praise for his disposition and character than for his attainments.[2] We can well believe, from the tittle-tattle concerning the affair at Geneva which John Vincent brought to Cotin, that Bruno's

---

[1] *Centum et viginti articuli—Ad Filesac.*

[2] Du Boulay; *Hist. de la Univ. de Paris.—Biog. Universelle, art. Filesac.*

unfriends had not been idle, either among professors or students. Liberty to philosophize freely was insecure at Paris, and the eighth war of religion was at hand. Indeed Bruno was on the point of leaving Paris " on account of disorders " [1] when the disputation took place.

We may suppose that there was tension in the air when, according to custom, the pupil, John Hennequin, took the big chair to read Bruno's theses, while their author, as moderator, took a lower seat. Hennequin must have been a lad of courage to take up a cudgel for his master's and for truth's sake against every astronomer and mathematician of his age. He belonged to a great family, nicknamed " the big-pots." [2] The glib young Gascon, Raoal Callier, who started the fray, might have been just the kind of impertinent youth to make a successful advocate had he not abandoned the law for the better prospects of courtly office. He was related to Rapin, the poet-scholar.

Man is a combative animal, and the students of Paris were as keenly interested in an intellectual fencing-bout as were the ancients in the palæstrum, our Georgians in a cockfight, or the youth of our own day in the athletic field. We can imagine the crowded hall; the seniors sardonically restless, only half-attending to the new doctrine; the youths full of the ebullient prejudice which always accompanies ignorance and is ready to demonstrate its force by noise. The behaviour of the Professors, so different from their former entreatment of Bruno, disgusts him, and it would have been below his dignity, as a former professor, to reply to Callier. The students have an opportunity to begin a " rag," and carry it out to their entire satisfaction. After the manner sanctioned by its antiquity, they were wont to

[1] *Cfr. Cent. et vig. art. ; A d Filesac* and *Doc. ix.*
[2] " La grande maignée." Auvray ; *op. cit., p.* 301, *note.*—Bibliothèque Nat. *MS. fr.* 31,411, *dossier Hennequin, fol.* 117.

express their contempt for any novelty by "turning up their noses, gibing, blowing out their cheeks and banging at the desks";[1] but on this occasion they surpassed themselves. For Aristotle's science had been attacked; and therefore they were insulted as Christians. "I have not taught in direct opposition to the Catholic Religion," Bruno told the Inquisitors, "but I was judged to do so indirectly at Paris, where I was permitted to engage in a disputation under the title of '120 articles against the Peripatetics' and other popular philosophers, printed by permission of the Heads."[2]

Latitudinarian England had proved itself indifferent to the new science; Calvinistic Geneva had persecuted its apostle, and now Catholic France definitely rejected his theses before considering them, not without show of physical violence. He had resolved to leave disturbed France and try his fortunes elsewhere before that unhappy end to the disputation.[3] Shall he seek some generous asylum in Germany, Catholic or Protestant?

The intrepidity of the traveller in the sixteenth century was indeed admirable. He hardly noticed discomfort and he despised danger. Everywhere he had to run the risk of plague, ague, smallpox, treacherous landlords and wayside murder. In Germany he was usually called upon to share his bed with dirty, disagreeable wanderers; all classes sat together at the common table, and filthy fingers fished in the common bowl for the choicest pieces. Vermin were a matter of course.[4] Yet there was no lack of company. Courtiers and scholars, monks and merchants, serving-men and mendicants trooped all over Western Europe and jostled

---

[1] *De Lampade Comb., Dedicatio.*   [2] *Doc. XI.*

[3] *Centum et vig. articuli ; Ep. ad Filesac ;* repeated in *Acrotismus*, 1587.

[4] Gratarolus, G ; *De regimine iter agentium,* 1561, *p.* 19.—Florio, G ; *Second Frutes,* 1591, *p.* 95.—Spelman, W ; *A dialogue, ed.* J. E. L. Pickering, 1896, *p.* 42.

each other in every considerable town.[1] It was an heroic
age. Bruno was far too zealous a missionary to be
squeamish; German bandits could hardly prove worse than
British boors.

[1] Even in Erasmus' time many people spent their lives in perpetual
pilgrimage, not from piety, but from love of change. *De utilitate
colloquiorum, ad lectorem.*

CHAPTER XIII

AT WITTENBERG. WORKS PRINTED OR WRITTEN THERE

THE Clerk to the Inquisitorial Court, taking down Bruno's words, writes: " In the first instance I betook me to Mez, alias Magonza, a city of the Archbishop who is first Elector of the Empire."[1] He undertook a journey of between four and five hundred miles along roads neither very easy nor very safe to Mainz (Magonza being a corruption of *Moguntiacum*, the Latin name for the city, itself derived from Mogons, the local god of the Kelts when they held sway in that district). " Here I stayed twelve days ; but not finding such means of subsistence as I required either here or at Vispure (Wiesbaden),[2] which is not far off, I went on to Wittenberg in Saxony." Bruno omits to mention that his philosophic mission first led his steps to a university situated in the picturesque town of Marburg. The enlightened mind of Melancthon had liberated the human spirit, to some extent, in Protestant Germany. Perhaps he will fare better there than he did at either Geneva or Oxford.

Marburg lies on a hill crowned by a fine castle overlooking the Lahn, which flows below. Bruno would observe the beautiful church erected in the thirteenth century to contain the bones of St. Elizabeth of Hungary, a new town-hall and

---

[1] *Doc. IX.*

[2] Brunnhofer ; *G. B's Weltanschauung und Verhängniss, Leipzig,* 1882, says that the peasants round about Wiesbaden call it Wisbare.

renaissance palaces; but his interest lay in the university, founded 59 years before (1527) by Philip the Landgrave. Here surely he would be welcomed; for not only was it the first German university to be established by a prince and independently of papal privileges, but at this time it was under the protection and patronage of William the Wise, Landgrave of Hesse-Cassel. German universities usually reflected the fanaticism, moderation or policy of the reigning prince.[1] William was a man of independent mind and interested in Astronomy.[2] Much might be hoped for. How much of that hope was fulfilled remains recorded in the rolls of Marburg students. Petrus Nigidius, Rector of the University, wrote therein: "Jordanus Nolanus Neapolitanus, Doctor in Roman Theology, 25 July, year 86. The right of teaching philosophy in public having, for weighty reasons, been refused to him by me with the consent of the rest of the Philosophic Faculty, he blazed forth and insulted me in my house, as though I had acted in this matter contrary to the law of nations, the usages of German Universities and every exercise of the Humanities. And, on that account, he refused to remain a member of the University. His desire was readily granted and his name erased from the university-roll."[3] In a letter to the University of Wittenberg Bruno complains of having been restrained from lecturing publicly: a right recognised and used by all nations.[4]

Marburg was too fiercely Protestant to listen to one who inscribed himself "doctor in Roman theology." It had been the scene of the famous "Colloquy" or contest between Luther, Zwingli, Melancthon and other theological experts concerning transubstantiation.[5]

---

[1] Kolbe; *Marburgh in Mittelalter, Marb.*, 1879.

[2] G. B; *Orat. Valedict.* § X.

[3] *Vide* Berti, *op. cit., cap. XI, Il Bruno in Marburgo*, where the document is reproduced.

[4] *De Lamp. Combin.*   [5] Kolbe; *op. cit.*

At some later time the name, through which Nigidius ran his pen, was restored, and the words " with the consent of the rest of the Philosophic Faculty " were crossed out.

Probably the unfortunate wanderer was induced to try for better fortune at Wittenberg by the fact that a Neapolitan whom he had known in England—no other than Alberico Gentile, the jurist—was now lecturing there. " He gave me his support," says Bruno, " and introduced me to lecture on the ' Organon ' of Aristotle." [1] Bruno had arrived at a seat of learning which, at this time, gave more liberty to philosophical discussion than any other ; and students from all parts of Europe, including many Catholics, especially young Austrian noblemen and Poles, were to be found studying there.[2] The professors received him cordially, and he was allowed to take private pupils on account of his poverty. Such a welcome, following on the one he got at Marburg, filled him with gratitude, which, after he had resided about a year in the city, he expressed with dignity, yet not without an undertone of pathos.[3] In 1587 he printed an enlarged and improved edition of his " Compendious Architecture," issued to the world five years before. This is entitled " The Lullian Combination-Lamp," and is dedicated to the senate of the University. " You have received and maintained me," he writes, " you have dealt kindly with me up to this day. I was a stranger to you, a fugitive from the tumults in France, undistinguished by any royal recommendation, bearing no ensigns of honour, *unproved and unquestioned as to your faith*. Finding in me no hostility (for my desire is to follow the peaceful path of good will to all men), my sole claim the profession of philosophy and pupildom in the

[1] *Doc. IX.*

[2] Meynert ; *Geschicht. d. Stadt Wittenberg, Dessau,* 1845. " Stay with us ; go not to Wittenberg." " What make you from Wittenberg, Horatio." Hamlet, Act I, sc. ii.

[3] *De Lampade Combinatoria, Dedicatio.*

temple of the Muses, you took me heartily as a guest, and
descried my name worthy to be written in the book of your
university and myself to be numbered with the loftiest and
most learned among you. Wherefore I must acknowledge
this great University, this German Athens, as no mere
private school or ordinary guild of scholars, and as my very
own." He names professor after professor, among them
Grün, who held that theology cannot stand apart from
metaphysic,[1] with accompanying remarks of respect and
even of admiration.

The University, which later on was incorporated with
Halle, was founded in 1502, and had been the abode of
Luther, who spent half his days there and who, like Bruno
now, lectured on the 'Organon' as well as on Dialectic,
and later, on theology. Bruno never before breathed so
free an atmosphere as Wittenberg had generally enjoyed
since Luther's days up to those when he first came there:
there was no small measure of such religious toleration and
philosophic liberty as the sixteenth century understood.
"For a brief space," sang Pindar, "hath opportunity for
men ; but of him it is known surely when it cometh and he
waiteth thereon, a servant but no slave."[2] In his official
capacity the new professor would seem to have lectured on
Rhetoric among other subjects ; for what is supposed to be
the notes of his teaching—a summary of the *Ad Alexandrum*,
falsely ascribed to Aristotle, together with outlines of arguments and synonyms to be used by speakers—was printed
by John Henry Alsted, who acquired them in 1610.[3] The
first part of the work is nothing but a digest; the second
part, "The Art Of Making A Speech," is a kind of *memoria
technica*, with arguments and synonyms ready for use. But

---

[1] McIntyre ; *op. cit., p.* 54.   [2] *Pindar, Ode IV.*
[3] *Artificium perorandi traditum a J. B. Nolani Italo. Francof.*
1612.

he also employed himself very fully in more congenial and important work. The first volume printed at Wittenberg in 1587 has been already mentioned. The art of Lully was in high favour with Germans at that time.[1] " The Combined Lullian Lamp" had the double purpose of helping the thinker to find out all that was discoverable by sheer thought and of enabling the speaker to be ready in a discussion on any subject. The subtle distinctions made by the schoolmen had not advanced knowledge, however much they had provided a training ground for the mind, and Bruno and the men of his age, while they were discontented with ancient methods, had not yet learned the exact limitations of formal logic. Bruno loudly claimed for his Lullian method that it would be found a means of arriving at general causes and of enabling the reader to acquire much knowledge of different kinds as well as to retain all in his memory.

There followed the "Advance And Hunter's Lamp Of Logical Matters,"[2] a work of a similar character, dedicated to the Chancellor of the University. It has two parts, intended to be of logical and mnemonic value, and, like the works dealt with above, it embodies a portion of Bruno's teaching at Wittenberg. It is worthy of note that he maintains that the Divinity does not impart its own real nature. "In universal propositions, no one but a fool, even at the end of all his study, would maintain that he had achieved perfect knowledge. Aristotle himself, who, of all philosophers, ascribed power to the human mind, observed that the ultimate nature and differences of things transcend our faculties and are not to be rendered in our language; for the organ of our understanding is as impotent to discern

---

[1] Brucker, J. J; *Hist. Crit. Phil.*, V, *p.* 24.
[2] *De Progressu et Lampade Venatoria Logicorum, Vitebergæ,* 1587.

them as is the eye of a nocturnal bird turned towards
the sun."

In the same year appeared a much more important work
entitled *J. B. Nolani Camœracensis Acrotismus seu rationes
articulorum physicorum adversus Aristotelicos.* It is not
possible to render into English the full implications of this
title. Aristotle's treatise on cosmology is headed ἡ φ.
ἀκρόασις, and the Acrotismus is an attack on his cosmology. But Acrotismus conveys a double, perhaps a triple
signification: it shows that Bruno possessed far more than
the little Greek indicated in the "Ash Wednesday Supper."
Ἀκροτής and ακρόατης are also words used by Aristotle;
the first means an extremity, a height or summit; the
second, one who comes to hear a discourse.[1] In fact the
Acrotismus is a reprint of the "Hundred And Twenty
Articles," with the addition of the defence of them intended
to have been made at the College of Cambrai. *Camœracensis* is a doubly barbarous Latinization, the interpretation of which has been given already.[2] The title of the
work might be freely translated as "The Cosmology of
Giordano Bruno the Nolan, of the Cambrai; or the
arguments of articles on physics against the Peripatetics."[3]

The work opens with a letter "to the Parisians and other
philosophers of the most generous Kingdom of France and
to friends and defenders of the philosophy of direct perception." Probably Bruno had not learned that Henry
announced on January 1st that he did not intend to observe
the Edict of Beaulieu which granted the toleration of Protestants; but he would know that the French King was in

---

[1] Aristot. ; *Plant.*, 2, 9, 12 ; *Pol.*, 2, 12, 9.   [2] See page 61, n. 3.
[3] We read "e regione gymnasii Cameracensis" and "prope col-
legium Cameracense" in the *De Umbris* and *De compendiosa Architectura* respectively ; both works being printed by Gorbin.

universal odium. Yet his gratitude to the Valois was so great that the next item in the book is a reprint of his letter to Henry which had been prefixed to the " Hundred And Twenty Articles," the only change being the substitution of " most powerful King " for " greatest among Kings." The epistle to Filesac follows, with " The Awakener." Then come the important theses. The defence of these is very soberly put : there must be unalterable, universal meanings in Nature ;[1] the " matter " of Aristotle is a mere logical abstraction ;[2] body limits space and not space body ; space is room for movement and must be infinite ;[3] he agrees with Aristotle that space is filled ;[4] movement in space is the measure of time and not time the measure of motion ;[5] we know duration through change ;[6] division to infinity cannot be accepted, for a mathematical line is not infinite, only it may be indefinitely produced and is no sum, and we must stop at minimal bodies in physics, although they are too small to be apparent to sense ;[7] there must be an internal change in the inert to cause movement,[8] and the First Mover is not outside but within the entire universe, which is for ever moving, vegetating and living.[9] Tocco thinks he came closer to a clear conception of the laws which govern motion than did any man of his time.[10] Bruno speaks of the ether as ungenerated, incorruptible and immeasurable.[11] So far as he regards it physically, his conception of this enigmatic substance pretty closely resembles that which was accepted in the later half of the last century. But he may have supposed it to be a sort of sublimated, spiritual body of the Soul of the World.

---

[1] *Art. i.*   [2] *Art. ij.*   [3] *Art. xxix–xxxi.*

[4] *Art. xxxiij.*   [5] Compare the modern view of Bergson.

[6] *Art. xxxix.*   [7] *Art. xlij.*   [8] *Art. xlvi.*

[9] *Art. xlviij.*   [10] *Art. lxv.*

[11] Tocco, F ; *Op. lat. di G. B. esposte etc., Fir*, 1889, *p.* 118.

It was Bruno's habit to employ a pupil as copyist. In the Augustan Library at Erlangen there exist two codices of " Aristotle's Physics explained." [1] One of these is in an unknown handwriting; the other was written later by Besler, of whom more anon. This work, with all other manuscript treatises by Bruno, has been published recently at the charge of the Italian people.[2] Vitelli thinks it is the substance of lectures given at Wittenberg, but Stöltzle and Tocco believe it to belong to the period when he lectured at Paris.[3] Bruno introduces a good deal of his own teaching into this tractate, which deals with Aristotle's " Physics," " Generation And Corruption " and a part of his " Meteorology."

He also dictated a still more important work at Wittenberg, " The Lamp Of Thirty Statues," [4] of which there is at Erlangen both an earlier and a later and less correct copy, the latter done by Besler at Padua. This " Lamp " is referred to in a work which was published at Prague in 1588 [5] as the " Lampas Caballistica," " The Caballistic Lamp," " a work to appear shortly"; but it has only been printed recently. It is a logical and mnemonic work, somewhat on Lullian lines and not barren of Neo-Platonic speculation. It was intended to provide an instrument for the discovery of truth; the arrangement and much of the thought in it appears mechanical and artificial to the modern reader, but its fantastic " types," " images " etc. were calculated to popularise it at the time. The author avails himself of Aristotelian conceptions; but it is obvious that he is

---

[1] *Libri Physicorum Aristotelis, a clariss. Dr. D. J. B. N. explanati. Codices* 1215 *and* 1279.

[2] *State edition, Op. lat., cura Tocco & Vitelli, vol. iij.*

[3] *Vide* Vitelli, *G. B. op. lat., vol. iij ;* Stöltzle ; *Archiv für Gesch. d. Phil.,* 1890, *p.* 387 *sqq.*; Tocco ; *Op. ined. di G. B., p.* 99.

[4] *Lampas Triginta Statuarum ; State ed., vol. iij.*

[5] *De Specierum Scrutinis.*

developing his own line of thought and devising a theory of
the atomic constitution of the material world. Sometimes
he uses "language of accommodation" with philosophic
purpose, clothing his own views in the vestments of current
orthodox Christianity. All things "are accidents of one
substance," which is "essence of essences, soul of souls,
nature of nature," from which all things proceed and wherein
they coincide. The Trinity becomes a philosophic concept;
the Father is Substance; the Son, Universal Intellect; the
Spirit, the Soul of the World; or the Father may be said
to be Immediate Universal Intuition; the Son, Intellect;
the Spirit, Love with Power;[1] but these are merely distin-
guishable aspects of the One Absolute,[2] to whom past is
not past, nor is the future to come, but to whom eternity is
entirely present, all things together and complete.[3] He
repeats what he wrote in the "Seal Of Seals" and in the
"Transports": the loftiest knowledge advances progressively from sense upwards, but admits of philosophic and
theologic illumination in ecstasy. Soul and Body are conjoined; but they are not therefore indissolubly requisite to
one another, as is a citharist to his cither. Soul is of a
nature distinct from matter; but both are immortal substances. Even stones and the most imperfect things parti-
cipate in intellect.[4] As to the problem of personality, some
people think that particular things are manifestations of the
Soul of the World; others, that the Soul of the World is
divided into parts: " truly, it remains in doubt, *but I incline
to the first opinion.*[5] A little farther on, he says that multiplication falls on the side of brute matter, but the soul

---

[1] *Cfr. Doc. XI; De Imm., VIII, X, v.* 59 ; *De Monade, IV, v.* 21.
[2] *Op. Lat., iij, pp.* 44-57.   [3] *Ibid., p.* 45.
[4] *Ibid., p.* 53. Compare the modern philosophers Royce and
Taylor, especially the latter thinker's article, *Int. Journ. Ethics, Oct.*
1902.   [5] *Ibid., p.* 58.

remains one.[1] Still farther on, we read that the individual is as a spark of the Universal Spirit, from which he issues and to which he returns.[2] But while God, as absolute, works in and through us, He does not impart Himself to us in His most innermost nature.[3] Intellect is not a mere function of animal organs.[4] Incidentally, Will is treated of. There are grades of volition; material, composite and spiritual varieties may be distinguished,[5] the latter being free from matter and wholly intelligible. Evil is necessary, being the complement of good: without it, good could not be.[6] The perfection of the Whole depends on the perfection of its parts in relation to itself, and it is greater than they.[7] It is noteworthy that he accepts the divine mission of Christ, the Son of God, sent " to raise us up from brutality and barbarism to the practice of love."[8] He often writes in a way to which no orthodox Roman Catholic could possibly take exception, but it is clear that he sincerely believed the Church to need purgation from superstitions and that its doctrines may legitimately receive metaphysical interpretation from the wise. Here, as whenever he treats of religion as more than a means of preserving social order and stability, he would substitute the milk of reverence and the bread of philosophy for the fiery distillations of dogma, whether Catholic or Protestant. He accepts much that is " miraculous "; for all is miracle, and superstitious people are impressed chiefly by that which is not yet understood. But the Essence of Christianity lies in Love or in nothing, and this has been forgotten.

The work closes with the quaint observation: " Thanks

---

[1] Cfr. Causa, Dial. I ; Spaccio, Epist. Esplic.
[2] Op. lat., iii, p. 182. Cfr. pp. 46, 47, 50.
[3] Ibid., p. 59.   [4] Ibid., p. 48.   [5] Ibid., p. 160.
[6] Ibid., pp. 21, 23.   [7] Ibid., p. 108.
[8] Ibid., p. 158. Cfr. Docs. xi, xij, xiij.

be to God, we have finished the Art Of Discovery By Means
Of Thirty Statues."

To this period also belongs a dictated manuscript, preserved at Erlangen, which bears the date Mar. 13th, 1587.
It is entitled "Observations Concerning The Lullian
Lamp,"[1] and is a tractate on the method of "getting at
genera and species by definition, at predicates by judg-
ments, and at middle terms by demonstration," not without
mnemonic dodges.

Albums would seem to have been as fashionable among
reverential scholars in the sixteenth century as among
young ladies in the Victorian era. One, which belonged
to a certain Hans von Warnsdorf, is preserved in the
Public Library at Stuttgart, and contains a characteristic
entry in Bruno's firm, bold hand. It runs: "Solomon and
Pythagoras: What is it that anything in reality is? That
which it was. What was it? That which it is. There is
nothing new under the sun. Jordanus Brunus Nolanus,
Witebrg, 18 Sept."[2]

. . . .

Before reaching Germany, in the work which was not to
be taken "too assertively," the Nolan had written about
that "drunken" land; where "their shields are plates;
their helmets are pipkins and kettles; their swords, the
thigh-bones of salt beef; their trumpets, drinking glasses,
pitchers and flagons; their drums, barrels and tuns; their
field, a table to drink (I would say, eat) at; where their
fortresses, bulwarks and bastions are cellars, ale-houses
and brandy-shops, which are more numerous than their
houses";[3] "where Gluttony is exalted, magnified, celebrated

[1] *Animadversiones Circa Lampadem Lullianam.* State ed.,
vol. iij.
[2] Sigwart gives a reproduction of the handwriting, *Kleine Schriften*,
vol. i, Freiburg, 1889, p. 293.   [3] *Spaccio, III, ij.*

and glorified among the heroic virtues, and drunkenness is
numbered among the divine attributes,"[1] and so on, inter-
minably.   He now enjoyed, for the first time, the hospitality of a German University which, in spite of its beer and
groaning tables, was really alive, and he might exercise
true "philosophic liberty"[2] there.   Like Pius II, he revised
his judgment,[3] recognised the merit of existing German
achievement and declared that, when Germans should cease
to waste their energies on theologic futilities, directing
themselves to saner thinking, they "would become, not
men, but Gods."   Indeed extraordinary latitude was extended
to Bruno, for, as he says, he proclaimed certain doctrines
which uprooted the received teaching of centuries, and
by no means kept to science as accepted by theology.
But a storm was gathering, although the University still
continued an unusual toleration of opinions opposed to
those considered to be "right."

In 1580 the Lutherans of Germany issued the famous
"Formula of Concord," popularly known as that of Discord.
For there was a subtle undercurrent of Calvinistic opposition, and Philippists maintained the broader-minded principles of Philip Melancthon with customary intolerance of
any other.   The Elector Augustus of Saxony died in
February of the year of Bruno's arrival and was succeeded by his son, Christian I, a prince who succumbed
in a short time, like so many German rulers of his time,
to drink.   Christian's brother-in-law, John Casimir, regent
of the Palatine Lines, was busy coercing his own wife and
his people into Calvinism, and this naturally aroused the
indignation of Saxon Lutherans.[4]   It is difficult to get at

[1] *Spaccio, III, iij.*   [2] *Oratio Valedictoria.*
[3] Æn. Silv ; *op. omn. Basel,* 1571, *Ep. ad Gug. de Stein ; Ep. ad
Greg. Heimburg.*
[4] Bezold, F. v ; *Briefe d. Pfalzg. J. Casimir, München,* 1882.

the real motive forces of these religious quarrels, though, usually, religion masked political struggles between ruler, nobles and common folk, reaction from economical pressure and social and racial resentment. Christian and his adviser, Nicholas Krell, were credited by the Lutherans with being under the sway of John Casimir.[1] Krell worked steadily for the Philippists and against the Lutherans; he was resolved to overthrow the "Formula of Discord"; for the good reason that Melancthon had exalted the State and denied the right of ecclesiastical authority to dominion over the conscience. The squabbles of Protestant sects left Bruno cold. But, strangely enough, his friends and supporters were of the narrower, Lutheran body, and were daily losing ground. Recounting his life, he told his judges: "At Wittenberg, in Saxony, I found two factions—the philosophic faculty were Calvinists and the theologic were Lutherans. The old Duke was a Lutheran, but the son, who succeeded him at that time, was a Calvinist and favoured the opposite party to the one which favoured me ; wherefore I left."[2] None the less, he seems to have departed in fair amity with everybody ; a philosophic pin-prick was enough to arouse him at least to philosophic fury; his restless spirit needed little provocation ; his missionary zeal, too, was ever urging him onward ; perhaps, change had become a habit with him ; he would set forth to champion the truth and attack some new academic world.

Before he left Wittenberg, he gave a farewell address in praise of wisdom in general and of wise Germans in particular. It was delivered at the University on Mar. 8th,

---

[1] *Leben, Schicksal u. Ende d. D. N. Krell, Leipzig,* 1798 (documents reproduced).—Brandes, F ; *Kanzler Krell ein Opfer des Orthodoximus, Leipzig,* 1873.

[2] *Doc. IX.*

1588.[1] He exalted such Germans as Albertus Magnus, Paracelsus and the Landegrave William of Hesse, patron of Copernicus. Of Cusanus, he said that he would have equalled Pythagoras had not his genius been stifled under priestly garments. In the city of Luther some eulogy of the great Reformer was expected. While the dogmas of the warring sects repelled Bruno, he admired Luther for protesting against ecclesiastical tyranny and rejecting fetters for the soul forged at priestly smithies. " But whom," said he, " have we passed by? The mighty hero who resisted the voracious monster, half-fox, half-lion; that vicar of the princes of Hell who polluted the world by craft and force and cajoled men into superstitious and uncouth worship under the disguise of divine knowledge and the simplicity which is acceptable to God. . . . Whence comes he? From Germany, from the banks of the Elbe. . . . Out of the darkness of Orcus your Hercules dragged forth the monster with the triple crown, bursting open the steely gates of Hell, triumphing over the city guarded by triple walls and the nine-fold stream of Styx. Thou hast seen the light, O Luther; thou hast regarded it; thou hast heard the awakening spirit of the Lord and hast obeyed it; thou hast confronted and overcome the adversary girt about with power, and thou hast despoiled him."[2] What he now said, added to what appeared later in a Latin poem,[3] was probably the chief cause of the curious impression that by the " beast " of the *Spaccio* Bruno referred to the Pope.[4] Also a tradition seems to have arisen from this oration that he had written a " paneygric upon the

---

[1] *Oratio Valedictoria, Vitebergae habita,* 1588, *apud Zach Cratonem.*   [2] *Ibid.*

[3] *De Immenso, VIII, j, v. 67 sqq.*

[4] *Cfr.* Brunnhofer; *op. cit., p.* 245.—*Cfr. Conrado Ritterhusio suo G. Schoppius, F.R.S.,* given by Berti, Frith and others.

Devil."[1] Probably the farewell declamation affected his treatment at the hands of the Inquisition.

It would have been churlish in one who had been allowed to teach strange doctrine in the cradle of Lutheranism, without any enquiry being made into his own religious faith, had he abstained from some recognition of Luther as a liberating force and the enemy of ecclesiastical abuse. But Bruno confined himself to no conventional homage; he knew no mean; he expressed his gratitude in passionate praise of a man with whose opinions he had less of sympathy than of disagreement. While he regarded Luther as right in breaking up abuses, he was far from admiring Lutheranism. He considered the reformers to be men more ignorant than himself.[2] Yet perchance it had been well for him had he merely repeated the compliments he had already paid the University.[3]

With the praises of the Arch foe of Rome still hot in his mouth, he set forth confidently for Prague, the capital of a Catholic monarch and the seat of a Catholic University. But he was no Lutheran; he deemed himself a Catholic, justly asserting the right to read profound esoteric doctrines into the dogmas of his Church.

[1] Cfr. Keckern ; *Syst. Rhet. Spec., lib. I, cxviij, p.* 1647 ; *I. ij, opera, Edit. Genev.,* 1614; quoted by Bayle, P ; *Dictionary (in English ed.),* 1738, *p.* 158 *and n.* 22.

[2] *Doc. xij.*

[3] *De Lamp. Comb., dedicatio.*

CHAPTER XIV

THE University at Prague, however, had maintained more or less liberal traditions during its two centuries of existence; and, although reaction was afoot, by far the greater number of the people of Bohemia were Protestants of one kind or another; nor had the Jesuits yet got the upper hand. But the city had lost much of its privileged liberty, and was just sufficiently a place of compromise to serve as a residence for the Emperor Rudolf II. He had achieved the Bohemian crown in 1575 by merely pledging his kingly word to introduce a comprehensive Confession which should prove satisfactory to the whole Bohemian people — a superhuman undertaking which was never fulfilled. Yet, although the Catholics in power were gradually forcing the Protestants back into the Roman Church, there was provisional peace, and therefore the visit of Bruno to Prague was less dangerous than might appear. There was, indeed, more than one reason why he directed his steps thither. Rudolf might, perhaps, have been considered a widely cultivated man had he not chanced to be born a prince. He affected every known branch of knowledge and posed as its patron. His scientific and artistic collections were magnificent. The melancholy which oppressed his later years manifested itself at this time only in shyness and singular behaviour. He wasted much time over horoscopes and the search for the philosopher's stone; but his interest in the perversions of science, which attracted Dr. Dee and his seer Kelly to his court, by an easy transition was also directed to astronomy, and, later on, both Tycho Brahe and Kepler sought his patronage.[1] Bruno had already sounded Rudolf's praises at Wittenberg;[2] he hoped that his Lullian art and his astronomical views would be recommendations to the Imperial favour. Moreover, Fabrizio Mordente, whom he had admired and extolled at Paris, was now at Prague, where he held the appointment of Imperial Astronomer. Here also was William of St. Clement, whom he had known as Spanish Ambassador in France, and who was now accredited to the Court of Rudolf. The Ambassador was interested in the works of his countryman, Lully,[3] and was *persona grata* to Rudolf, who had been educated in Spain. Much, then, might be hoped for in Prague: little but disappointment awaited Bruno there.

He arrived about Eastertide, 1588. On June 10th he dedicated two little works, bound together, to St. Clemente. These he entitled " The Examination Of Forms And The Combined Lamp Of Raymond Lully, Doctor Of All Knowledge And Almost Divine." The work is little more than the *De Lampade Combinatoria*,[4] which was printed at Wittenberg. Bruno seems to have brought unsold copies with him, removed the dedication to the Wittenberg University, substituted one to St. Clemente, and inserted the tractlet on " Forms." But he promised that a profounder " Cabalistic Lamp " should follow, which, it would seem, never appeared.

Soon afterwards there appeared from the printing press

---

[1] Pelzl, F. M ; *Geschichte der Böhmen, Prague and Vienna*, 1782 ; Moritz, H ; *Die Wahl Rudolf's II etc., Marburg*, 1895 ; Maurice, C. E ; *Bohemia, London*, 1896, *chap. xv.*   [2] *Oratio Valedictoria.*
[3] *De specierum Scrutinio, dedicatio.*
[4] *De specierum Scrutinio et Lampade Combinatoria R. Lulli ; doctoris omniscii, propemodumque divini. Pragae. Excudebat Georgius Nigrinus.*

of Georgius Daczenus a work dedicated to the Emperor, and entitled "One Hundred And Sixty Articles Directed Against The Mathematicians And Philosophers Of The Day."[1] The dedication is lofty and bold. He tells Rudolf that he looks forward to "a religion of love which shall be no cause of controversy and above dispute, being the desire of the soul and required by the reasonable covenants of the nation and of society." He protests against conflicting sects and intolerance of every kind. But he did not limit opprobrium to those who, to use the words of a modern seer, are "wont to vilify the sun because it will not light their cigar," for he detested still more those who "enforce their own prejudices with fire and sword." Bruno's ideal was the transformation of Catholic Christianity, purged of parasitic absurdities, into a true progressive religion. He had not the knowledge or interest to criticize Christianity; but he saw how "authority usually binds and deceives in countless ways"; and that the thinker must set himself free from "subjection to any other mind."[2] "It is sheer prejudice to settle a matter with small consideration; it is an evil deed to follow obsequiously the lead of another man; corrupt, slavish and traitorous to the dignity of free men to consent and surrender; wholly stupid to believe because of wont and usage; and imbecile to assent to the opinion of the mob." "We wish this law to be vigorously observed, that reason is as true as it is necessary, and the authority of no men, howsoever true and excellent persons they may be, is admissible as an argument." "Thus do we go forth to the most delightful splendour of light, understand Nature (which is crying aloud to be heard) and follow wisdom (which we hold supreme above all) with singleness of spirit and an honest heart." He

---

[1] J. B. N. *Articuli centum et sexaginta adversus huius temporis mathematicos atque philosophos. . . . Ad divum Rodulphum II imperatorem.*   [2] *Articuli centum et sexaginta, dedicatio.*

speaks of a new spirit which shall animate the future. Of himself he says: "In the free field of philosophy I shall shelter me from the ever-moving flood and seek the society of them that open their eyelids." He asserts with the Kantists that all measure is determined by the prior measure of mind; and we seem to be listening to Descartes when we are told that "everything, however men may deem it assured and evident, proves, when it is brought under discussion, to be no less doubtful than are extravagant and absurd beliefs."[1]

A brief introduction follows the dedication, and then come 160 articles and 180 constructions which are but bare outlines of much which Bruno dealt with later in the *De Minimo* and *De Monade*. One object of the articles was to show that the propositions of Euclid can be intuited in three figures. Bruno's mathematics are crude and fallacious, but they have never received the attention of a capable mathematician; who, it is quite possible, might detect some germs of valuable ideas amid much inaccuracy and misconstruction. Very important is his statement that we must assume a physical unit which is not to be appreciated by sense any more than is a true sphere. He holds that mathematical science starts from multiple units according to the kind of mathematical consideration involved—a doctrine which he tried to develop later.

The Emperor rewarded him with less than, in all probability, he expected; a treatise on alchemy or astrology would have procured him a far richer reward. "I stayed six months at Prague, and whilst I maintained myself there I got a book on Geometry printed, which I presented to the Emperor, who gave me three hundred dollars; and, possessed of these, I left Prague."[2]

In 1576, Helmstedt in the duchy of Brunswick suddenly

---

[1] *Articuli centum et sexaginta, dedicatio.*   [2] *Doc. ix.*

found itself in a position which it failed to keep very many years. In that year a university was opened there which became one of the chief seats of learning in Germany.[1] Its founder, Duke Julius of that ancient house of Brunswick-Wolfenbuttel, which traced descent from Ason, marquis of Este, was a somewhat effusive, stimulating potentate who took the fancy of his people. His policy was conservative and directed by dynastic and personal motives, although his motto declared: "I spend myself in succouring others." A Protestant, he allowed his son and successor, Henry Julius, to become the nominally Catholic Bishop of Halberstadt at the age of fourteen; but it is to his credit that when he abolished monastic houses he abstained from enriching himself thereby.[2] The articles of this new university aimed at controlling angry controversialists. The establishment was adorned by fifty professors. Whether the constitution of the Academy attracted Bruno we do not know. All that he tells us is: "Providence, not Chance, conducted me to this place."[3] He matriculated Jan. 13th, 1589. Julius died shortly after his arrival, and Bruno was so far successful that some time after the funeral he was allowed to deliver and print a funeral oration. In it, he spoke of being an exile for truth's sake; he "had suffered from the hungry tooth of the Roman wolf, but is now in the enjoyment of complete freedom."[4] Bruno did not stop with the word "wolf": uncalculating, unguarded, headlong as ever, he casts the

---

[1] Ludewig; *Geschichte u. Beschreibung d. Stadt Helmstedt, Helm.* 1821.

[2] Heinemann, O. von; *Gesch. v. Braunschweg u. Hannover, Gotha,* 1886 *sq.*—Bodermann, E; *Herzog Julius, Zeitschr. d. hist. Ver. f. Niedersachen, No.* 932, *Hannover,* 1887. — Beste, J; *Gesch. d. b. Landekirche, Wolfenbuttel,* 1889.

[3] *Oratio Consolatoria. . . . Prima mens. Jul.* 1589. *Helmstadii apud Joh. Lucium.*   [4] *Ibid.*

Papal tyranny among the constellations, which here as in the *Spaccio*, are allegorically treated. There it is "the Gorgon's head, nourishing snakes for hair and infecting the world with the rank venom of ignorance and vice." Such words were not calculated to make any easier his desired reconciliation with Mother Church, nor would they add to the safety of that return to Italy which he soon had the temerity to effect.

He told the Inquisitors that he had delivered an oration on the death of Julius. In the margin of the document is the ominous record: "he was a heretic." "For this speech," adds Bruno, "his son and successor" (Henry Julius) "gave me 80 scudi."[1]

The new duke was a highly educated and many-sided man, who adopted Lutheran Imperialistic policy, but did not concern himself overmuch with the University and such like matters. We do not know if Bruno had any relations with him after the gift. But, as in the case of Henry III, he bore the prince's generosity in mind; and in 1591, when he was in Frankfurt, and later in the same year, when he was in Italy, two of his greatest works appeared dedicated to Henry Julius, duke of Brunswick and Bishop of Halberstadt.[2] The first contains a highly ornamented eulogium of the duke on the occasion of his marriage with Elizabeth, the sister of James I's consort, Anne of Denmark. His eulogies of such heretic princes were remembered against him.[3]

It may have been because he found so much attention paid to occult and astrological subjects at Prague that Bruno's interest was directed to the obscure operations

---

[1] *Doc. ix.*

[2] *De triplici minimo et mensura.—De monade, numero et figura. Item de innumerabilis, immenso et infigurabili, seu de universo et mundis.*   [3] *Docs. ix, xiii.*

of the mind in mathematics and those subtle sympathies in Nature concerning which the age was ready to believe almost anything. Magic meant to Bruno natural operations which are obscure and surprising but of which, eventually, we may hope to learn the real character and laws. His mnemonic system was regarded as a species of occult science, for, quite apart from the Black Art, magical sciences were recognised as properly occupied with mathematics, physical sympathies, obscure causes and effects, such divine subjects as inspiration and prophecy, judicial astrology, metaphysical speculation etc., Bruno had already exhibited interest in what the Church held to be a dangerous borderland between the lawful and unlawful: in England he had written concerning the extraordinary effects wrought by the One Spirit in all things.[1] He dedicated his *De Magia* to a pupil named Besler, a youth from Nürnberg, whose father had studied under Luther and whose brother gained distinction as a botanist. Besler continued to act as Bruno's copyist, and either accompanied or followed him to Padua.[2] In 1866 the manuscripts of nine treatises and a larger work of Bruno's were put on the market at Paris and are now in the Moscow Library. These, known as the Noroff MSS., are for the most part in Besler's hand; but a little was written by Bruno himself. A copy of the *De Magia* is at Moscow, dated 1590, and a later MS. by the same copyist is preserved in the Augustan Library at Erlangen, together with the two codices of "Aristotle's Physics expounded by the illustrious Jordanus Bruno the Nolan," of which one is from the same hand. All these

---

[1] *Causa, Dial. II, III.*

[2] For Besler, see Stölzle, Remigius; *Die Erlanger G. B. MS, Archiv für Geschichte der Phil.* iv, *p.* 573 *sqq.*—Tocco, F ; *Opere inedite di G. B, Napoli,* 1891.—Frith, I ; *Life of G. B, pp.* 343 *sqq.*—McIntyre ; *G. B, p.* 114 *sqq.*—Berti, D ; *Vita di G. B, Processo, Doc. xi.*

hitherto unpublished writings are now available in the State Edition.

De Magia " Concerning Magic " treats of mathematics as hidden or occult operations to be found both in Mind and in Nature. Action and reaction at a distance are accounted for on Neo-Platonic principles of universal animism and mutual influences. Many marvels of a miraculous nature are accepted as due to natural operations, the precise nature of which remains undiscovered.[1] Everything may be reduced to the antagonistic yet co-operative principles of love and hate, or attraction and repulsion. There is one Soul of the World, of which finite souls are passing phases, and all things are derived from the Divine, but exist in successively decreasing degrees of reality and truth.

There are also MS. excerpts from Agrippa and other authors with annotations by Bruno : all belong to this period.

"The Principles, Elements And Causes Of Things,"[2] dated Mar. 16th, 1590, is a work showing great respect for and acceptance of tradition. The magician is said to operate with his soul, and belief helps the effect ; wherefore the Son of God could not work miracles where there was incredulity.[3] Light is a spiritual substance which exists in all things.[4] Air, the principle which causes movement, is within the body of the world.[5] He expresses belief in planetary influences. He intended to study judicial astrology ; but he had little respect for the usual pretenders to that science and had nothing but contempt for conjuration, incantation etc.[6] The importance of this work lies in its full

---

[1] It is worthy of note that, while Bruno placed little value on the testimony of miracles, he accepted those of Christ without question, as well as His birth from a Virgin-mother. *Docs. xij, xiij.*

[2] *De Rerum Principiis et Elementis et Causis.*

[3] *Op. Latin.*, *p.* 455 ; *Cfr. Matth. xiii*, 58 ; *xvij,* 20.

[4] *Op. Latin.*, *p.* 513 *sq.*   [5] *Ibid., p.* 522.   [6] *Doc. xiij.*

acceptance of physical minimal particles or atoms, a view derived from antiquity and elaborated in the great Latin poem. The whole book is an adventure into the unknown: everywhere he crosses the borderland of exact knowledge.

Pursuing a similar theme, comes the " Lullian Medicine, Drawn Partly From Mathematical, Partly From Physical Principles." [1] It was dictated at Helmstedt immediately after the " Principles." There are two codices, one being an incomplete emendation of the other. Most of the work is derived from the rare medical works of Lully. [2]

One of the conditions under which professors might teach at Helmstedt was an obligation to set forth the " true ancient philosophy without disguise, display or innovation." [3] Bruno was nothing if not an innovator, especially in cosmology, and the subversion of ancient geocentric theory reflected severely on the Christian scheme. So one is not surprised to find a letter which exhibits him in trouble again. It is preserved in the Archives of the University, is written in Bruno's own hand and is addressed to a certain pro-rector Hofmann, who was at that time Professor of Philosophy and leader of a religious party. It runs : " Very Illustrious and Reverend Pro-rector : Jordanus Bruno, the Nolan, being excommunicated by the chief pastor and supervisor of the Church at Helmstedt " (one Boëthius), " (who, without any public defence allowed, made himself both judge and executor in his own cause) humbly protests to your Magnificence and the very potent dignities of the Senate against the public execution of a personal and highly iniquitous decree. He demands to be heard, so that he may know if

[1] De Medicina Lulliana, partim ex mathematicis, partim ex physicis principiis educta.

[2] Lutoslaski, V ; Archiv f. G. d Ph., II, p. 566.

[3] Bartholomèss, C ; op. cit., I, p. 170, n. 2.

the attack on his position and reputation be just; for, as Seneca saith, ' He who judgeth, hearing one side only, is not just, even should his judgment be so.' Wherefore he begs your excellence to summon the worthy pastor, in order that, if God please, he may show cause and prove his fulmination to be that of a good shepherd and not the effect of private malice."

We must not take this document any more than that of Geneva as implying that Bruno was a member of the Protestant Church; but such formal excommunication would carry serious disabilities with it; for what student would be bold enough to pursue his studies under the direction of a denounced heretic? There exists no notice of the appeal, which, we have reason to believe, was rejected. For Bruno's indignation would seem to be recorded in the *De Minimo* and *De Immenso*, on which he was probably engaged at the time. The "priest and grammarian" is embalmed therein like a fly in amber.[1] Hofmann has not the shadow of an idea concerning the philosophy he professes ; he poses as the Rhadamanthus of boys; why, the very crumbled dust of ancient philosophers is worth more than his living soul.

The prospect of making a living at Helmstedt disappeared. Bruno indicates that the gift of the duke enabled him to proceed to Frankfurt "to get two books printed, namely *De Minimo* and *De Numero, Monade Et Figura."* [2] He left Helmstedt towards the middle of 1590. A year later his enemy, Hofmann, after being ejected from his chair, had also to pack his goods and depart. Later still, Boëthius was also overthrown. So fiercely did academic passions rage in the sixteenth century!

---

[1] *De minimo, lib. V ; De immenso, lib IV, c. x.*
[2] *Doc. ix.*

CHAPTER XV

AT FRANKFURT AND ZURICH

THE Free City of Frankfurt-on-the-Main was one of the
most important places in Germany. The Golden Bull of
1356 constituted it the seat of Imperial Election. It was a
renowned centre of trade, and twice a year, at Eastertide
and at Michaelmas, merchants from every country were to
be found at its famous fair. It stood first in the bookselling
and printing trade of Germany. A member of the Protestant
party, its city-fathers found it commercially advantageous to
tolerate Roman Catholics and all the factions of the revolt
against Rome, even the Socinian faction. An evil reputation indeed must have preceded Bruno, for we find it
recorded in the Book of the Burgomaster, July 2nd, 1590,[1]
that when he begged permission to dwell in the house of
Wechel, the printer, it was "Resolved that his petition be
refused and that he be told to take his penny elsewhere."

Printers were erudite men in those days, and scholars
and statesmen foregathered at their shops, which were true
intellectual centres where the latest books were seen and
discussed, where news and ideas came in from abroad and
dilettante courtiers could meet and gossip. The printers
were in the habit, not only of lodging travelling scholars
while they were printing their books, but of taking travelling
nobles as boarders; for the great scholars usually preferred
seclusion to the honour and profit of receiving guests who
were likely to disturb their studies and households, even if

[1] *No.* 160, *p.* 48.

they should be well-paid for the service.[1] Sidney had been
the guest of the Wechels, and it is possible that Bruno was
enabled to get a footing with them by reason of the two
books he had dedicated to one whose chivalrous behaviour
on the field of Warnsfeld, followed by his death, not only
made him the idol of his countrymen but added additional
glory to a name which was already famous throughout
Europe. John Wechel contrived, in spite of the prohibition, to get Bruno received at the Carmelite monastery, and
provided him with means of support.[2] Jacobus Brictanus,[3]
a middle-aged man who was born at Antwerp, but who had
settled as a bookseller at Venice, told the Inquisitors that
he had met and talked with Bruno at Frankfurt and at
divers other places. Bruno had never spoken to him about
Christianity or Catholicism, but the Prior of this Carmelite
monastery told him that "he was chiefly occupied in writing and in the vain and chimerical imagining of novelties.
Heretic doctors read with him; for in that city they are
mostly heretical." The innovator and "awakener" could
not fail to produce misgivings and discomfort among the
good fathers, and one is not surprised to learn that when
Brictanus asked the Prior what manner of man Bruno
might be, he was told that "he was a man of fine intellect
and erudition—a universal man—but he" (the Prior) "did
not believe him to possess a trace of religion; adding that
he professed to know more than did the Apostles and could,
if he wished, make the whole world of one religion."[4] Asked
who were his intimate friends, Brictanus could not mention
any. So Bruno would seem to have experienced that
mental isolation which is the usual lot of the original, or

---

[1] Erpenii Thomae, *De Perigrinatione Gallica*, 1631, *pp.* 6, 12.—
Bourne, H. R. Fox, *op. cit.*, *p.* 91. [2] *Doc. ix.*
  [3] The Italians called him Giacomo Bertano (*Doc. j.*). How they
spelled his name in his native Flanders, I do not know.
  [4] *Doc. vi.*

even of the merely independent, thinker! Giambattista Ciotto, a young Sienese of 27, who kept a bookshop in the Merceria, the chief street of Venice, under the sign of Minerva, and through whose agency much evil was to follow, saw a good deal of Bruno during the fairs. But he, too, though later on Bruno frequented his shop in Venice, never heard him say anything which could arouse suspicion as to his not being a good Catholic.[1]

At the Fairs, Bruno would find himself face to face with all sorts and conditions of men, and in intellectual touch with all that was most vigorous in European thought and life.

The first work of Bruno's printed by Wechel and Fischer, *De triplici Minimo et Mensura*, was dedicated to Duke Henry Julius of Brunswick. The dedication was not by the author but by the printers. It is dated Feb. 13th, 1591, and states that Bruno was "forced by an unexpected event to leave the city when only the last leaf remained for him to finish, and, being unable to correct this as he had done to the rest of the work, he wrote asking us to complete in his name the labour forbidden to him by fate." We are in darkness as to what had happened. It may have been that the City Fathers were about to follow up their resolution by ejection;[2] or it may have been that an invitation from the lord of Elgg necessitated a hurried (and, perhaps, prudent) departure. John Henry Hainzell, of a literate Augsburg family, had just acquired the estate of Elgg, near Zurich. Hainzell studied alchemy, was greatly inclined to the uncanny and mysterious, and exercised a noble hospitality to thinkers and especially to those who claimed acquaintance with the border-land of exact knowledge.[3] Bruno now

---

[1] *Doc. v.*

[2] This is Sigwart's suggestion. Cfr. *Kleine Schriften I.*

[3] Sigwart, C. von ; *Kleine Schriften*, 1889, *I, p.* 123. Hainzell's passion for alchemy and alchemists proved his ruin.

wrote for Hainzell a last book on Lullianism and Mnemonics, which appeared at the Michaelmas Frankfurt Fair.[1]
He also taught at Zurich, a great trading-centre, the wealth
of which had been much increased since 1555 by the industry of Protestant Italians—silk-weavers who had been
exiled from Locarno. Although Zurich had no university,
it was the intellectual capital of Switzerland and the heart
of the Swiss Confederation. Here resided at the time a
freeman of the city, one Raphael Eglin, who became one of
Bruno's pupils. Eglin had been expelled from the Grisons,
whither he had gone to organize schools, and Bruno handed
over to him the substance of his lectures, which remained
unprinted until 1595, when Eglin had them issued from the
press of John Wolff of Zurich.[2] But the first edition contained only a portion of the lectures. Later, in 1609, when
Eglin was Professor of Theology at Marburg (the University
which had refused Bruno permission to teach) he had the
Summa reprinted with additions.[3]

Bruno spent three or four months with Hainzell, but we
find him back again at Frankfurt on Mar. 7th, 1591, when
he received permission to print the already printed work
De Triplici Minimo Et Mensura.[4] He stayed at his old
quarters, the Carmelite monastery, about six months.[5] In
the brief account of his life which Bruno gave at his trial, he
passed over the first visit to Frankfurt and his sojourn with
the lord of Elgg and recorded his second visit only. The
first visit was a very short although eventful one; to have
been the willing guest of one who indulged in dubious arts

---

[1] *De imaginum compositione.*

[2] *Summa terminorum metaphysicorum.* Bruno was lying in the
prison of the Roman Inquisition at the time.

[3] *Accessit ejusdem Praxis Descensus etc. Ex officina Rud.
Hundtwelkeri.* For Eglin, see Brunnhofer, G. B ; *Weltanschauung
und Verhängniss*, Leipzig, 1882, *p.* 81.

[4] *Censur Register.*   [5] *Doc. ix.*

might have prejudiced his case with the judges.[1] "Sometimes Prudence hides the truth with her skirts in order to escape blame and outrage."[2]

There is no record of permission having been given for the publication of *De Monade*, with its far more important and larger adjunct, *De Immenso*, or of *De Compositione*, but both volumes bear the date 1591, and we learn from Bassäus' Catalogue of Frankfurt books that they were ready for the Michaelmas Fair. The first of these volumes was dedicated, like the *De Triplici Minimo*, "to the very illustrious and reverend prince Henry Julius, duke of Brunswick and Luneberg, bishop of Halberstadt," and all were printed by the partners John Wechel and Peter Fischer.

In the Golden Book of Venice, wherein the families of the oligarchy were inscribed, stood the noble house of Mocenighi, so distinguished that it gave three doges to the State in the 15th century and one in the 16th. "One day," deposed Giambattista Ciotto, the bookseller, "Signor Giovanni Mocenigo, a patrician of Venice, when he was buying a recent work of Giordano's,[3] asked me if I knew him, and if I knew where he was staying. I told him that I had seen him at Frankfurt and believed he was still there; whereupon the said Sig. Mocenigo added, 'I should like him to come to Venice to teach me the secrets of memory and the other things which he professes, as one may see in this book.' To this I answered, 'It is believable that, if besought, he will come.' Some days afterwards, Sig. Mocenigo brought me a letter addressed to the said

[1] *Cfr.* G. B. *Op. Lat. (State edition), vol. III, p. xxix.*
[2] *Spaccio, II, iij.*
[3] From the MS. it would seem that Ciotto first said the work was the *Eroici Furori*—this name is erased and *De Minimo, Magno et mensura* (sic) substituted for it. Evidently Ciotto had no clear memory of what work it was.

Giordano, beseeching me to deliver it and saying that he wrote to ask him if he would come to Venice." [1]

Bruno's account runs: "Being in Frankfurt last year, I received two letters from Sig. Giovanni Mocenigo, inviting me to Venice to teach him the art of memory and discovery, with promises to treat me well, and that I should be satisfied with him." [2]

Now Bruno had not always misjudged concerning what might befall him. In England he wrote of "the procession of 50 or 100 torches in broad mid-day that would not be lacking in a Roman Catholic country." [3] But he had dwelt in Roman Catholic countries and been less subject to the molestation and oppression which he experienced at Geneva, Marburg and Helmstedt. Venice like Frankfurt was a centre of trade, and the love of lucre so prevailed over the love of God that heretics found a fairly safe asylum there. She was a city renowned for her intellectual and artistic force and the beautiful productions of her printers, to whom much liberty was allowed. Many of the books published in Venice were condemned by Rome, though, indeed, this was largely due to the efforts of a rival press to secure monopoly. Venice alone among Italian States had preserved her independence of foreign Catholic Powers; she alone had resisted resolutely and, in the main, successfully the encroachments of the Papacy on civil liberty. Lullism was at the time a fashionable craze among the rich young dilettanti of Venice; so there was prospect of lucrative occupation. [4] Bruno had received a renewed invitation from a member of a renowned and powerful house, and was offered protection. He may have known that Giovanni Mocenigo, a man now entering on middle life (he was 34 [5]), had been one of the Assessors

[1] Doc. v.   [2] Doc. vij.   [3] Cena, Dial. V.
[4] Sigwart, op. cit., p. 302.   [5] Doc. iij.

of the State to the Inquisition; if so, surely an invitation
from such a source ensured safety. Bruno never regarded
himself as other than a Roman Catholic. So secure did he
feel that even when he found himself trapped he felt no
serious misgivings. " I shall tell the truth," he said to the
Inquisitors. " Often I have been threatened with being
brought before the Holy Office and ever did I deem it a
joke; wherefore I am ready to give an account of myself."
He entertained the extraordinary delusion that he could
induce the Church to receive him again and allow him to
dwell unmolested and outside his order in his own beloved
province.[1] Not all his bitter experience had taught him
the invincible, terrific power which is achieved over the minds
and actions of most men by doctrines early instilled and fortified by habit, tradition, general consent and authoritative
pressure; how feeble is the mere intellect to overthrow
passionate bigotry or push aside passionate ignorance or
calm the resentment of menaced power.

He had written of himself as " citizen and servant of the
world, child of the sun and mother earth";[2] he was, he
said, no mere stranger and out of place in foreign lands,
but, as a member of the Divine Universe, could share its
life in any place. He said this with his head; his heart
throbbed for home. Venice might prove a stepping stone
towards his never forgotten and dearly loved Campagna.
Once in Venice, might he not, by discreet conduct and
working through men of influence, return to his native
soil? In a fatal moment he resolved to trust to the
honour of a Venetian patrician and to the historic independence of the Venetian State.

[1] *Docs. ix, x.*   [2] *Spaccio, Epist. Esplic.*

CHAPTER XVI

THE GREAT LATIN POEM AND LAST BOOKS

I. THE THREEFOLD LEAST

THE earlier Greek philosophers wrote in hexameters, and Lucretius, impressed by the intrinsic dignity of a cosmic conception, followed their example. Bruno, essentially poet as well as thinker, regarded with deep emotion the glowing life and stupendous intelligence displayed in an Infinite Universe. Science was to him Revelation, and, in the fulness of his heart, he renewed the attempt to combine poetry with science. It would be a great achievement, were it possible to unfold the secrets of the Universe in music and re-invest what we have painfully disinterred from Nature with the warm beauty of her life. But who shall endow the cold conclusions of logic with the passion of poetry? For the essence of poetry is emotion caught at its intensest moment; while metaphysical and scientific enquiry is abstract and impassive.

Three closely related Latin poems appeared in 1591 in two volumes. These contain much of their author's ripest thought. The first volume, which was for sale at the Frankfurt Spring Fair, was entitled " The Threefold Least And Measure Of The Three Speculative Sciences And The Principle Of Many Practical Arts." [1] The work is in five books divided into chapters, each of which begin with verses followed by explanatory annotations in prose. The two

---

[1] *De triplici minimo et mensura ad trium speculativarum scientiarum et multarum activarum artium principia.*

first books contain a restatement of the teachings of the *Causa*, somewhat improved and more detailed. The remaining three are chiefly mathematical. The main argument is concerned with the threefold unity of three speculative sciences, which are of God, who is "both the greatest and the least that may be"; of the unitary individual soul, and of the material atom or physical unit.[1] As successive works of Bruno appear one finds in them a gradual disappearance of mere Neo-Platonism and theory of emanation, less mere admiration of the transcendency of God and deeper contemplation of His immanence in Nature.[2] These Latin poems are chiefly concerned with the operations of a Living Universe.

Five years before Descartes was born, we find declared here that "whoso itcheth to Philosophy must set to work by putting all things to the doubt."[3]

The thinker seeks the Universal; he would have knowledge of some underlying principle, some supporting substance underlying the flux of things. Such a substance must be simple, that is to say, without parts, for if it had parts these would again require a single, simple principle or substrate. Thought necessitates the unchanging amid change, ever at one with itself. Differences of number, the opposition of good and evil, all contraries, in a word, must be at one, as Cusanus taught. The greatest must be at one with the least; the maximum coincide with the minimum. So is it with God. He is "a unit, the source of all numbers, wholly simple, the substance of magnitude and composition, a dignity above every phase, not to be computed, infinitely great."[4] "He is the unit of units."[5] But we must not

---

[1] Tocco, F ; *Op. lat. di G. B. exposte etc., Fir.*, 1889, *p.* 138.
[2] Tocco, F ; *Conferenza, Fir.*, 1886.
[3] *De minimo*, I, i.   [4] *Ibid.*, I, i, *schol.*
[5] "Deus est monadum monas," *ibid.*, I, iv.

regard the Absolute One as bare unity. In a work written just before this one was published our author writes: " In themselves things change, and, in the material world, are effects and imperfect. They are rather not-beings than beings, for they issue from the void and, so far from truly being, they depart into the void. Their true existence must be where they cannot but be, in that first cause and perfect principle wherein lies the will and the power for their production at pleasure. Wherefore their true being is in the Monad itself, wherein, consequently, they are truly known, in simplicity and concurrence; for there all things are one, without distinction or dispersion or number; but this in an ineffable way." [1]

Bruno regards the unit from metaphysical, physical and critical points of view.[2] Metaphysically considered, the soul is an eternal minimum, the possibility of change. He was resolved to treat fully of metaphysics and of the soul " if it should please God to bestow on him time." To our loss, it was not permitted. There are minima of spirit, which are not further reducible and wherein absolute spirit manifests itself. The relation of these minima to absolute spirit is not shown, nor could it be, since one term of the relation at least remains quite ineffable. Bruno would seem in another work to incline to the opinion that they cannot be regarded as mere parts or divisions of the one spirit, but " truly it remains in doubt." [3]

No less than minima of spirit, souls or centres of experience, must we posit minima in the physical world. Bruno definitely adopts an atomic theory. The material

[1] *Summa terminorum.* Cfr. Bradley, F. H ; *op. cit. chapters xiij–xv.*

[2] Lasswitz ; *G. B. und die Atomistik, Vierteljahrschrift für Wissenschaft. Philosophie,* 1884.—McIntyre ; *Op. cit., p.* 246 *sqq.*

[3] *Lampas triginta statuarum, op. lat., cura* Tocco and Vitelli, *p.* 58.

universe, he says, is composed of irreducible units or atoms, which enter into composition as do the letters of the alphabet into the formation of words.[1] It must be so, since there cannot be infinite divisibility ; for could we go on subdividing for ever there would be no substance : there must be some minimum which has no parts. And if it were not so, everything would be penetrable : there would be no resistance of body to body. Composition changes, but the absolute minimum or substance is immortal : it is the possibility of change. Physical differences depend on this possibility being realized in the composition of these simple, homogeneous atoms. Each minimum is the centre of an energy which is an external quality and which is endlessly extended. It is indestructible, endlessly in motion, and this activity it derives from the operation of final causes which issue from the individual soul or from the Soul of the World. Each minimum or least thing is also the possibility of its own maximum, drawing all the other minima it may into connexion with itself.[2] And most of all must this be said of the Unit of Units, wherein the maximum and minimum and all qualities coincide and are at one.[3] Bruno's Absolute is self-conscious Spirit, containing and knowing all that is within itself.[4]

An atom is spherical.[5] Atoms come into contact at points on their superficies, leaving curved triangular spaces between them.[6] Since they touch with a limited surface only, we must be careful to distinguish between *body* and *limit*, and not to confuse these as Aristotle does.[7] In other words, we must not confound mathematical intuitions with

---

[1] *De minimo*, I, ij, v. 26.   [2] *Ibid.*, I, iij, v. 22–29, 50–55.
[3] *Ibid.*, I, iv, v. 10 *sqq.*
[4] Carrière, M ; *Weltanschauung d. Reformationzeit, p.* 470.
[5] *De minimo*, I, xij ; xiv ; II, ij.
[6] *Ibid.*, I, xj.   [7] *Ibid.*, I, vij, v. 19–25 ; 40–43.

physical being. The physical atom is a constant centre of God's operation; that by means of which the complexity of nature becomes possible.

Critically considered, the minimum may be such absolutely or relatively. An absolute minimum, such as a mathematical point, is irreducible, in whatever way the mind approaches it; but a relative minimum, such as bone, cartilage etc. is reducible.[1] Sense is the source of our information, but it needs correction by reason.[2] Without a unit or minimum, there can be no measurement; and it is by the exercise of reason that we arrive at the conception of a unit; but we must not forget that indiscernibles possess differences in actual existence.[3] The minimal standard varies according to that which is measured; the unit of physics is very different from that of the surgery, and the unit of the physician lies far from that of the mathematician.[4] For each division of knowledge there is a minimum; there is the point for mathematics, unity for arithmetic, atoms for physics—the latter being simple in themselves and without difference.[5] These minima depend on the mind and purpose of the thinker.[6] In Nature numbers do not exist: "ten horses are not equal to ten men." Everywhere we find a minimum but not a maximum: the unit is a relative concept leading us on towards the last and greatest. Everything is unique, and change of any kind never absolutely repeats itself; there are no perfect geometrical forms in Nature;[7] for there is a constant exodus and immigration of the particles of every material body.[8]

It is definitely stated that the minimum, whether spirit or

[1] De minimo, I, x.
[2] Ibid., I, xiv, schol.
[3] Ibid., II, ij, v, i. sqq.
[4] Ibid., I, x, schol.
[5] Ibid., I, ix.
[6] Ibid., I, ix.
[7] Ibid., II, iv, v. 36 sqq.
[8] Ibid., II, v ; V, ij.

physical atom, is immortal.[1] From this and one or two similar remarks elsewhere, some writers have supposed that Bruno came at last to throw over the teaching of the *Causa* and to believe in personal immortality. Here, he speaks of the transformations of the soul as not following one another in haphazard fashion, but as depending on the kind of life which has been led. Taken *au pied de la lettre*, this is an explicit assertion of personal immortality. But one often has to read the real Bruno between the written lines, and, above all, to compare every one of his utterances on a subject before one can form a conclusive judgment as to his real meaning. He repeats in this work that there is one Soul of the World, manifesting itself in manifold forms, and the passage may be merely his way of expressing the " secret sympathies " of nature which produce such facts as heredity, the transmission of ideas through space and time, definite tendencies in matter and mind etc. etc. Professor McIntyre thinks Bruno came to accept personal immortality.[2] Tocco, the completest and minutest of Brunian scholars, once thought so too,[3] but, since he had access to the manuscript works which have now been published, partly under his care, he has completely changed his opinion. He maintains that, in Bruno's philosophy, while Matter is resolved into insensible, irreducible atoms, Spirit is not thus fractionized, but remains always one with itself in quality and substance.[4] It may be questioned whether Bruno ever regarded the atomic theory as other than a relative one for human knowledge. But Tocco charges him with inconsistency and dualism in applying one principle to brute-

---

[1] *De minimo, I, iv,* 10 *sqq.*

[2] McIntyre ; *op. cit., pp.* 307, 313 *sqq.*

[3] Tocco, F ; *Conferenza., Fir,* 1886.

[4] Tocco, F ; *Op. ined. di G. B, Napoli,* 1891. *Cfr.* the last few pages of his study of the *Lampas triginti statuarum,* and the Introduction, p. 7.

matter and another principle to mind. In the *Lampas*, written at Wittenberg, in the *Spaccio* and elsewhere, Bruno writes that neither body nor soul need fear death, since both are eternal and constant principles. But the reduction of the Universe to two distinct principles—matter and spirit, if in some measure anticipatory of Descartes, is not made absolute. There remains the all-inclusive, all-comprehensive Unity which is at once Divine Intuition and Divine Power and all things else. No category is really ultimate for the Nolan. If he divides matter and spirit, he does not finally divorce them. And he were a bold thinker to day who should be so assured of the certainties of science and of his own metaphysical power as to interpret electrons in terms of spirit or spirit in terms of electrons. Bruno's atoms would seem to be *virtually* active spirit under the direction of individual souls. Thus, animal centres of experience direct the atomic evolution of the body from the heart as a centre.[1]

With regard to Bruno's assertions, often so obscure, concerning immortality, we must remember that it was his wont, as indeed was necessary, even for an unguarded person, to speak in guarded language. He employs current conceptions to rise above them; he makes use of any aspect of the Pythagorean or any other philosophy which approximates towards his own and which will give his own view some measure of authoritative support; he is fond of suggestive mythology, and lures the learner onward with "language of accommodation"; for is there not in all things some trace of truth, more or less clearly discernible? The reflective student can usually penetrate through the mask, which is at once an incitement and a clue. Just here there are considerable difficulties in the way of interpretation. We have seen that, in the Wittenberg "Lamp," he

---

[1] *De minimo, I, ij, schol; iij, v.* 22-29, 50-55 ; *Causa, Dial. II.*

wrote of how some think particular beings to be particular
manifestations of the Soul of the World; others, that the
Soul of the World is divided into parts ; " truly it remains in
doubt, but we incline to the first opinion." [1] A little further
on he writes that multiplication falls on the side of brute-
matter, the soul remaining one.[2] Of an underlying identification of the individual centre of experience with the
Universal Experience, Bruno felt sure. And that implies
a higher, fuller immortality than mere personal continuance
with memory-synthesis, or mere continued being-in-flux
without memory. Yet neither of these is inconsistent with
Bruno's central conception. Probably he formed no definite
conclusion about matters which he would regard as of minor
importance and unsupported by conclusive evidence. Tocco
writes : " The individualisation of the soul is for Bruno a
fleeting event which in the infinite bosom of time has but
the stability and duration of a flash." [3] But assuredly
Bruno meant much more than this. As has been shown,
he identifies the human spirit with the Absolute Spirit in
the last resort, and of the Absolute Spirit he writes in a
work of approximately the same date that " past is not
present to it as past, or future as future, but the whole of
time is present to it wholly, at once and complete." [4] " To
die," he says elsewhere, " is to spring into life." And in
the great poem published at the autumn fair, after such
pieces of Pythagorean metaphor as, " the organs of a
horse may await those of a man and all other creatures
in regular or irregular progression" he immediately adds,
" present organic death has nothing to do with the countless forms of enduring life. Were the Spirit but aware of

[1] *Op. lat., ed.* Tocco and Vitelli, *iij, p.* 58.
[2] *Ibid., p.* 59. *Cfr. Causa, Dial. II ; Cabala, II, ij.*
[3] Tocco, F ; *op. ined. di G. B. p. vij.*
[4] *Summa terminorum metaphysicorum.*

this it would not suffer apprehension. For the wise fear not death, but may even desire and set out to embrace it. Every substance shall endure throughout eternity, have infinity for its dwelling place and all forms for its realization." [1]

Bruno's phrase " God is the monad of monads " or " unit of units," [2] which was afterwards employed by Leibnitz, together with the similarity of their views concerning every living being containing a vast number of other living beings, [3] and many other resemblances or pseudo-resemblances led to the belief that Leibnitz was indebted to Bruno. But this is quite a blunder : [4] Leibnitz derived nothing from the earlier thinker. The Monadology, compared with Bruno's more comprehensive philosophy, is not merely one-sided, but, in its theory of pre-established harmony, is far more patently and extravagantly unsound. The earlier thinker did not indulge in the construction of a Pluralistic Universe.

All the latter part of *De Minimo* is occupied with a hopeless attempt to remodel Mathematics on the concept of monads or the various mathematical minima which he would have to be irreducible. While he almost anticipated the innovation of Kant by enquiring into the conditions of knowledge and in perceiving the intuitive character of mathematics, he was by no means abreast with the mathematics of his own day, and he quite failed to see the direction which that science had already taken. He further committed the fatal blunder of forgetting his own

---

[1] *De immenso, I, j.*

[2] *De minimo, I, iv, schol.*   Leibnitz fell on the phrase quite independently.

[3] Cfr. *Cena, Dial. III ;* Leibnitz, G. W ; *Monadology,* § 70.

[4] Stein, L ; *Leibnitz und Spinoza, Ein Beitrag zur Entwickelunge-geschichter der Leibnizchen Philosophie,* 1890, *p.* 197 *sqq.*—McIntyre ; *op. cit., pp.* 224, 343 *sqq.*

distinction between limit or boundary and the physical body which it bounds. For example, he treats of the line as a file of atoms.[1] He tried to simplify geometry by making the greater part of it intuitively comprehensible through three vastly involved figures.

II. THE UNIT

At the autumn fair, Wechel and Fischer produced the remainder of the great poem, permission for the printing of which is not recorded in the Frankfurt Censorial Register. It was entitled " Of the Unit, Quantity and Shape, A Book Following The Five On The Least, The Great And Measure. Also Eight Books Concerning The Innumerable, Immeasurable And Infigurable, Or Of The Universe And Its Worlds."[2]   In fact, two volumes were bound up in one. The first of these, " Of the Unit," commences with laudatory verses addressed to Duke Henry Julius of Brunswick. Bruno contrasts the strenuous life of those who love truth with that led by pleasure-seekers and the idle rich. It is clear that the long struggle with obscurantists, the buffets of exile, persecution by academies, and the general ill-success which attended his mission had left their marks. The iron had entered into his soul. Yet he is still un-daunted, and sings with prophetic instinct: " Whatever cruel fate shall await me, the struggle began far back in boyhood, and, God be witness, I follow the truth unvan-quished, nor may death itself bear the smallest terror to me, nor in any wise do I blench before the violence of any mortal man."[3]   And later in the book, he sings: " I have

---

[1] *De minimo, V, v.*

[2] *De monade, numero et figura, liber consequens quinque de minimo, magno et mensura. Item de Innumerabilibus, immenso et infigurabile, seu de universo et mundis, libri octo* . . . 1591.

[3] *De monade, cap. I v.* 38-45.

fought: it is much. . . . Victory lies in the hands of Fate.
Be that with me as it may, whoever shall prove conqueror,
future ages will not deny that I did not fear to die, was
second to none in constancy, and preferred a spirited death
to a craven life."[1]   Here, says Brunnhofer, is Bruno's
epitaph.

There are many fine poetic passages, too often marred by
ugly neologisms, curious syntax and execrable prosody.
Apart from these, the sole interest of the book to the
modern reader lies in the singularity of that pronounced
occultism which held so much attraction for men of the
Renaissance. The scientific education of the day was not
built on the secure foundation of careful observation and experiment. Stress was laid on word and symbol, with curious
results. With greater sagacity, men put faith in intuitions
springing from the mind, like Minerva from the brain of
her Divine Father; but they knew little of the methods of
verification. Bruno draws largely from many sources in this
work, but chiefly from Heinrich Cornelius Agrippa of Nettesheim.[2] He tells us that the work deals with revelation, faith
and divination, and not with reasoned knowledge and experiment. He takes occasion to protest against dogmas which
" disturb human calm and the peace of ages, put out the light
of the mind and avail not in morals."

The work is, however, chiefly filled with a selection of
such mystical and philosophic lore as fell in with the
author's own conceptions and with a singular series of
geometrical constructions founded upon a theory of distinct
mathematical minima, and upon the numerical mysteries of
Pythagoras, all invested with metaphysical significance.
One is the perfect number, the source of infinite series.

---

[1] *De monade, cap. vij, v.* 128 *sq.*
[2] *De occulta philosophia. Cfr.* Tocco, F ; *Fonti pui recenti della
f. di G. B. in Acad. dei Lincei, Rediconti ser., vj, p.* 534.

Even so does an infinity of worlds proceed from one substance; the diversity of the universe and all its creatures
being due to the union of the One and the Many.

III. On Immensity

The *De Immenso* is a very great book indeed. It is a
prolonged hymn of wonder and praise and intellectual
exaltation, sung in the temple of immensity. Perhaps it
may be ranked with the *Causa* as the greatest of Bruno's
works. Essentially in line with the explict idealists of the
early nineteenth century, he always tries to unite his
idealism with scientific conceptions of the Universe.[1] The
spirit of kinship with which he regards the starry host
is that of a poet lately among us:

> " So may we read and little find them cold :
> Not frosty lamps, illumining dead space,
> Not distant aliens, not senseless Powers.
> The fire is in them whereof we are born,
> The music of their motion may be ours." [2]

De Immenso is a restatement of the cosmic teaching of
the great Italian works, often more detailed and more
precise. Like the *De Minimo* and *De Monade* it consists
of Latin verses and prose annotations thereon. Seven
years had passed since the first bold attempts to furnish
the world with a new cosmology. As presenting Bruno's
views in their final form, the work is of the highest importance; but, since these have been dealt with in the order
in which they were given to the public, it is not necessary
to do more than present a general notion of the work and
set down indications of advance.

He says there is an incessant unfolding of Nature in move-

---

[1] Höffding, H ; *Hist. of Mod. Phil.*, *tr.* Meyer, 1900, *vol. I, p.* 139.
[2] Meredith, G ; *Meditation under the Stars.*

ment; and the same motion never exactly repeats itself.[1]
Illusion must be corrected by comparing the report of one
sense with that of other senses.[2] In the *Cena* Bruno's
mathematics and astronomy had fallen below the standard
of Copernicus : here he corrects errors, reproduces a whole
chapter from the work of that wonderful Pole,[3] criticises
him, and sagaciously comes very near to the law discovered
by Galileo, that in rotary motion the direction of the axis
remains parallel to itself.[4] All planetary life in any sidereal
system is derived from the light and heat of its central sun ;
planets such as the earth, being cold, dark bodies.[5] He
has insight, before Kepler, Galileo and Newton confirm
his assertion, that the earth is not the heaviest thing
in Nature, where worlds move securely through space, he
believes of their own intrinsic energy.[6] There is no
essential difference between the heavens and the earth,
as Aristotle taught ;[7] or in essential nature, between sun
and earth.[8] There are not merely invisible planets
revolving round the stars,[9] but undiscovered planets revolving round our sun.[10] The sun is a solid body, but
with liquid material in it, which burns, and hence it has
a luminous atmosphere. In 1584, he regarded the sun as
being a *solid* metallic body, but now he conceives of its light
and heat as produced by the chemical changes in the *liquid*
parts of its body.[11] The incessant internal commotion due
to these chemical changes cause a rotation of the sun ;[12] and

---

[1] *De immenso, VI, xvij.*   [2] *Ibid., I, iv.*
[3] Tocco, F; *Op. lat. espos. e confront., pp.* 313 *sqq.*
[4] *De imm., III, x & schol.*
[5] *Ibid., III ; IV, vij v. 76 sq ; VI, v,* 5 *sq.*
[6] *Ibid., III ; IV, xv, v.* 12 *sqq ; VI, ix, v.* 12 *sqq.*
[7] *Ibid., IV, iij, v.* 27 *sqq.*   [8] *Ibid., IV, vij, v.* 18 *sqq.*
[9] *Ibid., I, iij, v.* 13 *sqq ; III, iv, v.* 102 *sqq ; VI, ij, v.* 7 *sq.*
[10] *Ibid., II, ix, v.* 127 *sqq.*
[11] *Ibid., IV, ix, v.* 32. *Cfr. Infinito, Dial. III.*
[12] *Ibid., III, v ; IV, vii.*

the scintillation of sun and stars is due to rapidity of rotation; but the phenomenon is not observable in planets,
which do not give out light, but only reflect it.[1]

He exhibits great interest in comets and shows that he
was closely following the observations of the astronomers of
his time; he casts aside the notion, which had prevailed
since the time of Aristotle, that they were slowly burning
vapours, set afire by the motion of the stars, and he
recognises that these wandering Arabs of the sky are
genuine members of the cosmic system and subject to
cosmic law. Meteors are also cosmic matter, wandering
through space; they are living beings.[2] He had but a
poor notion of the relative distances of the planets: he did
not think Jupiter or Saturn could be much farther from the
sun than the Earth is, or that their period of revolution
could be much longer than our year.[3]

Seven years before, he would seem to have believed the
stars and planets to be eternal, though subject to vicissitude;[4] but now he says that only the Universe as a whole
is eternal; its worlds decay and perish, their constituent
parts entering into fresh combinations.[5]

He attacks the superstitions interwoven with all religions,
and especially the creed of those Catholics who put the
Pope in the place of God.[6] He is still as filled with religious
enthusiasm and poetic fire as when his eyes were first
opened to transcendent truth; he rejoices now as then in
the confident vision of an everliving, infinite universe and
its innumerable choirs of flaming spirits dwelling under the
reign of ever-unfolding, spiritual law.

It is worthy of note that he refers sympathetically and
almost proudly to the daring sea-dogs of Britain who had

---

[1] *De immenso, IV, vij,* 1 *sqq; IV, viij.*   [2] *Ibid., V, ij.*
[3] *Ibid., V, viij.*   [4] *Cena, Dial. V ; Infinito, Dial. II.*
[5] *De immenso, II, v, v.* 1 *sqq.*   [6] *Ibid., I.*

braved the might of his own monarch, Philip of Spain, and prevailed against him.[1]

IV. On Images, Signs and Ideas

At the same autumn fair appeared the last work given to the world by Bruno himself. There is no record extant of permission for its publication ; but it is mentioned, with the date of its appearance, in Bassäus' Frankfurt Catalogue of 1592. "The Arrangement Of Images, Signs And Ideas "[2] is preceded by a dedicatory letter to Heinrich Hainzell, the " distinguished and most generous" lord of Elgg. Bruno informs Hainzell that this is one of his most important works, having for its object the description of how images, signs and ideas may be so ordered in the mind as to sub-serve a general scheme for the discovery and arrangement of truths and for the fixing of them in the memory. The greater part of the treatise is in prose, but there are excur-sions into verse. There are three books, the first consisting of two sections. The author extracts all that he considers of first importance from the *De Umbris*, *Cantus Circæus* and *Sigillus*, condensing and improving without greatly altering. The work is indeed an important one, for, although Neo-Platonic distinctions are adopted, Neo-Platonic doctrine is widely departed from, and a position is taken up which is, in essence, that of the great German Idealists. " The simplest operations of arithmetic are very easy," he says, yet " to do these is to do everything ; to say them is to say everything. . . . Herein the whole light is more

---

[1] *De immenso, VI, xx.*

[2] *De Imaginum, Signorum et Idearum Comp., Frcf. ap. Jo. Wechelium et P. Ficherum consortes,* 1591. We know that it was the last work published at Frankfurt from the *De Monade, Cap. III, schol.* and from the work itself, *III, vij.*

present, clear and obvious to our intelligence than is the
outer light of the sun to the eyes. . . . Shall I call it a
power, however, because so few know and understand ? . . .
Because the eye beholdeth other things, itself it doth not
see.   But what is that eye which beholdeth other things in
such wise that it may perceive itself ?   It is that eye which
seeth all things in itself, and which even is all things." [1]
At the commencement of the book we come across a
passage where, couched in scholastic terminology, is the
identification of thought and thing, intellect and substance,
memory and nature, knowledge and fact. " Ideas are the
cause of things prior to the things, the vestiges of ideas are
the things themselves, that is to say, they exist in things ;
the shadows of ideas are derived from things, that is to say,
they are subsequent on them."

He again records his belief in mystic intuition, writing of
" the interior intuition which is both the light and that which
it illumines, differing from external intuition as a mirror
which only reflects would from a mirror illuminated of its
own nature . . . wherein object and sensitive subject
are one." [2]

That same Pythagorean fallacy is repeated which runs
through all Bruno's work and all the philosophy of his
time, viz., that, since simple numbers can be clearly conceived and are without contradiction, they represent the
ultimate constitution of the Universe and possess objective
existence.

He perceived the unity of the fine arts and that knowledge is a constructive art ; and one may infer from the
following passage that he found keener enjoyment in sight
than in hearing : " There be men who find harmony through
the eye ; others, though in less measure, through the ear.

[1] *Prefatory letter to Hainzell.*
[2] *De Compositione, I, sec. i, c.* 1

The minds of such as be true poets, musicians, painters and philosophers are akin; for all true philosophy is at once music, poetry and painting; true poetry hath both music and philosophy in it, and music and philosophy are a kind of divine wisdom and painting."

V. A Philosophical Lexicon

The "List Of Metaphysical Terms For Taking The Study Of Logic And Philosophy In Hand"[1] was published at Zurich four years after the lessons, of which it is a digest, were given in that city, and fourteen years later Eglin had them reprinted at Marburg with the addition of a " Proposition Of Descent Or The Unfolding Of Being."[2] The first part was written perhaps with the encyclopædic efforts of Aquinas and Albertus Magnus in his mind and certainly with the fifth book of Aristotle's Metaphysic serving as a guide. It is a crude but bold attempt at a philosophical dictionary.[3] The additional part is an application of the definitions (of the first part) of Neo-Platonism.

Here, as elsewhere, Bruno employs the language of the schools in order to rise above the conceptions it conveys. The work throws great light on his attitude towards religion. He says that, according to the Schoolmen, faith is implicit in babes and common folk and explicit in the wise and learned. God acts in time and space, but is above time and change, and with him liberty and necessity are one. Everything, however far it may be from being good in

---

[1] *Summa terminorum metaphysicorum ad capessendum Logicae et Philosophiae Studium, ex Jordani Bruni Nolani Entis descensu manusc. excerpta ; nunc primum luci commissa ; a Raphaele Eglino Iconio, Tigurino: Zurich,* 1595.

[2] *Accessit ejusdem Praxis Descensus seu Multiplicatio Entis ex manuscripto. . . . Marpurgi,* 1609.

[3] McIntyre, *op. cit., p.* 113.

itself, is nevertheless a means to good. We can observe Will operant in Nature (*voluntas naturalia*) as a self-moving principle, intelligent and prescient. God is not merely transcendent; but, in fact, operates through Nature and is in Nature. Wherefore thorough investigation of Nature can never give what is base or false. Philosophic truth is certitude, procurable by setting forth from the gates of sense. It cannot be at variance with theologic truth, as the upholders of the Twofold truth maintained, although the latter is given by revelation from a superior intelligence (*Summa sub evidentia*).

VI. The Fastenings of Kind

During his second and longer stay at Frankfurt, Bruno wrote with his own hand "The Fastenings Of Kind,"[1] which he never finished. A part of this was copied by Besler, pretty certainly at Padua, and detail was added. Both MSS., which were discovered in Paris during the last century, are now preserved at Moscow with the other "Noroff Manuscripts."

This treatise is on Moral Science from an objective point of view, the passions being dealt with in the cold, detached manner of an impartial observer. The different kinds of love which bind the human spirit are discussed, and sexual attraction is discussed in a singularly straightforward, naturalistic way, unrelieved by the smallest dash of sentiment. Here and there, passages from the Italian works are repeated. As in *De Magia*, an attempt is made to reduce the attractions and repulsions to be found in Nature no less than in human feelings and emotions to the contrary and opposite principles of Love and Hate. As with Dante, Hate is regarded as Love inverted. After

[1] *De Vinculis in genere.*

all, these two final contraries turn out to be one at
bottom.

Bruno opines that the fear of hell is more dreadful than
the place itself would be: it is a powerful chain to the
human mind, acting through the imagination.[1]

Tocco's judgement of this quite unfinished work is that
it "shows an experience of life, a sobriety in speculation
and a delicacy of observation far from common."[2]

[1] Bruno ; *Op. lat. cura Tocco & Vitelli, III, p.* 638.
[2] Tocco, F ; *Op. ined. di G. B., p.* 257.

CHAPTER XVII

AT VENICE AND PADUA

THERE had been a time when the human spirit, braced by the discovery of ancient letters and of a new world, enjoyed no small measure of freedom under Popes who were themselves distinguished sons of the Renaissance; but such liberty was never formally authorised and established, and the shock which Protestant aggression gave to the Catholic conscience and the dwindling power and purse of the Roman theocracy had by this time caused a complete reversal of Papal policy. Bruno, in spite of the persecution he had endured at the hands of minor officials, believed in the sweet reasonableness of a Church which tacked and temporised so often in the past, and which was even now governed by so many wise statesmen, had the adherence of so many scholars and numbered so many sincere priests. Filled with his own sincerity and a belief in the triumph of truth, the lessons of his life in Naples, Geneva, Paris and Germany were lost on him. Candid and of generous and open mind, he judged the rulers of the Church by his own high liberal standard and that of a few like-minded friends. He had not the least doubt as to the genuine Catholicity of his own belief, and that he only needed access to high authority to be restored to the bosom of his Church. Mocenigo sent him more than one pressing invitation[1] and probably promised him ample protection.[2] At length, it may be after some misgiving and swaying to and fro, desire to

---

[1] *Docs. v, viij.*   [2] Sigwart; *op. cit., p.* 30.

revisit Italy and dwell once more among Italians prevailed, and one fatal day in the autumn of 1591, he set forth for Venice.

Bruno could not have been long in finding out the mental limitations, perhaps the niggardliness also, of his new pupil. It is suggestive that Mocenigo told the Inquisitors : " he was for some time in lodgings, but for the most part in Padua." [1] But he was singularly inept at reading character. That of Giovanni Mocenigo is pretty fully revealed in his denunciations [2] and in the letters of Lauro Settizonio (G. B. Leone) [3] which Ciotto published for him. A man no less cunning than vain, as grudging as treacherous, as shifty as superstitious, an incapable dabbler, shallow-brained and managed by his confessor, though Bruno fought shy of too close an intimacy at first, we shall find him yielding to his solicitations later and taking up his abode with him.

There was a daily public boat-service between Venice and its University-town ; the distance was not more than about twenty miles. Bruno availed himself of this to return to the city where nearly fourteen years before he had found the University deserted by reason of plague. He now stayed three months at that ancient and renowned seat of learning, getting his bread by giving private lessons to a circle of German students.[4] Men of all ages and from all countries—from Scandinavia and Cyprus, Sicily and Spain, Britain and Poland were wont to foregather at the old palace of the Signoria which Venetian conquerors had restored and modernised by the hands of Sansovino and converted into the University building. The subjects taught therein were rigidly prescribed ; but free treatment of them was accorded to the famous public lecturers,

[1] *Doc. i.*   [2] *Docs. j, ij, viij.*
[3] *Lett. famil. di Go. Battista Leone, Ciotto, Venezia.*
[4] *Doc. vj.*

and troops of Protestants might be observed, making their
way to the University or to a tutor's rooms; and these
"not of suche students alone as most commonlie are
brought up in our universitees (meane mens children sent
to schole in hope to live upon hyred learning) but for the
more parte of noble mens sonnes, and of the best gentil-
men: that studie more for knowledge and pleasure than
for curiositee or luker."[1] The presence of wealthy students
was advantageous to the private lecturer; moreover, a
student was "bound to no lectures, nor nothing else but
what he lyst himself to go to."[2] But many of them
"lysted" to rioting and "feates of arms."

Bruno had Besler for company,—Besler acted as his copyist,
—and he met men whom he had known in Germany; con-
ceivably, men, also, whom he had known in England.
Strange that he did not take alarm at what was being
said about his presence in Italy! The scholars in Frankfurt marvelled at his temerity.[3] What the Germans in Italy
thought, we may read in a passage of a letter written by
Havekenthal of Brandenburg (Valens Acidalius), who was
studying at Bologna, to Michael Forgacz of Bavaria, who
was at Padua. "Tell me," he asks in a letter dated January
21st, 1592, "tell me of yet another matter. It is said that
Giordano Bruno the Nolan whom you knew at Wittenberg
is living among you at Padua. Can this be so? What
manner of man is this, an exile, as he was used to admit, to
dare to re-enter Italy? I marvel, I marvel, nor can I
believe it, although I have it from a sure source. Tell me, is

---

[1] Thomas, William; *The historie of Italie, a boke excedying profitable to be redde*, 1549, *p. 2; quoted by* Clare Howard, *English
Travellers of the Renaissance*, 1904, *p.* 53.

[2] Hoby, Sir Thomas; *The Travels and Life of Sir T. H., written
by Himself*, 1547–1564, Ed. E. Powell, *Camden Soc., Ser. iij, vol. iv*
1902, *p.* 10.

[3] Ciotto's evidence, *Doc. v.*

this news false or true ? " How far Havekenthal's astonishment extended to Italians, we do not know ; but it is clear that many-tongued rumour was at work among Germans in Italy, for on Mar. 3rd Havekenthal wrote : " I marvel no more concerning that sophist, for, every day, all sorts of incredible stories are reported here." [1]

Bruno would seem to have felt no fear. He had been dwelling in freer lands than Italy and did not realise the changes effected by the enforcement of the decrees of Trent. Nay, he went on with studies which the Church regarded as at least questionable. He was employing Besler in copying *De Vinculis* and ancient, unprinted works ; among them being the " Seals of Hermes and Ptolemy," a work which was found in his possession at Venice and which he was careful to state had been praised by Albertus Magnus,[2] the " Universal Doctor " of the Church. He confesses that he had not seen too closely into the contents of these books ; indeed this particular one he had not read. He was philandering with perilous material, preparatory to a study of judicial astrology.[3]

Whether or no Mocenigo's taste for secret knowledge included hankerings after the " Black Art " is not apparent. He was eager to get Bruno into his house at Venice, and offered tempting terms. " He would support me well and I should be satisfied with him," says Bruno. In a fatal hour the unsuspecting thinker put his head into a noose. He accepted the offer of a treacherous and incapable dabbler, returned to Venice in March, 1592, and took up his abode with Mocenigo in the little Campo of S. Samuele, on the Grand Canal, just opposite the palace where our Browning died.

---

[1] Acidalius, Valens ; *Epist. a fratre editum, Chr. Acid.,* 1606, *p.* 10.

[2] *Doc. xiv.* *Cfr.* Albertus Magnus ; *Physicorum Mineralium, lib. v.*   [3] *Doc. xiv.*

At first, it would seem that all went well. He frequented booksellers' shops and chatted with the learned people whom he met there. Ciotto would seem to have heard no heretical talk, and Brictanus said that "Giovanni had not spoken to him on such matters."[1] The fame of his abilities spread in Venice. There were literary clubs of a social character there as elsewhere in Italy, and the most distinguished circle was wont to assemble at the hospitable house of Andrea Morosini, the historian, a man now "in the middle of the journey of our life"—he was 35. Here were to be met all the cultivated patricians, Fra Paoli Sarpi, the famous printers and every Venetian of note who was interested in things of the mind. Morosini was a broad-minded Catholic, and, from the leanings of some of his guests, may have given his evidence with due caution and reservation. Anyhow, he related at the trial that "For some months past certain philosophical books had been on sale at Venetian booksellers, bearing the name of Giordano Bruno, a man reputed to be of varied learning. I understood from what I heard in Venice and from what Gio. Battista (Ciotto) the bookseller said to diverse gentlemen, and especially to myself, that this man was here and that we might desire to get him to our house, where certain gentlemen and also prelates are wont to come for the discussion of literature and above all of philosophy. Wherefore I said that he should get him to come; and he did so several times, debating on various learned matters. I have never been able to infer from his reasonings that he held any opinion contrary to the faith, and, so far as I am concerned, I have always considered him to be a Catholic—and at the least suspicion of the contrary I should not have allowed his presence in my house."[2]

"Many patricians and literary people gathered together

[1] *Doc. vi.*   [2] *Doc. xv.*

there," said Bruno, " and I have also entered into discussion with some librarians ; but I do not recollect particular persons, for I did not know who they might be "[1]—a wary statement, designed, it may be, to protect others as well as himself. But he appears to have exercised some measure of caution outside Mocenigo's doors : " Never since I have been in Venice have I taught heretical doctrine, but have only discussed philosophy with many patricians, as they can tell you."[2]

Indeed, now that he was in Italy, Bruno was making persistent and pathetic efforts to be received again into the " Christian, Apostolic and Roman Church." He meditated presenting his case to the New Pope, Ippolito Aldobrandini, Clement VIII, who, having achieved no small reputation for wisdom and temperate policy when he was papal legate, was elected to the tiara on Feb. 2nd 1592. Bruno knew the new Pope to be a man of gentle character and broad intelligence, anxious to secure the best minds for the service of the Church, and, indeed, for a time Clement acquitted himself as a wise and tolerant pontiff. But the Protestant rebellion so re-awakened the slumbering prejudices of Catholicism and the Roman theocracy found itself so threatened on every hand that the establishment of unbending authority had become essential to safety. Clement, who was truly pious, confessing his sins every day, was speedily acted on by the Curia, and finally Cardinal S. Severino led him into a policy of inflexible severity. Bruno exhibits a childlike belief in the reasonableness of men and that the world could be persuaded to share his philosophic outlook: the Roman Pontiff only required an intellectual appeal to perceive the value of his views and to extend to him benevolence and toleration. He says: " I was about to proceed hence to Frankfurt again to get certair of my works printed, and

[1] *Doc. xvij.*　　　　　　　　[2] *Ibid.*

especially one on the seven liberal arts,[1] together with other
of my printed works, both those which I confirm and those
which I do not confirm, and place myself at the feet of His
Beatitude (for I have heard that he loves upright men), and
to explain my case and to try to be absolved for my mis-
behaviour and allowed to wear the clerical habit, but free
from monastic authority, whereunto I have spoken during
these last days to many Neapolitan Fathers of my order who
were here" (rather a perilous proceeding, perhaps!) "and
particularly Father Superior Fra Domenico of Nocera,
Father Serafino of Nocera, Father Giovanni, who comes I
know not whence, save that it is in the Kingdom of Naples,
and yet another of Atripalda, who left off his habit but resumed
it; I don't know his name; in religion he was called Brother
Felice."[2]   He repeated to his judges his desire to return to
the Church, but to be relieved of the bonds of monastic
obedience.[3]

In a singularly cramped handwriting there is confirmation
of Bruno's statement.   Father Domenico writes : " In this
very month of May, on the Holy Feast of Pentecost, as I was
coming out of the Sacristy of the Church of St. John and
St. Paul, I observed a layman bow to me.   At first I did
not know him; but when he spoke to me saying, ' Come
into a private place,' I remembered him as one of our
brethren in the province of the kingdom, a man of letters,
Brother Giordano of Nola by name.   We withdrew to a
quiet place in the aforesaid church, and there he told me
the reason of his leaving our province and of the cause of
his unfrocking; being excommunication by Fra Domenico
Vita, Provineial at the time.   He told me of his sojournings
in many Kingdoms and at Royal Courts and of his important

---

[1] The *Trivium* or grammar, rhetoric and dialectics, and the *Quad-
rivium*, or arithmetic, mathematics, astronomy and music.
[2] *Doc. ix.*
[3] *Doc. xvij.*

work in lecturing, but that he had always lived as a Catholic. And when I asked him what he did in Venice and how he subsisted, he said that he had been in Venice but a very short time and had his own sufficient means; and that he wished to live quietly and set about the writing of a book he had in mind, and then, through important patronage, he would present it to His Beatitude and obtain his pardon together with satisfaction of conscience for what he had told me about. He hoped to stay in Rome, to devote himself to literature, to show what he was made of and, perhaps, to deliver some lectures."[1] During Lent he seems to have gone frequently to the noble church of St. John and St. Paul, the Westminster Abbey of Venice, and also to the smaller mediæval church of S. Stefano which was close by his quarters.

These efforts are quite interpretable. The original thinker had found no country which was not hostile to new ideas. After his stormy experience he sought a haven in the Church to which he had once given a love which he had never quite lost, a church that had ennobled itself by periods of tolerance and even by active help in the liberation of the human spirit. Above all he desired to be able to return to his own beloved district—" to my Province "—without the odium of apostacy; but, at no price with the renewal of cloistered life and discipline.[2] He says that he confided his desire to Mocenigo as well as to Fra Domenico, and " he promised to help me in all things which were right." Blind belief that all men who might appear to be friendly towards him were no less sincere and single minded than himself! Filled with his own ideas, he relaxed whatever modicum of caution he had exercised in Venice in the intimacy of guest and teacher with host. Strozzi gave the youthful traveller, Henry Wotton, excellent advice when he told him to " keep an

[1] *Doc. x.*   [2] *Doc. xvij.*

open countenance and a shut mouth"[1] in Italy. Bruno said far too much to a man of just sufficient intelligence to misunderstand and misrepresent; one whose affectation of a love of learning, friendliness and generosity disguised a stupid, superstitious mind, a treacherous heart and a mean, sordid disposition. Such blindness is well-nigh inconceivable.

Either, with depraved religious zeal, perhaps at the instigation of the Inquisition, Mocenigo had set a trap for Bruno and enticed him from Germany to hand him over to the Holy Office when he had accumulated sufficient evidence; or he was dissatisfied with the lessons he received. He may have hankered after instruction in the Black Art and taken a mean revenge when he found this not to be forthcoming. Probably, in any case Mocenigo's confessor had something to do with his action and took advantage of the pupil's discontent to egg him on and to direct his procedure. The reader will be able to form his own surmise from the facts to be produced. Mocenigo wrote to the Inquisitors: "I am compelled by my conscience and the order of my Confessor;"[2] and again: "Since you have favoured me with so much forbearance by pardoning my error in delaying my tardy accusation, I pray you to excuse it before these Illustrious Lords, since my intention was good; *for I could not get at the whole matter at once;* nor did I know the vileness of the man until I had kept him in my house some two months . . . *and then I desired to get the better of him and by my dealings with him could be certain that he would not make off without my knowledge. Thus I have always assured myself of being able to make him come under the censure of the Holy Office. This I have succeeded in*

[1] "I pensieri stretti e il viso sciolto," Wotton, Sir Hy., *Life and Letters*, ed. L. Pearsall Smith, *Oxford*, 1907, *vol. ij, p.* 382.

[2] *Doc. i.*

doing." [1] This looks as if Mocenigo, advised by his confessor, had spread the net. On the other hand, his statements are such twistings of truth ; he was such a double-dealer and so artful that his desire " to get the better of Bruno " may have arisen from disappointment and spite, and his confession to his spiritual director a means to that end, while his statement to the Inquisitors may have been a dodge to wriggle out of an uncomfortable animadversion of the Authorities and to set himself right again. As a former Assessor at the sittings of the Inquisition, he had intimate knowledge of its methods and was probably in sympathy with them. So shallow a soul may have been the mere obedient instrument of his confessor.

At first things had seemed to go smoothly. At the trial, Bruno volunteered the statement that he confided his desire to be restored to the bosom of the Church to Mocenigo as well as to priests, and that Mocenigo promised to do his best for him.[2] He could not but be assured, by this time, of the mental poverty of his pupil, but rash and blind as Bruno's expectations were, Mocenigo must have been a master hand at dissimulation. He did his best to instruct a shallow person, expounding what he was engaged for, and more.[3] Either the pupil wished to dabble in secret arts which Bruno scorned, or he wished to worm out enough evidence concerning the Black Art to make a good case for the Holy Office to deal with. It was a futile attempt. The Nolan " despised conjuration and never attributed any efficacy to it." He had not even studied astrology, though he confessed to his judges that he had told several people that he wished to examine and see if there were anything in it should he get the necessary means and leisure and could find some quiet place; conditions which had never yet been in his power.[4]

[1] *Doc. ij.*   [2] *Doc. ix.*   [3] *Doc. vij.*   [4] *Doc. xiij.*

Mocenigo, bent on betrayal, went to Ciotto. Booksellers had to be careful, for their avocation was a somewhat dangerous one, although many works highly objectionable to the Church were sold quite freely; the State being by no means so subservient to ecclesiastical authority as to interfere rashly with a trade which added to the riches and reputation of the Commonwealth. Being learned men, they knew something of the contents of their wares. Ciotto certainly, and Brictanus probably, had Bruno's books on their shelves. Before the Inquisition such witnesses might well falter. If they gave their evidence a colour favourable to the prosecution they might have to excuse the fact of selling heretical books; if they were taken to be favourable to the accused they might find themselves in the same plight with him. The impression one gets from the evidence of Ciotto and Brictanus is that they stated what they knew quite faithfully and simply. Ciotto said: "I was about to start for the Frankfurt Fair last Easter when Signor G. Mocenigo found me and asked me if I were going thither. He said 'I have him (meaning Giordano) here at my expense. He has promised to teach me many things and has had a quantity of clothes and money from me on this account. I can bring him to no conclusion. I doubt whether he is quite trustworthy. So, since you are going to Frankfurt, keep this in mind, and do me the service to find out if anyone has faith in him and if he will carry out his promises.' By reason of this, when I was in Frankfurt I spoke with several scholars who had attended his lectures when he was in that city and were acquainted with his method and discourse. What they told me amounted to this, that Giordano made strong professions of memory and other similar secrets, but success with anyone was never seen, and his pupils in this matter and others similar to it were far from satisfied. They said more. They did not know how he could remain in Venice, for he is regarded as a man without religion. This is all I gathered, and I told it to Ser Giovanni when I returned from the fair, whereto he replied, 'I also had my doubts of this; but *I wish to find out what I can draw from him of the instructions he has promised me, not to lose altogether what I have given him, and then I shall hand him over to the censure of the Holy Office.*'"[1] Mocenigo also pumped the Flemish bookseller, Brictanus, and declared that he, " in particular, spoke of him to me, declaring him to be an enemy of Christianity and our faith, and that he had heard him utter great heresy."[2] Brictanus, when examined, utterly refuted this statement.[3]

According to his own showing, the pious patrician's next step was to consult his confessor, who advised him to denounce Bruno to the Inquisition. Any feeble-minded, muddle-headed intriguer could set its terrible, remorseless machinery in motion. Bruno seems to have become aware that mischief was brewing. He tried to slip through the net which was closing in. He considered that he had discharged himself of even more than all the obligations which he owed his host. He told his judges: " I therefore resolved to return to Frankfurt and get certain of my works printed, so last Thursday (21st May) I took leave of him to go away, and, according to what he said, he believed I was not going to Frankfurt, but to teach what I have taught him and others. He insisted on my remaining; but I was equally set on going. He began to complain that I had not taught him what I promised. Then he used threats, saying he would find means, if I did not remain of my own free-will, to compel me. Next night (Friday), seeing that I was determined to go and that I had settled up my affairs and arranged for the transit

[1] *Doc. v.*   [2] *Doc. i.*   [3] *Doc. vj.*

R

of my belongings to Frankfurt, after I had gone to bed, he came in, on the pretext of wishing to speak to me, and was followed by his servant, Bartolo, and, if I mistake not, five or six others, whom I believe to be gondoliers of the neighbourhood. They made me get up and brought me to a garret and locked me in: Ser Gion himself saying that if I would remain and teach him the terms for the memory of words and geometry as from the first he had required, he would have me set free, but if not there would be very unpleasant results. I replied that it always seemed to me that I had taught him enough and more than I engaged for, and that I was far from deserving such treatment. He left me there until the following day, when a captain entered with men whom I did not know, and made them take me to a cellar in the basement where they left me until night-time, when another captain came with his squadron and brought me to the prisons of the Holy Office."[1] Later on, Bruno declared: " He not only wished me to teach him all I know, *but desired to learn what I am unable to teach anybody*, and has constantly threatened me in life and honour if I did not give him my knowledge."[2]

Mocenigo impounded all Bruno's money, clothes, manuscripts and books and handed them over to the inquisition. One Matteo Avanta, captain under the Council of Ten, effected the arrest and removed him to the Prison of the Inquisition, behind the walls of the Prison, to the west of the Bridge of Sighs and facing the Ducal Palace. For on that very day, May 23rd, Mocenigo had denounced his guest to His Very Reverend Paternity, the Father Inquisitor for Venice.

The small-brained man is usually crafty and malicious. There is abundance of stupid misunderstanding, artful perversion and odious fabrication in the three documents

---

[1] *Doc. vij.*   [2] *Doc. xiv.*

successively submitted to His Very Reverend Paternity.
Statements which are obviously truthful are skilfully inter-
twined with others less obviously false. The first precious
document informs us that the Nolan "at various times
when he has talked with me at home said that Catholics
are much to blame in holding that bread becomes flesh;
that he is an enemy of the Mass; that no religion pleases
him; that Christ was a wretch; that he might very well
foretell his being hanged, since he did evil to seduce the
people; that there is no distinction of Persons in God,
which would be an imperfection; that the world is eternal
and that there are infinite worlds, and that God unceasingly
makes infinities because he wills as much as he can (*sic*);
that Christ worked miracles in appearance and was a
magician; the same of the Apostles, and that he might
be given the mind to do as much and more; that Christ
shewed he was unwilling to die, and put it off as long
as he could; that there is no punishment of sins, and
that souls, created by the operation of nature, pass from
one animal to another, and that, even as brute beasts are
born of corruption, so are men, who are born again after
deluges. He set forth a design to form a new sect, under
the name of the New Philosophy; said the Virgin could
not have brought forth a child, and that our Catholic faith
is full of blasphemy against the Majesty of God; that the
disputes and revenues of friars should be stopped, because
they befoul the earth; that they are all asses and their
doctrines asinine; that we have no proof that our faith is
endorsed by God, and that to abstain from doing to others
what we are unwilling they should do to us is enough for
a good life; that he is in favour of all other sins, and that
it is a marvel God endures so many heresies of Catholics;
he says he desires to apply himself to divination, and all
the world would follow him; that St. Thomas (Aquinas) and

all the doctors knew nothing, and that he could enlighten
the first theologians in the world so that they would be
unable to reply." Mocenigo then says that Bruno told him
the Inquisitors at Rome had prepared 130 charges, and that
he made off while they were being presented because he
was said to have thrown his accuser, or him whom he
believed to be such, into the Tiber.[1] He adds that Ciotto,
Brictanus and Morosini can confirm his statements. He
believes Bruno is possessed by a devil, asks for a speedy
trial, and presents three printed works by the accused and
a manuscript on the Deduction of the Universal Predicates
of God [2] and certain hasty memoranda made by himself.[3]

Searching questions would seem to have been put to the
Denouncer, for another statement, dated the 25th May, runs:
" On the day when I held Bruno locked up, I asked him if
he would fulfil his promises concerning what he proved
unwilling to teach me in return for my many acts of kindness and gifts, so that I might not accuse him of so
many wicked words to me against our Lord Jesus Christ
and the Holy Catholic Church." Truly an astounding
piece of self-revelation ! The short-witted man discloses,
not only avarice, but the hypocrisy of his religious zeal,
in weighing his coppers against his Christianity. The
precious document continues: " He replied that he had
no dread of the Inquisition, for he had offended no one
in his way of living and could not recall having said
anything wicked; and, even if he had done so, he had
said it to me without any witness being present, and
therefore he did not fear that I could injure him in that
way, and, even if he should be handed over to the Inquisition, they could only force him to resume his habit. ' So
you were a monk,' said I. He replied, ' I only took the

---

[1] Compare Cotin's statement, page 35.
[2] Not known to exist.   [3] *Doc. i.*

first habit, and therefore, in any case, I can readily adjust matters.'" This dramatic account of how Bruno let slip that he had been a monk, how Mocenigo caught at it and how Bruno lied concerning the final and irrevocable vow hardly tallies with Bruno's own account that he had consulted his host as well as many priests as to his getting to the Apostolic Chair and being allowed to live in peace, wearing the clerical habit, but not under monastic rule.[1] " I followed up with, 'And how can you adjust your affairs if you do not believe in the most Holy Trinity ; if you say such wicked things of our Lord Jesus Christ ; if you hold our souls to be made of filth and everything in the world to be guided by Fate, as you have told me on several occasions ? You must needs first adjust your opinions, and the rest will be easy ; and, if you wish, I will give you all the aid I can, that you may know that, although you have so broken your word and been so ungrateful for all my kindness, I still wish in every way to be your friend.' At this he only prayed me to set him free; if he had packed his things and told me he wished to leave, he did not mean it, but wished to bridle my impatience to be taught, wherein I perpetually tormented him, and, if I would set him at liberty, he would teach me all he knew; moreover, he would disclose the secret of all his works to me alone; also, that he meditated writing others, which should be beautiful and exceptional ; he would be my slave with no further reward than what I had given ; and, if I wanted all he had in my house, it should be mine, for in every way he owed everything to me: all he wanted was a little book of conjurations which I found among his writings."[2] This was " The Seals of Hermes and Ptolomy" which Albertus Magnus, universal doctor of the Church speaks about and which Besler copied at Padua for Bruno, who had not yet read it.[3]

[1] *Doc. ix.* [2] *Doc. ij.* [3] *Doc. xiv.*

CHAPTER XVIII

THE TRIAL

THE evil lead given in the fourth century by the fifteen ineffective edicts against heresy in order to weld the Empire into unity and protect it against those blind, scarcely conscious centrifugal forces which were apt to fight under the more legible ensigns of religious differences persisted throughout the Middle Ages. But it was not until the Thirteenth Century that an organised Inquisition was first instituted and the Church, holding the keys of heaven and hell at its girdle and conscious of the duty of maintaining its own supremacy and some sort of unity in Europe, acted with free authority and made a systematic attempt to fetter opinion. Its proceedings became secret and mysterious; the victim disappeared as if the earth had silently swallowed him, and the issue was only apparent when he was restored to the public gaze in a procession of priests and godly men conducting him to the stake. Written accusations were accepted of anyone, and, while the accused might demand a written account of the charges brought against him, the names of the accuser and of witnesses were with-held.[1] After a period of greater tolerance, at the instigation of Don Inigo Lopez de Recalde, better known as Ignatius Loyola, founder of the order of Jesuits and a man wholly devoted to the service of God, Paul III yielded to the entreaties of Cardinal Carafa and instituted the Roman Inquisition, 21st July, 1542, on the improved, severe and

[1] Bulls of Innocent IV, *Cum Negocium* and *Licet sicut accepimus.*

searching Spanish model. It is noteworthy that within a few months of this event Copernicus published his subversive theory and set afoot the long war between Science and Orthodoxy,[1] dedicating his book, with quite unconscious irony, to the Pope.

The Roman Inquisition became more and more active and terrible. On Oct. 21st, 1567, Carnesecchi, who had published no books but had expressed his opinions to friends, was beheaded and his body burned. On July 3rd, 1570, after four years of imprisonment, Antonio Paleario was strangled and his body burned because he sympathised with Protestants beyond the Alps and declared that it was unlawful for the Vicar of Christ to put heretics to death. The Roman Inquisition triumphed throughout Italy, save only in the Republic of Venice, which would not allow it to enter its territory and jealously watched such spiritual encroachments of the Ruler of the Papal States, wherein it perceived a menace to its own independence. This is probably why Bruno thought himself safe in Venice.

At Venice there sat with the Inquisitors the Patriarch, invariably a patriot, and at least one of three *Savii all' eresia*, Assessors of the State, who were changed every year and who were under the direction of the Governor, himself usually a just and humane man. While, in the Roman Inquisition, the whole Court and all witnesses and officials were sworn to secrecy, here, the representatives of the State were compelled to reveal the proceedings to the Doge and Senate, and had the power to suspend the proceedings if Venetian laws were not wholly respected or if secret instructions had been received from the Government. The Court could not be opened without the formal sanction of an Assessor being given;[2] and torture was rarely applied.[3]

---

[1] *De Orbium Cœlestium Revolutionibus.*
[2] *Doc. xiii, prœmial.*   [3] Berti; *Vita di G. B., capitolo xv.*

It is believed that, at that time, the Inquisitors met at the Patriarchal Palace on the opposite side of the Rio di Palazzo to the prison and a little higher up. They sat under the presidency of the Patriarch.

On Tuesday, 26th May, 1592, the Holy Tribunal met to consider the case of Bruno. The judges were Laurentio Priuli, the Patriarch, who had been Venetian Ambassador at Paris during Bruno's first visit, ten years before, and who may have heard of or even seen him there; Ludovico Taberna, the Apostolic Nuncio, the Very Reverend Father Giovanni Gabrielle of Saluzzo, and Aloysio Fuscari the Assessor. Ciotto, having been sworn, gave evidence which, so far as his direct knowledge of Bruno went, was wholly favourable. But he had heard the prisoner spoken ill of at Frankfurt. That was all he knew or could say concerning Giordano; if he knew more he would tell it. As was customary he was sworn to silence and the Court rose.

It did not reassemble until Friday, the 29th, and was composed of the same members as before. Brictanus, the Flemish bookseller, an older man than Ciotto by twelve years (he was 37), knew nothing at all of Bruno's views except hearsay. After adjournment for the mid-day meal, Bruno was brought in. He had lain three days in his cell. The Clerk of the Court describes him as of ordinary height, chestnut-coloured beard, and looking his age, about 40. Ciotto had described him as little, slenderly-built, with a black beard. We know from Eglin and Alsted that he accompanied his earnest and rapid speech with lively gestures; he had the changing expression of a Southern Italian. Admonished to tell the truth before cross-examination, he burst out, " I shall tell the truth. Often have I been threatened with the Holy Office and I deemed it a joke; so I am quite ready to furnish an account of myself." Then, in answer to questions, he commenced that story of his life and wanderings which has been incorporated in these chapters, until "the hour was late, when he was sent back to his place with the usual warning."[1]

The Inquisitor required Mocenigo to furnish more matter: he must write down "with extreme carefulness all that Bruno had said against our Catholic faith." The document is a subtle commingling of truth with its distortion. Dated the same day of Bruno's first examination, it affirms that Bruno had pronounced the priesthood degenerate from Apostolic practice, "manifesting violence and not love towards heretics. The world could not remain in ignorance and without a good religion. Truly the Catholic religion was more acceptable to him than others; but all needed much reform. Soon the world would take its own reform on itself, for it could not continue so corrupt. He hoped much from the King of Navarre, and therefore he was anxious to publish his works and get credit; for himself would lead that coming time. He would not always be poor, but would enjoy the goods of others. There is greater ignorance than ever was afore-time, since men now teach what they do not understand, namely that God is a Trinity, which is impossible and blasphemous against the Majesty of God. When I told him to be silent and hasten on with what he had to do for me, because I was a Catholic and he a Lutheran, and I could not abide him, he replied, 'Oh, you will see what your faith will do for you,' and, laughing, 'await the Judgment, when the dead shall arise you will get the reward of your righteousness.' And on another occasion, he said, 'This Republic has a reputation for great wisdom; it should deal with the monastic revenues in the French manner; there the nobles enjoy the monastic revenues and the friars live on broth. The friars of to-day are all asses, and to let them enjoy so much wealth is a great sin." (This stroke

[1] *Doc. vii.*

was certain to tell.) "Also he told me that ladies pleased him well; but he had not yet reached Solomon's number; the Church sinned in making a wickedness of that which was of great service in Nature, and which, in his view, was highly meritorious."[1]

Next day, Saturday 30th May, Bruno was again fetched from prison. The Apostolic Nuncio was represented by his vicar, Dom Livio Passero.[2] Bruno, having been sworn to tell the truth, continued the concise, matter of fact and straightforward story of his life, making a natural mistake here and there about the length of time he stayed at this or that place. Parenthetically, he observes that he does not endorse all the works he has written—a statement which he repeats later on, adding: " I have uttered myself and handled matters too philosophically, wrongly, not sufficiently after the manner of a good Christian, and, in particular, I have taught and maintained in some of these works philosophical doctrines concerning what, according to the Christian faith, should be attributed to the power, wisdom and goodness of God; founding my doctrine on sensible experience and reason and not on faith." He goes on to say, probably in reply to a question: " This is a general observation; for details, I will look up my writings; for I cannot now recollect any particular passages or teaching; but I will reply to questions as they shall come back to me."[3] We gather, then, that he was allowed to refer to the seized books. After a lengthy sitting, he was given the customary serious warning and taken back to his cell.

Next day the officers of the Inquisition obtained a deposition from Fra Domenico which confirmed Bruno's statements about their conversation together. The Court sat again on the 2nd June, another State Assessor, one Sebastian

---

[1] Doc. viii.

[2] Cigogna ; Iscrizioni Venete, iv, p. 417.

[3] Doc. ix.

Barbadico, giving the requisite permission and watching the case. Bruno furnished a complete list of his works, and drew the attention of his judges to the fact that, as their titles and contents should prove, they were purely philosophical. We see that he still believed that "judicious theologians" would recognise the validity of the claim of the intellect to free and independent enquiry, "provided it does not dispute divine authority but submits to it."[1] Putting into practice his demand for " philosophic freedom," he set forth his deepest convictions with manly sincerity, spirit and pluck. "I have ever expounded philosophically and according to the principles of Nature and by its light; not chiefly considering what must be held according to Faith; and I believe that nothing can be found by which I can be judged rather to animadvert on religion than to uphold philosophy; although I may have set forth much impious matter occasioned by my own natural light. . . . Never have I taught anything directly contrary to the Catholic Religion, although I was judged to have done so indirectly at Paris, where, indeed, I was allowed to maintain certain discussions entitled 'A Hundred and Twenty Articles against the Peripatetic School and other commonly accepted Philosophers'; and this was printed by permission of the Authorities. I was allowed to expound on natural principles without prejudice to truth in the light of faith, in which way one can read and teach the works of Aristotle and Plato; for they are indirectly contrary to the faith in the very same manner—much more so, in fact, than the philosophy I propounded and defended, the whole of which is expounded in my last Latin books published at Frankfurt and entitled *De Minimo, De Monade* and *De Immenso*, and, in part, *De Compositione*. In these my object and doctrine may be specifically read, which is, in a word: I hold the

[1] *Cfr. Causa, Dial. IV.*

universe to be infinite as result of the infinite divine power;
for I think it unworthy of divine goodness and power to
have produced merely one finite world when it was able to
bring into being an infinity of worlds.[1] Wherefore I have
expounded that there is an endless number of individual
worlds like our earth. I regard it, with Pythagoras, as a
star, and the moon, the planets and the stars are similar to
it, the latter being of endless number. All these bodies
make an infinity of worlds; they constitute the infinite
whole in infinite space, an infinite universe, that is to say,
containing innumerable worlds. So that there is an infinite
measure in the universe and an infinite multitude of worlds.
But this may be indirectly opposed to truth according to
the faith.

"Within this universe I place a universal Providence,
whereby everything lives, grows, acts and abides in its
perfection. And I understand this in a two-fold way: one,
after the fashion of the spirit which is completely present
in the whole body and in every part thereof. This I call
Nature, the shadow and record of the Divine. The other
manner is the inconceivable way in which God, an essence,
presence and power, is in all and above all, not as part, not
as spirit, but unspeakably.

"Now, I understand all attributes to be one and the same
in Deity, and, with theologians and the greatest thinkers, I
conceive of three attributes; power, wisdom and goodness;
or, mind" (intuitive Power), "comprehension and Love.
Things are through mind; they are ordered and are distinct through intellect; they are in harmonious proportion
through universal love, in all and above all. There is
nothing that doth not shine in being, any more than anything is beautiful without the presence of beauty; wherefore
nothing can exist shorn from the divine presence. But

[1] Cfr. Infinito, Proem. Epist.

distinctions in the Divinity are made by the method of Discursive Thought and are not reality.

" I understand, with Aristotle, that all which exists depends on the First Cause, so that to call it a creation is not contradictory, as St. Thomas explains. Whether understood as external or in time, all is the effect of the first Cause and is not independent."

Bruno next, supporting himself by quotations from Holy Writ and Virgil, endeavours to reconcile the doctrine of the Trinity with his philosophy. That attribute or essential characteristic which the Church calls the Father is Will or Power ; the Son or the Word is the intellect, understanding ; the Holy Spirit is love—the life of the universe, the Soul of the World, " whence issues all that has life. All things, souls and bodies, are immortal as to their substance,[1] nor is there any other death than dispersion and re-integration."[2]

Asked if he held Father, Son and Spirit to be One in Essence but distinct Persons, he replied that he had doubted in private concerning the distinct personalities of the two latter. Indeed the term Person was declared by St. Augustine to be new in his time. He had doubted the doctrine from his eighteenth year, but had never denied, or taught or written against it. Asked if he had doubts concerning the First Person, he replied " Never " : he had always held the doctrine of the faithful Christian in that regard. In answer to interrogatories, he said he had doubted and wrestled in spirit concerning the incarnation, but had never doubted that the Son was one in essence

---

[1] He would seem to use the term substance in its Aristotelian, logical sense to express substrate or the ingredient, one knows not what, of concrete being as such, and not in the scholastic sense of the nature of the individual thing.

[2] *Cfr. De minimo, I,* 1, *v.* 4; *De immenso, VIII, x; De monade, IV.*

with the First Person, while the Spirit, if indistinct as to
essence, was not inferior, since all the attributes of God
are also those of Son and Spirit. He had merely quoted
the opinions of Arius in his youth at Naples as being those
of Arius.

The time had come to adjourn for the mid-day meal and
Bruno was taken back to his cell after the invariable
warning.

On reassembling the Nuncio was represented by his
Vicar, as he had been on May 30th, and the Patriarch by
his Vicar. Questioned, Bruno repeated his admission that
much objectionable matter might be extracted from his
works; but never had he impugned the Catholic faith. He
had always claimed to reason by natural intelligence and
not as a theologian.[1] He had reasoned philosophically
and had merely quoted the heretical opinions of others.
He repeated that he had gravely doubted the Word becoming flesh. The examination being pushed he said: "To
make clearer what I said this morning, I have held and
believed that there is a distinct Godhead in the Father, in
the Word and in Love, which is the Divine Spirit; and, in
Essence, these three are one; but I have never been able
to grasp the three being really Persons and have doubted
it. Augustine says, 'we utter the name of Person with
dread when we speak of divine matters, and use it because
we are obliged;' nor have I found the term applied in the
Old or New Testament." As to the Incarnation, he thought
the Divine Word was present in the humanity of Christ;
but he could never comprehend the union of the Infinite
Real with the finite in the way in which body and soul are
one single reality, but had swayed to and fro as to the
ineffable manner thereof, and never as to the authority of
Scripture which declares the Word was made flesh and is

[1] *Cfr. Causa, Dial. III; Eroici, Dial. I, i.*

so in the Blessed Sacrament. Pressed he said that, speaking theologically, Divinity could not be united with the human except as supporting it (*assistentia*), but he did not infer that Christianity was not divine.

As to miracles, he held them to be genuine witnesses to the Divinity ; but a yet greater witness was the law of the Gospel. He had always accepted the doctrines of the Church as to transubstantiation,[1] and had shown his respect for the Mass by absenting himself therefrom, he being excommunicate. He had never held the opinions of Protestants or sat at their Communion table or discussed anything but pure Philosophy with them, whereby they deemed him to be a man without a religion.

He was asked concerning the statements of Mocenigo that he had denied Christ's divinity and asserted him to have been a malefactor, the author's name being withheld. "I marvel," he exclaimed, "that you should ask such a question. Never did I say or think such a thing about Christ. I believe as Holy Mother Church does concerning him." The document relates how, "as he said this he grew very sorrowful" and, returning to the subject: "I cannot conceive how such things can be imputed to me." He held that Christ was begotten, by the Spirit, of a Virgin-mother : when the contrary should be proved of him, he would submit to any penalty. He believed in the Sacrament of Penitence and the damnation of such as die in mortal sin. He had repeatedly tried to be absolved and accepted by the Church. "I have held and still hold the immortality of souls, which are kinds of existence specially due to substance.[2] That is to say, speaking Catholically, the intellec-

[1] Cfr. the statement in Cotin's diary, *sub* Dec. 7th 1586, quoted on p. 185.

[2] He uses the scholastic term *substantiae subsistentiae*. *Cfr. Doc. xi.*

tual soul does not pass from body to body, but goes to Paradise, Purgatory, or Hell; but I have thought deeply, as a Philosopher, how, since the soul does not exist without body and does not exist in the body, it may pass from body to body even as matter may pass from mass to mass; which, if not true, bears a close resemblance to the opinion of Pythagoras." It is obvious that he would claim for the initiated the right to hold theological doctrine in a different sense from that in which the uninitiated take it.

Whereupon the Court puts the sardonic question: "Are you a skilled theologian and acquainted with Catholic decisions?" Answer: "Not much,[1] having pursued philosophy, which has been my avocation." Had he poured scorn on theologians? No; on the contrary, he had condemned Protestant teachings so far as they departed from those of Rome, and had always upheld the theologians of the Church, St. Thomas Aquinas before all. He had read heretical books and animadverted on them. As to the doctrine of good works, he quoted passages from his own writings, which maintained that works, no less than faith, were necessary to salvation. Since he gave the precise page, it is evident that the books lay on the table or that he was allowed them in his cell for the preparation of his defence.[2]

Had he said that monks did not make their lives conform to those of the apostles? "'I have said nothing of the kind, nor held that view,' and therewith," says the Inquisitorial record, "he threw up his hands and was agitated because such questions were asked of him."

The judge-prosecutors pushed him hard with Mocenigo's charges, which they brought forward one by one. Bruno

---

[1] It is true. Later in the examination he attributes to Joachim of Flora a doctrine which Joachim expressly repudiated.

The *Causa* is erroneously inserted for the *Spaccio* in the MS.

remembered saying that the preaching, example, and miracles of the Apostles effected more than the Church's appeal to force to-day does; but his works showed that he supported the discipline of the Church against heresy. Closely pressed as to the different method of the Church in Apostolic times, he replied that perhaps hearts were harder to-day, and so, although there were exemplary Christians, our wicked and perverse generation would not listen.

Asked if Christ wrought his miracles by magic, he raised both hands and cried out: " What is this ? Who invented these devilries ? I have never even thought such a thing. O God! what is this ? I would rather be dead than have said anything of the kind." The gibe concerning the Last Judgment which Mocenigo attributed to him was then brought up, and Bruno exclaimed: " I have never said these things. My Lord, look through my books. They are profane enough; but you will not find a trace of this; nor has it entered my head."

Asked as to carnal sin, he had spoken of fornication as the smallest of such sins and joked about it in frivolous company. He had never blamed the Church for its moral code, but accepted its teaching on the subject. Changing the subject, the Court then informed Bruno that he must not be surprised at the questions which were asked, for he had dwelt in heretical countries, had had many dealings with heretics and had attended their sermons. Such was their comprehension of the impressionability and lack of personal force of the great original thinker before them ! He had admitted, they said, enough to make the allegations against him credible. These were enumerated. Let him take heed and make full, open and faithful confession in order to be received into the bosom of Holy Mother Church and be made a member of Jesus Christ. But it would be a marvel if persistence in his obstinate denial did not lead

S

to the usual end of the impenitent. The Holy Office was desirous of bringing to the light, by its piety and Christian love, those who were in darkness, and of deliverance from the crooked way to the straight path of eternal life. At last it must have been clear, even to Bruno, that the noose was tightening. " So may God pardon me," he replied, " every one of my answers to every question has been true so far as my memory has served me; but, for my greater satisfaction, I will again pass my life in review, and, if I have said or done anything against the Catholic Christian Faith, I will frankly confess it. I have said what is just and true, and I shall continue to say it. I am certain the contrary shall never be proved against me." He put a vastly different interpretation on the Catholic Christian Faith and what he had written about it to that of the Church itself.

Next day (June 3rd) the Court reassembled, the Patriarch and Nuncio being again represented by their vicars. The interrogatories of the previous day were again read over and Bruno was asked if he were guilty with regard to any of the charges indicated. He replied that he had indeed broken fasts, which were not kept by heretics, for he did not know the appointed days except when among Catholics: he had had scruples, but punctilious observance would have excited ridicule. He was of opinion that every faithful Catholic should adhere to the Calendar; but he called God to witness that he had not offended in this respect because of despising such observances. He had attended the sermons of Protestants out of intellectual curiosity, and had never sat with heretics at their breaking of bread or at their other usages. Pushed on this point he replied: " Wherein I have erred, I have told the truth, and you will never find that this is not so. There are plenty of Catholics in those parts who drop their own religious observances without becoming heretics." Cross-examined concerning the divinity and birth of Christ, he repeated his former statement, adding, " what I have held, I have told you. I never talked on the subject. I volunteered admissions to clear my conscience." Frankly, the doctrine of the infinite nature and infinite humanity of Christ could not be understood in the same way as the unity of body and mind in the one individual. He was far from being with Joachim of Flora in understanding the human nature of Christ as a quaternity, additional to the Trinity.[1] The whole subject was one bristling with difficulties, and, however fallacious his premises might be, he had not fallen into heretical conclusions. Pressed as to his having derided the Miraculous, Christ and the Sacraments, he repeated his former denials and referred his judges to his Latin poem, which would show that he had done justice to the Clergy. He had never held that man was of purely animal origin, though he had quoted the opinions of Lucretius and Epicurus ; nor could such a charge be drawn from his writings. He had contempt for conjuration and the like ; but, nonetheless, still desired to study judicial astrology. Never had he taught that the world is governed by Fate and not by God's providence ; nay, he had always held that there is a Divine Providence and that the will is free, which is the antithesis of Fate. True he had praised heretics and their princes for their human virtues, but not for their religious opinions ; moreover, the praise of Princes is demanded by etiquette. Cross-questioned about the King of Navarre, he said that when conversation turned on that monarch he had expressed his belief that his profession of heresy was made with an eye to the throne. He had seen but did not know him or his ministers ; but he had said that, if the new monarch followed the edicts of his predecessors, permission might be obtained

[1] Bruno was in error ; Joachim did not hold this view.

for him (Bruno) to lecture publicly, which the former king
had allowed. With regard to his compliment to Elizabeth,
he neglected to point out that if he had called her *diva*
he had also called Rudolf II *divus*. He had no recollection
of having said that he wished to be " captain " and secure
the wealth of others ; his was no martial disposition, and
what he wanted was not wealth but to follow philosophy
and the sciences.

Throughout the day, the Court had repeated, in varied
forms, questions which had been asked before and to which
the prisoner had surely replied sufficiently. It was now
demanded of him if he abjured and hated his heresies.
Bruno answered : " I hate and detest all the errors I
have at any time committed as regards the Catholic Faith
and decrees of Holy Church, and I repent having done,
held, said, believed or doubted anything Catholic. I
pray this Holy Tribunal that, aware of my infirmity, it
will admit me into the bosom of the Church, providing me
with remedies proper to salvation and shewing mercy."
We shall see how he received both.

The facts as to his flight from Naples were now extracted
from him, and he was removed to his cell.

At a short sitting the next day, whereat the Nuncio and
Patriarch themselves were present with the Father Inquisitor and the State-Assessor, Barbadico, the evidence was
read over to Bruno who replied that it was accurately
reported and he had nothing to add. Asked about Divination, he explained about the transcription found among his
belongings. Asked if he had an enemy, he replied he
could think of none, except Mocenigo, against whose tru-
culent and vindictive behaviour he inveighed, exposing what
he supposed to be its cause.[1]

---

[1] *Doc. xiv.* The examination of Bruno is given in Berti, *Docs. vij,
ix, xi, xij, xiij, xiv, xvij.*

It was not until three weeks later that the judges re-assembled, Thomas Morosini now representing the State. The prisoner was not brought before the Court, but the entirely favourable deposition of the distinguished patrician and scholar, Andrea Morosini was taken. Ciotto was called and confirmed Bruno's statement that he intended to present a book he was writing to the Pope in person.[1]

After two tedious months in a prison-cell, doubly lacerating to a spirit so enamoured of freedom and so restless, not to speak of the doubt and dread which would attend any solitary prisoner of the Inquisition, Bruno was brought again before the same authorities as on the last occasion; with the addition of a second State-Assessor. He was asked if, having had time to reflect, he could tell the truth better. No, he had nothing to add. He was informed that his protracted and contumacious apostasy placed him under the grave suspicion of the Holy Chair (so there had been communications with the Pope and Curia). Perhaps there was more than appeared behind the statements he had made. He must purge his conscience. The prisoner replied that his confessions and writings were indeed such as to rouse suspicions of heresy; he had always felt remorse and wished to amend his ways, wherefore he had sought a less irksome path than that of returning to strict monastic rule and had hoped to make himself acceptable to His Holiness, so as to live in more freedom, yet as a Catholic priest. There had been no slight intended to the Faith, but dread of the rigours of the Holy Office and love of liberty. But, he was told, "had your desire been sincere you would not have lived so long in France and other Catholic countries and here in Venice without having consulted some prelate; whereas you went on teaching false and heretical doctrine up to now." Bruno referred the

[1] *Docs. xv, xvj.*

judges to his deposition to prove that he had indeed consulted prelates and Catholic Fathers. His conduct in Venice had been without fault; he had discussed philosophy with many patricians, as his judges might ascertain ; he had expressed his disapproval of Protestantism; he designed to be absolved so as to live, but not cloistered, among the monks of his native province. He believed Mocenigo, and he alone of men, was his accuser. Being told that he had been so long time an apostate and dwelt so many years among heretics that he might easily be 'a wicked man, wherefore he must prepare to purge his conscience, he replied that it might be he had erred more than he could recollect, but truly, though he had thoroughly searched himself for faults, he could not find them. He had readily confessed all he knew of; he was in their Lordships' hands; he did not know what the needful penalty might be; he was ready with his soul to receive it.

His great scheme of getting the ear of an enlightened Pope through high influence and the presentation of an explanatory and illuminating book had failed, like all his many attempts to reconcile himself with the Church. Traitorously delivered to the Inquisition, at first he felt little or no fear, for he was convinced of his own integrity and blindly self-assured of his own essential Catholicity. But now he felt with the Theban King—

> " All I can touch
> Is falling, falling round me, and o'erhead
> Intolerable destiny descends."

He cast himself on the mercy of the Inquisition. Falling on his knees he humbly demanded pardon of God and the Court. Might any punishment be given privately, and public disgrace not attach to the habit he had worn. If his life were spared he promised so to reform it as to outbalance all previous stain. The Sacred Tribunal ordered him to rise and asked if he had thought of anything more to reveal. There was nothing.[1] So the prisoner was again removed to his cell to meditate and the judges went to dine. This was the last appearance of Bruno before the Venetian Inquisition.

[1] *Doc. xvij.*

CHAPTER XIX

BRUNO AND THE INQUISITORS. THE REPUBLIC AND THE POPE

LET us pause to examine a little more closely the conduct of the Inquisition, and the line taken by the prisoner.

Like the proceedings of the Venetian Three, those of the Inquisition were shrouded in secrecy and silence, and the Court was shielded by the terror which it inspired.[1]

Every witness, every official was muzzled by a sacred oath. Morosini in his history makes no mention of Bruno. The judges allowed their prisoner no advocate.[2] The onus of proving his innocence fell on him alone; but he had no means of communicating with the outer world; the names of his accuser and of witnesses were withheld from him,[3] and he was given no opportunity of cross-examining the witnesses, who were heard and questioned by the Court only. His prosecutors were his judges, and they were past-masters in the art of luring the victim on until he made some fatal admission. They were ecclesiastics who professed that the sufferings of our mortal life weigh as nothing compared with eternal blessedness or the tortures of the damned. "Eternum servans sub pectore vulnus," Eternal Justice gave authority for the suppression of humaner instincts and for loosing those primitive instincts

---

[1] Lea, J. C ; *Hist. of Inquis. in Spain*, 1906, *vol. ij, p.* 470.

[2] Masini, Eliseo ; *Sacro Arsenale, ovvero Pratica dell' officio della Santa Inquisizione, Bologna,* 1665.

[3] Bulls of Innocent IV, *Cum negocium* and *Licet sicut accepimus.*

of cruel absolutism and crushing retaliation which are so heartily aroused in the most cultured minds when some darling prejudice or wonted privilege is assailed.

Yet the Court seems to have acted with caution and with honest intention, according to its lights. The inquisitors practically restricted their enquiry to the charges contained in Mocenigo's denunciations and conducted it with as much moderation as was usual in the civil courts of the period. The Court was more painstaking than is many a modern Court of Justice. The case presented difficult points, so the prisoner's philosophical doctrines were lightly skimmed over. Perhaps they were merely put aside for the present. The judges would naturally be perplexed, and it may be for this reason that they communicated with Rome.[1] For, unlike the rebel-churches, the heretrix of Imperial Rome has always secured by organization and subordination that its ministers shall deal only with those matters in which they are fully competent.

On the whole, the depositions would seem to have been carefully and accurately recorded.[2] They were read over to the prisoner, who thus had opportunities of discovering and correcting any injurious mistake. An easy evasion by Bruno of the charge of having broken his obligation to celibacy was fought shy of by the judges, for sexual immorality, even in the priesthood, was never pursued during the Counter-Reformation, or at any time, with that implacable rancour with which heresy was hunted down.[3]

---

[1] *Doc. xvij.*

[2] Fiorentino; *Lettera al Prof. Spaventa, Giorn. Nap., N.S.,* 1879, *pp.* 450–51.

[3] Peccant nuns, however, were far more severely dealt with. An examination of the *Index Expurgatorius* to-day will show that its great object is not the suppression of vicious literature but of anything which impugns the authority or doctrine of the Church.

But, as the trial proceeds, we find the attitude of the
judges becoming more and more sinister; accusations are
brought up again when they have been answered and
apparently disposed of; less and less is the mask of im-
partiality maintained.

What was Bruno's attitude? The Canon Law recognised
two sorts of apostasy—*a fide* and *a mandatis Dei*—that of
unbelief and that of violating monastic vows. He considered himself guilty of having violated the latter and less
apostasy only; and this was within the sole jurisdiction of
his Order, and the Inquisition had nothing to do with it.[1]
The Roman form of the Tribunal was not allowed in Venice;
he felt himself secure, and when dragged before the Venetian
Court, he was confident, fearless, and franker than was wonted
even with innocent persons. Untaught by so long and bitter
experience, he believed that such highly qualified scholars
and thinkers as the men who tried him would be as devoted
to the pursuit of truth as himself, as eager for "large draughts
of intellectual day," as tolerant and broad-minded, and as
ready to follow the "Divine Counsellor within them."[2] He
remembered only the long periods of intelligent toleration
by which the Church had distinguished itself, and he forgot
the Council of Trent. He boldly expounded his philosophy
and science; he might be mistaken on this or that point, but
he believed he presented what intelligent men would discover
to be truth, or at least a reasonable view of God and of
Nature. So, the first man since the triumph of Christianity
to return openly to the independence of the old Greek
thinkers, he claimed the right to expound philosophy as
essentially superior to theology and independent of it. He
maintained his right to think for himself; he would not
passively receive the opinions of others. He referred his
judges to his latest works. He was anxious to subscribe

[1] Bartholmèss; *op. cit., II, p.* 226.   [2] *Spaccio, III, ij.*

to Catholicism, which he believed to contain high truth and to be necessary for human guidance and the maintenance of social order. He tried to show that he was truly Catholic at heart and believed the main teaching of Holy Church, though he had attacked the superstitions of Catholics and Protestants alike in his writings. For in that very *De Minimo*, to which he dared to refer his judges, he had written of having been saturated from childhood with lunatic meanings held by the professedly holy man and based on a false conception of truth.[1] He is possessed by consuming passion for truth ; must declare truth to all men of understanding. How strange to him that Catholic perverters in high places do not see how far they have departed from the ineffable light ! Will they not soar again from the abysmal depths of mere superstitious credulity, communicate afresh with God, who declares Himself in the open book of Nature and in the human heart, and reform themselves into a truly universal and better instructed Church ? Otherwise Bruno believed they would contrive their own ruin ;[2] there would be no universal Roman sanction for social order and civic authority. Witness the dissensions among Protestants ![3] And without constituted religion how could society flourish ?

But, although anxious to subscribe, he must be allowed to reveal his own philosophic vision ; he will not have his soul in fetters. Without recalling one single word of his philosophic and scientific creed, he admitted the essential truth contained in Christian dogma and practice. His inmost conviction, expressed elsewhere, but concerning which he was discreetly silent at the trial, was that, while there are immediate experiences which cannot be restated in thought, theological dogmas are defective truth at best,

---

[1] *Cfr. Oratio Consolatoria.*
[2] *Spaccio, III, ij.*   [3] *Ibid., II, i.*

though very necessary and of supreme practical importance.[1] His temperament was scientific, not pietistic, though extremely reverent; he fought shy of all fanatic ways, yet, like all the men of the Renaissance, he discovered traces of truth in every singular creed. Ancient cults had a certain charm for Bruno; the religion of the Classic world was tolerant; it glorified humanity, it rejoiced in the fulness of life; the " Bacchic rout " of its deities set forth the persistent power and vital immanence of the Godhead;[2] the ancient Egyptians had also seen God in Nature. Christianity was inferior in so far as it had become a cult of ascetic saints and dead men's bones; so far as it mutilated human joy and noble activities.[3] It had become obscurantist, and the Pope had pushed his pretensions unduly.[4] Yet the emphasis it laid on Divine love raised it above other imperfect adumbrations of the One Perfect Light. Only a purgation of the excrement, superstition, and a granting of complete tolerance to the qualified and judicious thinker were needed.

The opposition between Revelation and reason had been clearly discerned at a very early period in the history of the Church. Tertullian affirmed the former to be " credible because inconsistent; assured because impossible. I believe it because of its absence of reason." Later, in order to secure freedom for human reason, certain schoolmen [5] maintained that Truth is twofold and contrary, the content of reason occupying a different sphere from that of Faith. They enabled the human intellect to pursue its own course; but the distinct and superior claim of Faith was acknow-

---

[1] Gentile; *G. B. nella storia della cultura*, *p.* 78, *n.* 2; *Spaccio*, *I, ii.*

[2] *De Immenso, VI, ij; Spaccio, III, ij.—Cfr.* Spaventa, B; *Saggi di Critica*, Napoli, 1867, vol. i, p. 225.

[3] *Cfr. Cabala; Asino Cillenico.*

[4] *De Immenso, VIII, i, v.* 67 ; *Oratio Valedictoria.*

[5] William of Ockham and Duns Scotus to wit.

ledged. The doctrine had not yet been impugned, and
Bruno frequently distinguished between Catholic and Philosophic doctrine in his defence. But he did not accept though
he did not disclaim it. Of the line of Lully and Cusanus,
he took a higher ground. Lully had maintained the possibility of demonstrating Catholic truth by the exercise of
reason ; Cusanus had made some attempt to explain away
the current theology ; Bruno scorned theologic subtleties
and disputes ;[1] his conviction was that dogma was the
mere symbol of reason, and that intuition and reason, so far
from being opposed, are the two sides of what should be the
great and growing body of organised knowledge.

As early as the second century certain followers of
Aristotle began to interpret the Hebrew Scriptures in
terms of Greek Philosophy. Later, Philo systematized
allegorical renderings of them. Tertullian, Augustine and
the early Christian apologists availed themselves of the
doctrine of "language of accommodation."[2] St. Thomas
Aquinas, whom Bruno especially respected, expounded and
Dante popularized the doctrine that both Scripture and Holy
Church condescend to the weakness of human faculty.[3] The
best minds in the Middle Ages took the symbolic view that
the world was subtly and mystically interpenetrated by the
Divine Spirit, which revealed itself in many imperfect forms ;
they regarded Virgil as inspired in the same way as Isaiah,
though less fully and persistently. Classic mythology was
symbolic to Dante and others ; an uncertain twilight, penetrated by flashes from the high white star of truth. This
belief, Bruno accepted. Authority still reigned in the Re-

---

[1] *Artic. Cent. et sexag. Dedicatio.*
[2] Tertullian ; *Adv. Marc., II,* 16.—St Augustine ; *Gen. xviij*, as
well as other writers.
[3] Aquinas ; *Summ. Theol., I,* 1, 10; *I,* 19, 11 : *I²*, 4, 7 ; Dante,
Paradiso, III, 40 *sqq.—Cfr. Spaccio, II, ij.*

naissance, and Bruno defended himself by quoting Virgil, the Bible, the Fathers and Pythagoras. But such philosophy was not for the vulgar; "Let simplicity and moral fable remain." [1] So we find Bruno, fortified by example, not infertile in gloss nor wanting in reservations. Such expedients are not entirely unknown in attempts to reconcile dogma and reason. He endeavoured to make his peace with the Inquisition; he took care not to expound the sense in which he accepted heaven, purgatory and hell; he did not develop the veiled hint, given in the Spaccio, as to the Divine Virtue merely communicating itself in the person of Christ. [2]

Roman Christianity was the organized and historic bond of unity among the western peoples; he had been born and bred in the Catholic Faith. It was a system entwined round his heart by early associations; branded into his brain by that early appeal to the senses which is as of reality itself. It had buried itself in the depths of his nature, become bone of his bone and flesh of his flesh. Deprived of corporate communion he had been for years doubly an exile from home. Catholic authority had judged him to sin, and, as a good member of human society, as a good Catholic, he accepted the judgment, however mistaken it might be. And, while he would not sacrifice any assured philosophic conviction, he was in deadly peril; his chance of being received into the bosom of the Church was now narrowed down to what might happen at this trial. Surely at worst, he might hope for life and be allowed a life of quiet study if he did what he had always purposed doing—confessed his fault? [3] He fell on his knees and submitted, but he did not retract. Seven years before he had written: "As to my faith I hold it a most proper thing to declare and affirm with theologians

[1] *Spaccio, III, iij.*   [2] *Spaccio, III, ij.*
[3] *Cfr.* Gentile, *op. cit., cap. ij, La genuflessione.*

and those who are concerned with the laws and institutions of the people."[1] No one was ever firmer in also maintaining his right to hold and declare his own conclusions.
But he tried to reconcile irreconcilables. Pouring new wine
into old bottles is an ingenious but not always a successful
experiment. The Church had become less lenient than of
yore to esoteric interpretation of its doctrines.

. . . .

The case was by no means easy to deal with. Philosophical and theological problems of a very intricate nature
were involved, and where precedent rules, caution is indispensable. The Venetian Inquisition was in communication
with the Holy Office at Rome, and here, on September 12th,
a Congregation assembled under the presidency of Cardinal
Santoro di Santa Severina, who represented the Pope.
Santoro, a Spaniard, had distinguished himself by purifying
the Church in the extirpation of heretics. In earlier days
he had persecuted in Naples; he had hailed the massacre of
Parisian Huguenots with satisfaction and pronounced that it
made the Feast of St. Bartholomew "a famous and a very
joyous day." He loved humanists little better than heretics;
but it is to his credit that he and Cardinal Colonna saved
the tomb of Cecilia Metella from the destructive energies of
Sixtus V.[2] It is not surprising that, with such a zealot in
the chair, the Congregation resolved to get the heretic away
from Venice (a State which was politic and too commercially
affected not to be somewhat Laodicean in regard to heresy)
and to deal themselves with a difficult and dangerous person
who would appear to have set up philosophy against established truth. They despatched a missive to the Venetian
Inquisition, demanding that the prisoner should be sent to
the Reverend Governor of Ancona, by whom he would be

[1] *Eroici, Argomento.* Cfr. pp. 173, 174 of this work.
[2] Balzani, Count Ugo; *Camb. Mod. Hist.*, 1904, *vol. iij, pp.* 443, 4.

forwarded to Rome.[1] Perhaps it was not religious zeal alone which prompted this action. Rome never missed a politic opportunity of asserting Papal claims over a government which so often defied them and with which there was an enduring territorial dispute.

Five days later, September 17th, the letter was read at a sitting of the Venetian Inquisition, Tommaso Morosini being the State Assessor present. It behoved the Sacred Tribunal to act warily: they waited until the next Roman post arrived; so that it was not until eleven days later that the Vicar of the Venetian Patriarch, the Father Inquisitor and Morosini appeared before the Doge and Council.[2] The Vicar professed that they had not liked to bear the prisoner away to Rome without informing the Council first. This was a device to disguise the aggression of Rome: Venetian consent had to be sought for extradition. The true bias of the judges now appears. They urge that Bruno is not merely guilty of heresy, but a leader therein; he had written books in which he praised Elizabeth of England and other heretical princes and in which there was much that was inimical to religion, even if taken philosophically; he was an apostate monk, who had dwelt many years in those heretical parts, Geneva and England, and he had been pursued for heresy before at Naples and Rome. The Vicar added that he desired the matter should not be delayed, for a boat was just about to set off. The Doge refused to be hustled: he replied that the matter should receive due consideration.[3] It was not the first time the Venetian government had had difficulties with the zealous Inquisition; when Sixtus V was Inquisitor in the city they had demanded his recall by Rome.

In the afternoon of the same day the Father Inquisitor came again, and was put off with the statement that, seeing

[1] Doc. xviii.   [2] Doc. xix.   [3] Ibid.

the matter was an important one and the Council being occupied with many grave matters, they had not been able to decide about it.[1]

A few days later, Oct. 7th, a copy of the Roman demand was sent by the " Three," together with secret instructions to Donato, Venetian Ambassador. The " Three " sign themselves $+117$, -2 and -6. The request could not be complied with; for the demand was an infringement on the Authority of the Venetian Inquisition, and if complied with, a very bad precedent would be set. Moreover it interfered with the liberty of Venetian subjects. The Ambassador is to convey this to the Cardinal with due compliments.[2]

Donato replied on the 10th that he would carry out these commands: should any incredible argument turn up, he would deal with it discreetly.[3] Three months passed, during which Bruno lay in his prison cell at Venice and there was diplomatic fencing between Pope and Ambassador at Rome. On Dec. 22nd the Nuncio returned to the charge. He appeared before the Venetian College, repeated some of the heretical charges, and added another calculated to appeal to commercial instincts: some of Bruno's books purported falsely to have been printed at Venice. His Holiness desires to have the prisoner in Rome to expedite justice and begs the Doge to extradite him. The Nuncio was followed by Donato, who had returned to Venice. He recounted his interview with Clement; he had told the Pope that justice was invariably done at the Venetian Inquisition; for the Pope was always represented there by his Nuncio, who could always obtain instructions from Rome, and, in fact, did so; he failed to see any necessity for extradition. Whereat the Pope appeared to be satisfied, and never mentioned the subject again. But Severina and

[1] *Doc. xx.*   [2] *Doc. xxi.*   [3] *Doc. xxij.*

T

the Inquisitors were not men to be easily put off. The
Nuncio now spoke again, urging that the man was no
Venetian but a Neapolitan, charged long ago at Naples and
Rome with the gravest offences. On previous occasions,
more than two dozen cases had been sent on from Venice
to the Holy Roman Tribunal, which, the Nuncio reminded
the College, was the head one. The man was merely a
friar, and therefore the desire of the Pope should not be
denied to him ; moreover the culprit was a notorious
heresiarch and guilty of vile offences which he (the Nuncio)
would not speak about, as only the matter of faith was to
the point. Undoubtedly the Venetian Inquisitor should deal
with ordinary cases arising within the Venetian State, but
not with this grave case, begun aforetime in Naples and
continued in Rome.[1]

The Nuncio was informed that their Lordships would
confer, and he was assured that it was desired to give His
Holiness every satisfaction possible.[2]

The Government was somewhat perplexed. The Papacy
had increased its temporal power by consolidating the
States under its rule, and, at the same time, the carrying out
of the Decrees of Trent had added to its spiritual prestige.
An open rupture with Rome was very undesirable, but the
Venetian Republic must be kept inviolate from the ever
recurring attempts at aggression which marked the policy
of the Pope. So the government consulted with the pro-
curator, Federigo Contarini, an ingenious lawyer, to find
a way out. He appeared before the College on Jany. 7th
1593. After recounting facts as to the first processes
against Bruno, he added that he escaped to England,
where he lived after the custom of that island, and afterwards (sic) in Geneva, leading apparently a licentious and

---

[1] There is no mention of the alleged Vercelli process.
[2] *Doc. xxiij.*

diabolical life (sic). But the legal mind requires that a certain balance shall be held; so, after this, when stating that "his heretical offences are very grave," Contarini adds, "although, for the rest he has a mind as excellent and rare as one could wish for, and is of exceptional learning and insight." Venice prided herself on fostering learning; so here is also an indirect compliment to the State. After this preamble, since Bruno is a foreigner and no subject, and the case having been begun elsewhere, the wishes of His Holiness may very well be complied with, especially as there have been precedents, and His Holiness is reputed to be very prudent. There is yet another argument: he avails himself of Bruno's desire to reconcile himself with the Pope. He understands, by report, that the prisoner, on being informed that the case was coming to a conclusion, replied that he had resolved to present a petition showing his earnest desire to be remitted to the justice of Rome; but this may be mere pretence, designed to delay the evil day. A bit of self-revelation follows. With professional caution he entreats the illustrious Signory to keep his report absolutely secret for public as for private reasons. May we suspect that these reasons were that Bruno had particular supporters in Venice whose favour the time-server did not wish to lose? He goes on to say that he will always be ready at the command of His Serenity and in the service of his country. Whereupon the Doge must have been much relieved; for now there was a clear way open out of a difficulty, not unattended by the diplomatic advantage of appearing to yield up a foreign monk who had formerly escaped from justice and no Venetian subject, and of being graciously disposed to His Holiness. He complimented the clever lawyer on his activity and promptitude in the public service.[1]

Doc. xxiv.

Later on in the same day, it was resolved by the Three to notify the Nuncio and the Venetian Ambassador at Rome that, it being found suitable, especially in such an unusual case as that of an escaped prisoner from the Neapolitan and Roman Inquisitions, to give satisfaction to His Holiness, Bruno shall be delivered over to the Nuncio. On the 9th Jany., a letter signed like the former one in a secret code, was sent to Paruta, now Ambassador at Rome, instructing him to make capital out of the transaction ; he is to represent to the Pope that the extradition is an expression of the filial reverence the Republic bears for His Beatitude, and to commiserate with him on his recent illness and express the joy felt at his recovery.[1]

The compliments were returned: on the 16th Paruta replies that the extradition was news to His Holiness, who expressed himself as highly gratified. Clement diplomatically added that he greatly desired to be in harmony with the Republic, and he hoped that, thenceforward, it would not give him very hard bones to gnaw, lest he should be accused of yielding too much to his great affection. The Nuncio responded with correct expressions of devotion.[2]

So the prisoner was consigned to the Nuncio and forwarded by sea to Ancona, whence he was transported along a fork of the Flaminian Way and along that historic and splendid approach to Rome. Released from eight months of captivity in a cell, some gleam of hope may have visited him as he breathed the keen wintry air and saw the ever green valleys of Central Italy and the sun playing on the waters of the Tiber. There lay before him dismal years to test his sincerity and firmness and the final, ironic pageantry of a triumphal parade to the stake.

[1] *Doc. xxv.*   [2] *Doc. xxvij.*

CHAPTER XX

THE ROMAN PRISON. FINAL SCENES.

HE was cast into the Prison of the Roman Inquisition, Feb. 27th 1593.[1] Here he lay seven long years. For the greater part of this time there is absolute silence concerning him, and some Italian critics deem the absence of existing documents significant.[2] During the short rule of the Roman Republic in 1849, the Secret Archives of the Vatican were searched backwards from February 1600, but time only admitted of records up to Nov. 1598 being examined. To day we are assured that no further documents exist there.[3]

Bruno would lie unvisited, save by Officials of the Inquisition and chosen priests, scriptures in hand, come to exhort him to repentance. Neither books nor writing materials were allowed. Prisoners were often put into irons. If they remained obstinate in heresy, milder measures were sometimes tried and promises held out; or, if they were supposed to conceal their views, they were put to the torture. Campanella was tortured twelve times, the twelfth lasting forty hours.[4] During this barbarity a notary took down what the sufferer said, and, if he were silent, torture was re-applied. The mildest punishment

---

[1] *Roman Docs. iii.*

[2] Luigi, Annibale; *Due Artisti ed uno scienziato, Atti della R. Acc. delle sc. mor e pol, Napoli, xxiv, pp.* 468 *sq.*

[3] *Archiv f. Gesch. d. Phil., vj, p.* 344 *sq.*

[4] Levi, D ; *G. Bruno, Torino,* 1887, *p.* 369.

which an apostate monk might hope for was perpetual imprisonment. The Inquisitors were instructed to be merciful. Their manual speaks of the Institution as not desiring the death of the sinner, but rather that he should turn from his wickedness and live.[1]

The earliest of the documents still preserved in the Archives of the Holy Office at Rome bears the date Jan. 14, 1599,[2] The Congregation consisted of eight cardinals, seven coadjutors and the official notary. Eight heretical propositions had been extracted from Bruno's books and from the process by the Commissary and Bellarmin. These were read, and it was decided that certain ones, not named in the document, should be selected, so that it might be seen whether he would abjure them. A search was to be made in the process and in his works for other heretical propositions.

Among the Congregation were Cardinal Santoro di Santa Severina and the great Jesuit luminary Robert Bellarmin. Santoro had been a candidate for the Papacy; so sure was he of election that he had chosen his title—the same assumed by his rival Aldobrandini; his naturally bitter temperament was not thereby improved. Bellarmin was one of the first learned men to weaken the mediæval conception of Papal empire; but he was unaware of the real nature and importance of the new principles he invoked; he was always ready to employ his vast erudition and intellectual dexterity in the service of obscurantism; he it was who took the main responsibility on himself of denouncing the Copernican theory, who distinguished himself by persecuting Sarpi and Galileo and who added certain works on Natural Science by distinguished men to the Index.

[1] *Sacro Arsenale ovvero Pratica dell' Officio della S. Inquiz*, Bologna, 1665, *p.* 294.

[2] *Given in Berti's Vita di G. B.* 1886, *p.* 441.

We gather from a further record of a Congregation held on Feb. 4th, whereat six cardinals, seven coadjutors and the notary were present, that Bruno had expostulated concerning the eight propositions deemed to be heretical, whereupon the Pontiff (who, it may be observed, was falling more and more under the influence of the more bigoted and therefore the more energetic members of the College of Cardinals) " decrees and ordains that it be intimated to him by the Father in Theology Bellarmin and the Commissary that all these propositions are heretical, and not now declared so for the first time, but by the most ancient Fathers of the Church and the Apostolic Chair. If he shall acknowledge this, good ; if less, a term of forty days shall be allowed." The later part of these minutes is not in the notary's hand and has been corrected.[1] What the propositions were, we do not know.[2] For all the papers of the trial as well as Bruno's MSS. have mysteriously disappeared. Yet, however doubtful, it is quite possible that Bruno's trial did not commence before the sitting of Jany. 14th ; the first in which there is a recorded reference to him. For it was decided then that the propositions which Bellarmin and the Commissary had already selected should be read and acted on.

But why was there in this case a delay which was unprecedented and unparalleled ? On Monday, April 5th 1599, a visitation of the Prison is recorded. Among twenty-one other names appears that of Bruno, " apostate from the order of Preaching Friars"; the dates of incarceration are given, and only one prisoner had been kept confined so long as a little more than a year and eight months, most of them only a few weeks or days. The problem remains unsolved. Gentile believes that Bruno may have referred to his books

---

[1] Berti, op. cit., p. 441.
[2] Tocco endeavours to reconstruct them. See his Conferenza, 1886, p. 86.

to refute Mocenigo and that the works published abroad were sent for and carefully examined, which would take time.[1] As McIntyre remarks, the books were not hard to come by, "and it would not require six years to find enough material to condemn him if that were desired."[2] But was it desired, ardently desired? Fanatics may be, and often are, conscientious and painstaking; the doctrine of the Two-fold truth was not yet officially condemned; the relationship philosophy should bear to theology, a thorny subject, not officially determined, and Clement was by nature conciliatory and diplomatic, one who would perceive the value of de-monstrating by example the liberal bearing of Rome towards thinkers could Bruno but be brought to bridle his tongue and make himself subservient to the Authority of that Church which he had never renounced. Brunnhofer thinks that the "Seven Liberal Arts" may have been already written and have proved in some measure acceptable to Clement, as furnishing a plausible alliance between philo-sophy and religion. There could hardly have been anyone at once so powerful and so friendly to Bruno as to have intervened on his behalf. Perchance, however, some of the Princes of the Church may have perceived the essential sincerity of the man in believing he was genuinely Catholic, and the strength of his desire for reconciliation. But, in the absence of documents, speculation is idle. The Church has never acted precipitately; its wont is to await the unfolding of events and act at the appropriate season. And doubtless it had its own good reasons for delay.

Forty days had been granted, but more than nine and a half months were allowed to pass—evidence both as to the skilful dialectic, courage and firmness of the prisoner and the no less persistent effort of the theologians to break

---

[1] Gentile; *G. B. nella storia della cultura*, 1907, *p.* 75.
[2] McIntyre; *op. cit., pp.* 88, 89.

him down. For the times, the lenity shown was phe-
nomenal. But it must not be forgotten that the Inquisitor's
manual directs that "if the culprit deny the indictments and
these be not fully proved and he, during the term assigned
to him to prepare his defence, have not cleared himself from
the imputations which result from the process, it is necessary
to have the truth out of him by a rigorous examination."[1]
The case of Campanella shows what "rigorous examination" meant. Whether the sardonic irony of torture was
applied to the man who had sung of heroic enthusiasm and
held it the acme of human greatness to rise above all
sensibility to pain[2] we do not know. If so, he remained
steadfast and unsubdued.

On Dec. 21st Bruno was brought in person before
the Congregation, which numbered nine cardinals, six coadjutors and the notary. He was "heard concerning all
his pretensions." " Says that he ought not to renounce
nor will he do so ; there is nothing for him to renounce and
he knows not what he should renounce. The very illustrious" were still patient (Santoro and Bellarmin were
among them) ; they ordered that his "blind and false
doctrine should be made manifest to him, and appointed"
Hypolitus Maria[3] and Paulus Vicarius[4] "to deal with the
said brother and point out to him the propositions to be
abjured, so that he may recognise his errors and amend
and recant; and do him all the good they can as soon as
possible."[5]

The Pope himself presided at a Congregation held on
January 20th 1600. It was reported that Bruno was
settled in his resolve not to abjure, asserting that he had

---

[1] *Sacro Arsenale, p.* 154.   [2] *Spaccio, II. iij.*

[3] Ippolito Maria Beccaria, no less a person than General of the
Dominicans.

[4] Paolo di Mirandola, his vicar.   [5] Berti, pp. 444–6.

never propounded any heretical doctrines and had been badly interpreted by the servants of the Holy Office. An appeal of his to the Pope was presented and opened but not read.[1] Among the Catholic dignitaries who had visited and failed to convince Bruno was Cardinal Baronius,[2] Clement's confessor, from whom he was wont to obtain daily absolution,[3] and who may have reported his impressions concerning the prisoner to the Pope. It was at once decreed that "further measures be proceeded with, sentence passed and the said Brother Jordan handed over to the secular arm."[4] There is a further record of this having been done on Feb. 8th.

There are reasons for the final condemnation which readily suggest themselves, though those for the long delay which preceded it remain a mystery. The apostate monk demanded free enquiry into truth, unprejudiced and unaffected by theologic authority. And he was regarded as a heresiarch, the possible leader of a new sect, the fomenter of a new discord within the Church that had already suffered so much in purse, prestige and power from the sectaries of the Reformation.

The sentence was publicly declared the next day. Gaspar Schopp, a scholar and recent convert to Rome, was present. He was informed that the culprit had been about two years in prison. He says the Cardinals and Coadjutors were assembled together at the Monastery of the Minerva. The Governor of Rome represented the secular arm. Bruno was brought into the Hall of the Inquisition and forced down on his knees. Sentence was

---

[1] For the purpose of preparing the petition writing materials would be allowed him.

[2] *Conr. Ritterhaus suo G. Schoppius, vide* Berti, *op. cit., Appendice I.*

[3] Struvius, B. G ; *Bib. hist. lit, Jenae,* 1754, *vol. I, fasc. v.*

[4] Berti ; *op. cit., p.* 447.

pronounced, and therein his life, studies and opinions were recounted, as well as the zeal and brotherly love of the Inquisitors in their efforts to convert him.[1] In the latter part of the last century copies of documents relating to Bruno and the Inquisition were, by sanction of the Pope, given by Canon Giovanni Battista Storti to Raffaelle De Martinis, a worthy priest. The document containing the sentence is mutilated just at the place where it should begin. Storti gave a few words of the condemnation: these run: "You have said that the transubstantiation of bread into flesh was great blasphemy." But Storti adds: "This *note* (sic) is not in the Archives to-day. G. C. S."[2] Gentile believes that the Canon was under orders.[3] It is suspected by many that the record of the sentence was deliberately and designedly destroyed and false colouring given to the fact. One able critic writes: "The sad conclusion is that one can place no confidence in the Heads of the Holy Office"[4] This may be so. Schopp repeats the travesty of Bruno's views, as given by Mocenigo, almost word for word, and, although he attributes these to the work entitled "The Shadow of Ideas," he reproduces the denunciation so accurately that there can be no doubt about these charges having been repeated in Court for the edification of those not behind the scenes. Therefore one may well believe that it was convenient to suppress the terms of the condemnation; for Schopp heard that when the Nolan was only eighteen he began to doubt and subsequently denied Transubstantiation; he was also

---

[1] Berti; *op. cit., Appendice I, Conrado Ritterhusio suo G. Schoppius.*

[2] De Martinis, R; *Giordano Bruno, Napoli*, 1886, *pp.* 207 *sqq.*

[3] Gentile, G; *G. B. nella Storia etc.*, 1907, *pp.* 71 *sqq.*

[4] Luigi, Annibale; *Due Artisti ed un scienziato, Atti Della R. Acc. delle sc. mor. e pol, Napoli, xxiv, pp.* 468–69.—See also *Archiv. für Gesch. d. Philos. IV, pp.* 348–50.

charged with denying the Conception of Christ by a
virgin, the publication in London "of a libel concerning
the Triumphant Beast—which is to say the Pope," (sic!)
and other manifold "terrible and most absurd doctrines"
among which we find those of an eternal universe and
innumerable worlds. All this should have been duly set
forth in the precious document of which no trace can be
found. "Then," says Schopp, "he was unfrocked, excommunicated and handed over to the secular arm."[1] The
office of formally stripping a priest of his insignia and
station should have been singularly unpleasant; but it
was by no means unprofitable. The general register of
Pontifical expenses bears the record that the bishop of
Sidonia received 27 scudi for "the degradation of Giordano
Bruno, heretic."[2] The Governor of Rome was addressed,
in the usual formula: "take him under your jurisdiction,
subject to your decision, so as to be punished with due
chastisement; beseeching you, however, as we do earnestly
beseech you, so to mitigate the severity of your sentence
with respect to his body that there may be no danger of
death or of the shedding of blood. So we, Cardinals,
Inquisitor and General, whose names are written beneath
decree."[3] By this hypocritical form, Holy Church was
wont to secure its purpose while veiling its infamy. "When
all these things were done," writes Schopp, "he said not
a word except in a menacing way, 'Perchance your fear
in passing judgment on me is greater than mine in
receiving it.'"[4] The officials of the Governor then con-
veyed him to the city prison by Tiber-side, nearly

---

[1] Berti, *op. cit., Appendice I, Schopp's letter.*
[2] Fiorentino, F ; *Op. lat. di G. B, state edition, I, p. xix.*
[3] Frith ; *op. cit., p. 302 ; also Sacro Arsenale ; Schopp's letter.*
[4] The Count di Ventimiglia, a pupil of Bruno, gives the same testimony. Berti, *p.* 326, *note* 1.

opposite to the castle of St. Angelo,[1] a considerable distance from the Minerva.

So great was the horror of causing the death and eternal damnation of an impenitent sinner that eight days of grace passed by before the sentence was carried into effect. But, on the 12th February the *Avvisi*, a wretched and ill-informed attempt at giving news, informed the Roman world: " To day we believe there will be witnessed the doing of a most solemn act of Justice (nor do I know if it be not already finished) on a Dominican monk of Nola, a most obstinate heretic, who on Wednesday, at the mansion of Card. Madruccio (sic) was shown to be the author of diverse horrid opinions, in which he remained obstinate and does so still, notwithstanding that theologians visit him daily."

The sentence was carried into effect on the ninth day after the trial " without the shedding of blood." For many years the only account of the tragedy was that of Gaspar Schopp, and Catholic apologists declared the letter to be a forgery and that Bruno had only been burned in effigy.[2] It was long suspected, however, that some document relating to the execution might be found in the Archives of the Brotherhood of Pity of St. John the Beheaded, who were wont to accompany heretics to the stake and use the last chance of moving an obdurate soul and ensure to it " a happy journey." It was stoutly denied that any such record existed, and examination of the Archives was refused to many of the most eminent Italian scholars. But when Crispi was in power he desired to inquire into the

---

[1] Berti ; *op. cit., Appendice I.*—Pognisi, A ; *G. B. e l'archivio di S. G. Decollato, Torino*, 1891, *p.* 62. The prison was called the " Tower of Nona."

[2] Desdouits, Théophile ; *La Légende tragique de J. B, comment elle a été formée, son origine suspecte, son invraisemblance, Paris*, 1885.

[3] Pognisi, *op. cit., p.* 63.

finances of the Brotherhood. They thought that, as so
many applications had been made concerning Bruno, this
was what Crispi was at, and forthwith, in order to avoid
further inconvenient investigations, the Royal Commissioner
was informed of the presence of an entry concerning him in
their registers. In fact, the Company was discovered to
have registers of the roasting to death of 25 other people
during the sixteenth century, and some of these " solemn
acts of justice " were aggravated by atrocious cruelty.[1] The
journal of the *Provveditore* records,[2] " Justice done on an
impenitent heretic. At the second hour of the night information came that justice would be done on an impenitent
friar in the morning. Hence, at the sixth hour of the
night, the Comforters and the chaplain assembled at
S. Ursula and went to the prison in the Tower of Nona,
entered the chapel, and offered up the winter-prayers. To
them was consigned the man Giordano Bruno, son of
Gni. Bruno,[3] an apostate friar of Nola in the Kingdom,
an impenitent. He was exhorted by our brothers in all
love, and two Fathers of the Order of St Dominic, two
of the Order of Jesus, two of the new Church and one
of St. Jerome were called in. These with all loving zeal
and much learning, showed him his error, yet he stood
firm throughout and to the end in his accursed obstinacy,
setting his brain and mind to a thousand errors and vain-
gloryings; and he continued steadfastly stubborn while
conducted by the Servants of Justice to the Field of
Flowers (*Campo di Fiori*), and there being stripped and
bound to a stake, was burned alive. Throughout, our

---

[1] Pognisi ; *op. cit., p.* 23.

[2] The entry is dated Thursday 16th ; it should read 17th.

[3] We do not know if Giordano's father, who was alive in 1586,
still lived, and of his mother we only hear in the examination at
Venice.

Brotherhood sang litanies and the Consolers exhorted him
to the very last to overcome his obstinacy. But thus ended
his agony and his wretched life." [1]

Short inadequate notices have been found in the contemporary issues of news. One runs: "Thursday was burned alive
in the Field of Flowers that Dominican Brother from Nola,
a pertinacious heretic, with a gag on his tongue because of
the vile words he spoke without wishing to listen to the
Comforters or others. He has been twelve years in the
prisons (sic) of the Holy Office, from which he was liberated
on another occasion." Yet another account, bearing 19th
Feb. for date, announced that: "Yesterday morning in the
Field of Flowers was burned alive that wicked Dominican
Brother from Nola, of whom we have given news before; a
most obstinate heretic who, in his whims, concocted diverse
dogmas against Holy Faith, and particularly against the
Most Holy Virgin and the Saints. The vile man obstinately
made up his mind to perish in these. He said that he died
willingly and was a martyr, and that his soul would ascend
in the smoke to Paradise. To-day he knoweth if he spake
truth." [2] The two accounts would appear to differ as to the
tying of the tongue, but probably Bruno was gagged when
he could not be restrained in uttering " wicked words." For
it would seem that the Count of Ventimiglia, a disciple of
Bruno who was present at the trial, said that, before his
death, the sufferer urged him (the Count) "to follow his
glorious footsteps and to flee from prejudices and errors," [3]
and Cantù, without naming his authority, writes : " It is
narrated that when the crucifix was offered him he refused
to kiss it, and that he repeated the words of Plotinus, ' Vast
power was needed to reunite that which is divine in me with

---

[1] Pognisi ; *op. cit.*, p. 62.

[2] *Libri " Avvisi e di Ritorni,"* quoted by Berti, *op. cit.*, pp. 329,
330.   [3] *Ibid., p.* 326.

that which is divine in the universe.'"[1] Schopp, writing to his Protestant friend Conrad Rittershausen, this very 17th February, 1600, tells him that when the heretic "was led to the stake to-day, although already dying, when the crucifix was held out to him, he turned his face aside in disdain." At last he had come at the actual worth of dialectic doublings and glozings and of an official Religion of Love. He had done with all that now, mocked by the imbecile zealots who, almost from Calvary, have converted the symbol of self-sacrifice into an engine for letting loose all the devils that lurk in the human bosom to rage and rend.

He had sung of despising death;[2] he had written of being "so deeply possessed by other thoughts as not to feel the last agony."[3] That he was victor over the grave we know; that supreme confidence in a rational universe so filled his soul that his senses were dead to the torment of the stake, we may piously hope.

So closed a life marked by supreme unity of purpose—to know the truth and declare it.

He perished in jubilee year. The men of all countries flocked to Rome. Fifty cardinals were assembled there. Processions, confessions, kneelings at altars went on all day. Rome resounded with penitential psalms. Tradesmen and harlots did a busy trade. Men went along the broad new streets and marvelled at them and at the new cut by which Sixtus V had joined the Lateran with the Vatican ; at the new population where a waste had existed ever since Robert Guiscard burned half the city of Hildebrand to the ground ; at the great buildings. Little notice was taken of the fire lighted that early morning in the Field of Flowers. It was no startling novelty; only a minor

---

[1] Cantù, Cesare ; *Gli eretici d' Italia*, 1867, *p.* 62. The quotation is from Porphyry's Life of Plotinus.

[2] *De immenso, I, i.*   [3] *Sig. Sigill.*

excitement thrown in with the other allurements of a holiday. The culprit made his painful way over the tufa stones with bared feet. He was chained by the neck and wore a white sheet emblazoned at the corners with the cross of St. Andrew and illuminated here and there with devils and red flames. He was accompanied by a procession of priests, singing litanies, exhorting him to repent, and thrusting the crucifix to his lips; the Brotherhood carried torches and the officials of the Governor of Rome acted as guard. Arrived at the open space where the fashionable frivolity of the ancient city was once wonted to crowd into the Theatre of Pompey, the ruins of which still guarded the Field of Flowers, all the rabble of Rome who now dwelt around it were assembled at this "Roman holiday." Narducci discovered at the Vatican that the precise spot where Bruno was burned was in front of a house at the corner of the Campo di Fiori and the Vicolo Balestrari, where there is a stone inscribed with Latin verses and put up by the Superintendent of Streets in the fifteenth century.[1] That Jubilee was remembered; for it celebrated the success of Clement's foreign policy and the submission of Catholics to the yoke of discipline. Bruno's small part in it was forgotten, almost from the moment when, in accordance with the official direction concerning heretics, his ashes were scattered to the winds.

The strange delay in dealing effectively with him was repeated in the case of his writings. They were not placed on the Index until $2\frac{1}{2}$ years later (Aug. 7th, 1603). Since in Catholic Countries the possessor of proscribed works placed himself in grave peril, original specimens have become very rare. His books never achieved popularity. The English deists who rediscovered him in the early part of the eighteenth century tried to make much of him and failed.

[1] Levi; *op. cit.*, *p.* 390, *n. i.*

U

His name practically disappeared. Then, in the vigorous
youth of German Philosophy, Jacobi recognised his genius,
and this was generally acknowledged by German thinkers,
though his works were not closely studied. Hegel and
Schelling found in him a kindred spirit. In 1847 a Frenchman, Christian Bartholmèss, furnished with scanty material
laboriously collected, attempted a biography and gave the
world a well-considered criticism of his published works.
Since then, in Germany, France, England and especially in
Italy, research has been made and valuable monographs
have appeared. During his researches, Ranke came across
a portion of the record of the trial at Venice. Valuable
documents were afterwards discovered and scholars, such
as Fiorentino, Berti and Tocco, devoted years to the examination of Bruno's life and works. After the unification of Italy,
his countrymen caught fire. A complete edition of his writings, including unprinted manuscripts, was issued volume
by volume. For a time there was a veritable " Brunomania."
The man more " God-intoxicated " than Spinoza even, was
hailed in the eighties by materialists and monists and hide-
bound scientists claiming to be metaphysicians as their
harbinger in the 16th century. The general enthusiasm
reached its climax on the 9th June 1889. Thirty thousand
folk assembled, most of whom could never have read Bruno
or have formed any sound judgment as to his merits : they
only knew he had been martyred by the Papacy. And to
the ordinary Roman, who from time immemorial has never
been able to abide a Pope or subsist without one, that was
occasion enough. All followed the Syndic to the Field of
Flowers, where a monument had been erected to the
memory of yet another great Italian ; and this statue of
the Nolan was unveiled. There was much feasting, and
the guests hurried from dinner back to the monument to
illuminate it. It is said that Leo XIII fasted throughout

the day, and cast himself prostrate at the Statue of St Peter. He issued an address to the Curia which was read in the churches. One discovers therein an impotent echo of that species of Christian charity and understanding which was exercised so freely of old time. He denounced Bruno as "a man of impure and abandoned life: a double renegade, a heretic formally condemned, whose obstinacy against the Church endured unbroken even to his last breath. He possessed no remarkable scientific knowledge, for his own writings condemn him of a degraded materialism and show that he was entangled in commonplace errors. He had no splendid adornments of virtue, for as evidence against his moral character there stand those extravagancies of wickedness and corruption into which all men are driven by passions unresisted. He was the hero of no famous exploits and did no signal service to the state; his familiar accomplishments were insincerity, lying and perfect selfishness, intolerance of all who disagreed with him, abject meanness and perverted ingenuity in adulation." [1]

Reading this, one thinks of the famous exclamation of Galileo, " E pur si muove." Amid the hysterics of the herd on the one hand and, on the other, the denunciations of dogmatists in fanaticism of fear, " the heavens journey still and sojourn not " and " philosophic liberty " pursues her path of peace unconcerned.

Surely an ironic smile plays on the lips of Clio, the Muse of History, as she registers the vagaries of " succession and vicissitude." Rarely has old Time, that antic fool with a bitter wit, seemed more sardonic than in his dealings, during life and after death, with this man of so rare personal force. Bruno was endowed with the fatal combination of a mind of enormous power and almost unrestricted range and a de-

---

[1] Given by the late Prof. R. Adamson in his Development of Modern Philosophy, 1903, vol. ij, p. 23.

ficiency in those self-regarding virtues which we hold in so high esteem to-day. One of the most original thinkers, or rather let us say, one of the most penetrative of seers, that gift of practical wisdom in the conduct of his own life which makes the safe and successful man, was withheld from him. He experienced little but protracted buffetings from adverse fate. And the man who, in many respects, marched genera-tions ahead of his fellows had the evil fortune to influence directly only one great thinker. But that thinker was Baruch de Spinoza, and, after all, to influence Baruch de Spinoza was much. And the intrepid constancy of the martyr for the right to think is more. It raises the human measure for faithfulness and strengthens reverence for what is of highest and best in man. Bruno fell like a first blossom of spring, foredoomed to be withered, to fail of its function and to fall. But it is the promise of a thousand to follow, which shall not fail but fructify.

INDEX